The Age of Scientific Sexism

The Age of Scientific Sexism

How Evolutionary Psychology Promotes Gender Profiling and Fans the Battle of the Sexes

Mari Ruti

Bloomsbury Academic
An imprint of Bloomsbury Publishing Inc

B L O O M S B U R Y
NEW YORK • LONDON • NEW DELHI • SYDNEY

Bloomsbury Academic

An imprint of Bloomsbury Publishing Inc

1385 Broadway	50 Bedford Square
New York	London
NY 10018	WC1B 3DP
USA	UK

www.bloomsbury.com

BLOOMSBURY and the Diana logo are trademarks of Bloomsbury Publishing Plc

First published 2015

Library of Congress Cataloging-in-Publication Data
Ruti, Mari.
The age of scientific sexism : how evolutionary psychology promotes gender profiling and fans the battle of the sexes / Mari Ruti.
pages cm
Includes bibliographical references and index.
ISBN 978-1-62892-379-7 (pbk. : alk. paper)– ISBN 978-1-62892-380-3 (hardback : alk. paper)– ISBN 978-1-62892-381-0 (ePub)– ISBN 978-1-62892-382-7 (ePDF)
1. Sex (Psychology) 2. Mate selection–Psychological aspects. 3. Sexual attraction. 4. Sex differences (Psychology) 5. Sexism. 6. Evolutionary psychology. I. Title.
BF692.R87 2015
155.3'3–dc23
2014049113

ISBN: HB: 9781628923803
PB: 9781628923797
ePub: 9781628923810
ePDF: 9781628923827

Typeset by Fakenham Prepress Solutions, Fakenham, Norfolk NR21 8NN
Printed and bound in the United States of America

It is only a slight exaggeration to say that there is nothing about human life we hold less in common with animals than our sexuality. We can imagine a bird happening to make a nest out of a lady's shoe; we cannot imagine her getting excited about it. The shoe-as-nest holds onto a biological function; the shoe-as-fetish leaves that behind.

Jonathan Lear

CONTENTS

INTRODUCTION

Evolutionary psychologists routinely confuse theory with idle speculation. ... [Their] stories do not qualify as science, and they do not deserve the assent, or even the respect, of the public.

JERRY COYNE

1

I stumbled upon evolutionary psychology by chance. I was reading self-help guides on romantic relationships in preparation for writing my own treatise on love, which was, among other things, a critique of how the self-help industry manipulates straight women into thinking that they can control the course of their love lives by adhering to the right regimen of rules.[1] I found that most of these guides resorted to blatant gender stereotyping—what I will in this book call "gender profiling." Women were being seduced to believe that if they learned to profile men correctly, their ever-lasting happiness would follow. As has been the case at least since John Gray's 1992 *Men Are from Mars, Women Are from Venus*, self-help gurus were unshaken in their conviction that men and women live in vastly different psychological, emotional, and sexual universes, and that their relationship problems are due to their inability to understand each other's gender-specific needs, strengths, attributes, and confusions. There was little room for the possibility that couples might run into problems for the simple reason that they bring their unique personal experiences, unconscious motivations, existential struggles, histories of suffering, and points of vulnerability to the intimate encounter. Gender—and gender *alone*—was thought to be the cause of relationship troubles. Men and women were believed to fall nearly universally into the neat boxes of a rigid gender binary. And though there were occasional nods toward the idea that "some" men and women might deviate from the picture, the overall assumption was that the differences between them were self-evident, intrinsic, natural, and more or less immutable. The justification for this reasoning (when it was stated at all) was that our science—particularly evolutionary psychology—had "proven" its validity.

This is how I came to read up on evolutionary psychology. I decided to limit my research to arguments about sex, desire, and romantic behavior. And I chose to focus on books from the last two decades written for mainstream audiences by professional academics and researchers. That is, I was less interested in how evolutionary psychologists talk to each other in academic settings than in how they talk to non-academic readers. As my familiarity with the field increased, so did my astonishment: here was a *scholarly* field whose main aim seemed to be to convince non-specialist readers of the *scientific* validity of the worst gender platitudes of our culture. I discovered an entire field built on gender clichés of mind-numbing banality: while men are aggressive, women are nurturing; while men are autonomous, women are relational; while men need space, women need intimacy; while men are productive, women are reproductive; while men like sports, women like to cuddle; while men are willing to have sex with a telephone pole, women are coy and sexually modest; while men are attracted by youth, beauty, and feminine vulnerability, women are looking for men with power, status, and financial resources; while men are hardwired to cheat on their partners, women are the faithful sex; while men are aroused by porn, women need a lengthy courtship—flowers, conversation, expensive dinners, and flashy displays of devotion—to feel the slightest quiver of the needle. It was as if a time machine had dropped me in *Mad Men*'s world of high-powered male executives bedding their young female secretaries while their long-suffering wives wisely chose to look the other way. The trouble was that this was not a fantasy world designed to comment on the gender relations of an earlier, less enlightened era. Rather, it was objective science. Or at least that's what it tried to tell me it was.

As someone who has taught complex theories of gender and sexuality within the humanities for more than two decades, I found the world I had entered disorienting. This wasn't because its arguments were difficult to follow. If anything, they seemed absurdly, almost childishly, simpleminded. What kept startling me was that scholars—*any* scholars—could believe that a strictly dichotomous approach to gender could yield any meaningful information about men and women. Had we not spent decades deconstructing the toxic binary of men and women? Had we not constructed erudite theories of how men and women are socialized into differentiated gender roles, so that even when observable gender differences exist, it's impossible to attribute them to immutable laws of human nature? Had we not revealed the reductiveness of categorical thinking: its impossibility of capturing the intricacies of human experience, including the lived realities of gender and sexuality? Had we not emphasized the oppressiveness—the tremendous violence—of overgeneralizations in all areas of life, and in particular in the realm of gender, sexuality, race, ethnicity, and related identity markers? Had we not shown that a generous attitude toward others entails respecting their irreducible singularity? Had we not noted that when we reduce others to walking caricatures, we subdue what is most alive, and thus most interesting, about them? Had we not, in short, illustrated that profiling people on the basis of preconceived notions of any kind makes us unethical in our interactions with them? We had; we had definitely done all of this! But evolutionary psychologists either had not read any of our work or had refused to give it any credence. It was as if the post-68 intellectual revolution within the academy had never happened.

Nor had feminism made a dent. When it was mentioned at all, it was usually with considerable hostility. Third wave feminism—deconstructive feminism—seemed to be a completely foreign notion, which, I suppose, makes sense if you haven't moved past the idea that the binary of men versus women holds irrefutable value. Overt misogyny and heteronormativity were ubiquitous to a degree that is highly unusual in modern academic contexts. And there was little effort to hide the fact that evolutionary psychology has, until recently at least, been a white men's club recycling the same worn-out clichés about men and women since the time of Darwin. Indeed, what struck me most forcefully was the field's stubborn loyalty to Darwin's pronouncements about gender differences. While those of us in the humanities have long understood

that the best male thinkers of the Western tradition—from Plato
to Hegel to Kant to Nietzsche to Freud—tended to become a little
obtuse whenever they started talking about women, that even
the most brilliant minds found it difficult to transcend the gender
norms of their eras, evolutionary psychologists seem to earnestly
believe that what Darwin had to say about women was the actual
truth about them. This includes the gem of an idea that women
are angelic creatures with few sexual inclinations. In modern
evolutionary psychology this has been translated to the notion that
women are naturally sexually reticent. I'm not saying that evolutionary psychologists don't admit that Darwin was influenced by
Victorian morality in his assessments of female sexuality. As we'll
see, they do often admit this. But through a mysterious twist of
logic, they conclude that this doesn't matter, that even if Darwin
couldn't sidestep the gender prejudices of his time, his verdicts
about women were still *right*. And to this day some of them adhere
to these verdicts with a remarkable lack of critical distance.

2

I'm by no means hostile to science as such. I have no interest in
valorizing the humanities over the sciences in any general sense,
for I believe that each domain has a contribution to make to
our overall understanding of the so-called human condition.
I'm also quite interested in the possibility that new avenues of
academic inquiry could be opened up by a greater degree of
collaboration and intellectual exchange between humanists and
scientists. Crossing disciplinary boundaries is frequently the best
way to break intellectual impasses, and the boundary between the
humanities and the sciences (or the social sciences) certainly holds
potential for a productive crossing of this kind. But when it comes
to evolutionary psychological attempts to account for gender and
sexuality specifically, the obstacles seem insurmountable: from my
humanistic perspective, the enormity of the field's blind spots about
the deeply masculinist—deeply patriarchal—nature of its undertaking is both incomprehensible and unforgivable. There is, quite
simply, no excuse for it in the context of contemporary academic
knowledge production. This book is designed to illustrate why I

think this, not just because I'm a feminist and a critical philosopher, but because I don't appreciate sloppy reasoning.

Here a couple of qualifications are in order. First, I'm by and large not opposed to evolutionary thinking. I group Darwin among the greatest minds of Western history and I'm deeply grateful for the ways in which his discoveries freed us from the vise of religious dogma. Obviously, my objections to evolutionary psychology do not arise from theological scruples. I state this fact so plainly because I've learned that one way in which evolutionary psychologists intimidate their critics into silence is by accusing them of being creationists. The categorical either-or logic typical of the field causes some of its proponents to act as if those who don't believe that Darwin was right about *everything* were automatically anti-Darwinians. This is akin to saying that the fact that I think Freud was mistaken in some of his assumptions about women makes me an anti-Freudian—which anyone who has ever read anything I've written knows is not true. So let me be clear: I'm an atheist. I believe in the evolutionary origins of human culture. I just don't believe the first thing evolutionary psychology has to say about so-called innate, genetic gender differences.

Second, I do not wish to imply that all scientists working on gender and sexuality are guilty of the kind of reductive thinking I'll be criticizing in this book. Indeed, if I started this introduction by quoting Jerry Coyne—a population geneticist who condemns evolutionary psychology for being "idle speculation" rather than accurate science[2]—it is because I wanted to show that there are scientists who find many evolutionary explanations just as problematic as I do. One of the things that is so disturbing about the kinds of renditions of evolutionary psychology that I'll be looking at is that they tend to hide the fact that the field is hugely contentious—that for every evolutionary psychologist who claims to know the "truth" about men and women, one can point to another scientist who challenges (or even ridicules) this "truth." That such rifts within the scientific community are concealed from non-specialist readers can mislead such readers to think that what they are getting is a scientifically objective presentation of "facts," when in reality what they are being sold is an interpretation of (usually insufficient) data that is inconclusive at best and manifestly biased at worst. One of the aims of this book is to alert non-specialist readers to this reality—to show that when evolutionary psychologists profess to tell us how men and women differ from each other, they are frequently engaged in cultural myth-making; they are using their "science" to buttress a very particular social ideology about gender.

At the core of this ideology is the belief that every detail of human romantic behavior (what the field labels "mating behavior") can be explained by the evolutionary imperative to produce as many viable offspring as possible. That is, romance is a matter of sex and sex is invariably a matter of making babies. And it doesn't seem to much matter how the babies are made, as long as they get made successfully. Take Robert Wright's assertion, in his widely-read classic, *The Moral Animal*, that "a female, in sheerly Darwinian terms, is better off mating with *a good rapist*, a big, strong, sexually aggressive male; her male offspring will then be more likely to be big, strong, and sexually aggressive ... . So female resistance should be favored by natural selection as a way to avoid having a son who is *an inept rapist* (assuming it doesn't bring injury to the female)."[3] Wright is speaking of orangutans in particular, but goes on to specify that the same logic applies to other primates as well, which, of course include humans. His overall point is that female sexual resistance—or coyness—is a valuable evolutionary adaptation because it ensures that the vigorous genes of those males who are able to penetrate it make it onto the next generation: "For whatever it takes to penetrate resistance, the sons of strong resisters are more likely to have it than the sons of weak resisters. (This assumes, again, that the relative possession by different males of 'whatever it takes' reflects underlying genetic differences.)" (52–3).

Wright is basically arguing that it is advantageous for females to put up some sexual resistance because, that way, they can be sure that they end up mating with males who possess "the good rapist" genes—that is, "big, strong, sexually aggressive" males who have "whatever it takes" to penetrate female resistance. This in turn guarantees that their sons will also have these same strong-willed genes. God forbid a female would want to have a son who is "an inept rapist"! Wright attempts to qualify his depiction by conceding that it shouldn't be taken to mean that "a female primate, her protests notwithstanding, 'really wants it'" (52). Yet, as Wright continues, "what natural selection 'wants' and what any individual wants needn't be the same," so that "even when females demonstrate no clear preference for certain kinds of males, they may be, in practical terms, preferring a certain kind of male" (52). The implication here is that on some deeply instinctual level—a Darwinian level that drives an orangutan female to want to generate the strongest possible sons—she really kind of does "want it." And lest there is any doubt that the same reasoning could be applied to humans, Wright states, on the next page, "A common reaction to the new Darwinian view of sex is that it makes perfect sense as an explanation for animal behavior—which is to say, for the behavior of *nonhuman* animals. People may chuckle appreciatively at a male turkey that tries to mate with a poor rendition of a female's head, but if you then point out that many a human male regularly gets aroused after looking at two-dimensional representations of a nude woman, they don't see the connection" (53). Needless to say, Wright would like us to see the connection.

In evolutionary terms, the distance between a male turkey and a human male is much greater than that between an orangutan female and a human female, so that logic dictates that if it is possible to compare the behaviors of turkeys and men, it must also be possible to compare the behaviors of orangutans and women. This suggests that, from Wright's crudely Darwinian perspective, it might be advantageous for women to be raped once in a while, just to make sure that their sons will carry those oh-so-desirable rapist genes. What's more, Wright's wording implies that it is possible—even common—for a female to be raped without being injured, as if rape were just one sexual adaptation among others, and perhaps even a particularly efficient one. Indeed, given that Wright's larger evolutionary argument about gender differences hinges on the notion the men are "naturally" randy whereas women are "naturally" coy (reluctant, resistant, largely asexual), one could easily reach the conclusion that rape might sometimes be the only way for men to get what they want. In this book, I will show that Wright is not the only evolutionary psychologist to brandish the icon of the coy female, that the idea that women find sex vaguely distasteful persists, to this day, as one of the cornerstones of the field. But—as I will emphasize in Chapter 1—Wright's obsession with stripping women of the slightest signs of libido leads him to heights of misogyny that are genuinely astounding to those of us who are used to thinking that greater gender equality is a sign of social progress.

3

Wright makes no secret of his disdain for those who would like to build a more egalitarian society. But the gist of his message about rape is common in evolutionary psychology. David Buss, who doesn't seem to share Wright's antifeminist views, confirms, in *The Evolution of Desire*, that there might be evolutionary advantages to rape.[4] Among other things, he cites a study that found that the pregnancy rates of raped women are more than double the pregnancy rates of women who have consensual sex.[5] Other studies have argued otherwise, but what matters in the present context is that it doesn't seem to bother Buss that the authors of the study in question—Jonathan and Tiffani Gottschall—blithely discuss the "reproductive benefits of rape," as if there was no contradiction whatsoever between the realities of rape and the notion of "benefits."[6] More specifically, that evolutionary psychologists routinely align rape with "mating success"—as Buss himself does when he refers to another study that found that men who have many sexual partners also score high on sexual aggression (273)[7]— ignores all the ways in which rape is a crime that has nothing to do with sexuality, let alone reproduction, but rather with displays of domination. And what are we to make of Buss's rather astonishing conclusion that the higher pregnancy rate of raped women might be due to rapists choosing women who are "especially physically attractive," for attractive women, evolutionary theory tells us, are on average more fertile (274). Seriously? How, exactly, is this attractiveness determined?

Buss argues that scientists who have been brave enough to advance the theoretical possibility that men may have, over evolutionary history, evolved "rape adaptations" for reproductive success should be lauded. In his view, ideological considerations should not stand in the way of objective scientific research. In principle I agree. It's just that I don't for one minute believe that the evolutionary psychological research that is currently being conducted on human sexuality is value-neutral. Fortunately for me, Coyne is not the only scientist who concurs. Joan Roughgarden— an evolutionary biologist at Stanford—echoes Coyne's outburst about evolutionary psychology not deserving the respect of the public when she admits that Darwin's theory "is open to corruption by psychologists, yielding a stimulating fantasy."[8] Referring to the rape argument in particular, Roughgarden notes that the idea that all men are potential rapists is offensive enough to make many male scientists—Coyne among them—angry about the misuse of Darwinian theory.[9] Many women have of course been angry about other aspects of evolutionary psychology for a long time, but their objections have for the most part been ignored. The handy thing about adopting the label of "science" is that you can call anyone who disagrees with you "unscientific." And you can do this even when your own endeavor bears no resemblance to real science. This is why it's so important that some scientists have started to speak out, to acknowledge, as Coyne does, that evolutionary psychologists often "choose ideology over knowledge," which means that what they produce is "not science, but advocacy."[10]

Interestingly, Buss himself remarks that the so-called "orangutan rape strategy" that Wright valorizes might actually be quite unique in that it has not been observed among other primates closer to humans, such as bonobos and chimps (271).[11] Strangely, the evolutionary psychologists who promote the "can't-fight-nature" theory of rape seem to want us to believe that, when it comes to sexual behavior, human males are more like orangutans than bonobos and chimps even though evolutionary biology itself reveals that otherwise they bear a greater resemblance to the latter. Likewise, one has to wonder about the consistent portrayal of the human female as sharing the sexual reluctance of the orangutan female rather than the sexual eagerness and rampant promiscuity of the bonobo or chimp female. Why are so many evolutionary psychologists—Wright included—not admitting that the sexual behavior of humans might actually be quite similar to those primates that humans are most immediately related to, and that when this is not the case, the divergence might be explained by cultural factors, such as the various social and religious restrictions that have historically been placed on female sexuality? Why insist on the *naturalness* of human sexual behavior that our closest primate cousins do not exhibit? I can think of only one explanation: whether it realizes this or not, evolutionary psychology is protecting a very specific—and a very conservative—social mythology about human sexuality.

4

What is even more bizarre is that many of the authors of popular evolutionary treatises readily admit their biases *at the same time* as they claim that their science is absolutely dispassionate and unprejudiced. Wright, for instance, boasts that "male Darwinians may get a certain thrill from saying males are built for lifelong sex-a-thons. Scientific theories spring from many sources" (69). Along related lines, Geoffrey Miller, the author of *The Mating Mind*, writes, "One's understanding of human sexuality and human behavior depends, to some extent, on one's sex ... . some of my ideas have probably been too influenced by my sex, my experiences, my intuitions. The trouble is, I don't know which ideas are the biased ones, or I would have fixed them already."[12] Fair enough. But if this is the case, why continue to assert—in unashamed self-contradiction—that one's theories present a scientifically impartial truth about men and women? Why keep on insisting that one's science is devoid of personal bias, social ideology, or cultural corruption? It seems to me that one can't have it both ways: either one's science is biased or it's not. If one is going to acknowledge that the scientist's gender might have something to do with its results, then one can't simultaneously argue that one is producing objective science, except, of course, if one assumes that anything that is male is automatically objective. Miller notes that the recent entrance of women into evolutionary psychology has transformed the field.[13] If so, perhaps it's time to question some of the field's fundamental premises, including the ways in which these premises seem to reflect the sexual fantasies of (some) male scientists—who, let's be frank, usually spend more time buried in their research than in women's skirts.

My point is not that evolutionary psychology is biased because it is being produced by men, though some of the male authors I surveyed certainly left themselves open to this charge. There are many female researchers—Helen Fisher among them—who seem to agree with the main outlines of evolutionary psychology, though they do often contest aspects of it, such as the emphasis on female coyness.[14] The matter cannot therefore be reduced to some kind of a male-female binary. And in any case, such a reduction would war against the crux of my argument, namely that gender dichotomies get us nowhere. I would never want to suggest that male scientists aren't capable of producing good theories or that female scientists will automatically get it "right." Rather, my argument is that evolutionary psychology as a field remains permeated by enormously traditional modalities of thinking that have gone largely unchallenged since Darwin. The mantra of the field, even now, seems to be—to borrow from Donald Symons's 1979 classic *The Evolution of Human Sexuality*—that "there is a female human nature and a male human nature, and that these natures are extraordinarily different."[15] One may understand why Symons might have held this view in the 1970s, but what is much less intelligible is why so many of the field's advocates still do. As a matter of fact, they seem to do so all the more vehemently the more our social environment has started to reveal how very untenable it really is. Simply put, the more modern men and women deviate from the evolutionary mantra, the more desperately (some) evolutionary thinkers seem to want to assert it as the "truth" about human nature.

What is so damaging about much of evolutionary psychology is that it seeks to place the stamp of scientific approval on some of our culture's most entrenched gender stereotypes. It wants to persuade the rest of us that the rhetoric of Mars-Venus, the rhetoric of "men *this*, women *that*" that infiltrates every corner of our social world, has a genetic basis. I will return to the broader cultural ramifications of evolutionary psychology in the final chapter of this book. Here I merely wish to note that the most commonly circulated evolutionary explanations of heterosexual romantic behavior repeatedly commit the same mistakes: they equate human sexuality with reproduction; they build "scientific" hypotheses on the basis of a predetermined, socially conditioned understanding of gender differences; and they exaggerate these differences to the point that they completely lose track of the multiple ways in which men and women are alike. And when it comes to homosexuality, evolutionary psychology is truly in the Middle Ages, for a theory that reduces all human sexual behavior to the reproductive impulse obviously cannot account for same-sex desire except as a kind of evolutionary "dead-end." If the sole purpose of life is to pass your genes onto the next generation, then the only sexuality that is rationally defensible is reproductive heterosexuality. As a result, when evolutionary psychology tries to explain homosexuality, it comes up with one shaky scenario after another, including the idea that, in prehistoric times, homosexual men were guys who failed to reproduce because they couldn't attract women. Homosexuals, then, are just failed heterosexuals—folks who are forced to have sterile sex with their own kind because they can't engage the interest of the "opposite" sex.[16] Charming.

5

In this context, it may help to recall that evolutionary psychology has always had trouble with socially sensitive issues. And its objectivity has long been called into question. For instance, when Arthur Jensen, back in 1969, argued that the fifteen-point difference in IQ tests between whites and blacks (blacks scoring lower) might have a genetic cause, some of his fellow scientists got so furious that Jensen ended up having to revise his research agenda, devoting his energies to studying bias in IQ testing instead. Even more famously, when E. O. Wilson published his 1975 landmark study, *Sociobiology*, some of his eminent Harvard colleagues, including Richard Lewontin, Stephan Gould, and Ruth Hubbard, protested on the pages of *The New York Times*, accusing him of bad science, biological determinism, and an ultra-conservative racist social agenda.[17] One of my questions in this book is why the same upheaval hasn't happened with gender profiling.

To be sure, the same people who were upset about Wilson's racial generalizations were also upset about some of his statements about gender roles, such as the following: "In hunter-gatherer societies, men hunt and women stay at home. This strong bias persists in most agricultural and industrial societies and, on that ground alone, appears to have a genetic origin ... My own guess is that genetic bias is intense enough to cause a substantial division of labor even in the most free and egalitarian future societies ... Even with identical education and equal access to all professions, men are likely to continue to play a disproportionate role in political life, business and science."[18] Wilson here suggests that our genes condemn us to gender inequality—and that women are going to be inferior to men in the key areas of politics, business, and science—no matter how hard we try to change things for the better. It would be difficult to deny that he is, in this instance at least, guilty of biological determinism of the worst kind (while, ironically enough, deriving his "genetic" argument from his observations of *social* arrangements rather than from any actual biological data). And it hardly helps to point out, as Ullica Segerstrale does in her *Defenders of the Truth*, that Wilson redeems himself by admitting that "this is only a guess" (211). As far as I'm concerned, if your science consists of guessing, then perhaps you should rethink your research methods, particularly when it comes to something as important as predicting the future of gender relations.

I'm not surprised that some people got annoyed at Wilson back in 1975. But what *does* surprise me is the relative ease with which evolutionary psychologists continue to promote gender profiling in today's society—a society that has in other aspects tried to move beyond stereotypical thinking, if not always in practice, then at least in its official rhetoric. Among other things, we have learned not to make assumptions about people based on race, ethnicity, nationality, religion, income, and so on, because we know that such assumptions are a pitifully simplistic way of making sense of the world, not to mention immensely hurtful to those who are forced to carry their burden. Though racism, for instance, remains an enormous problem, few of us are *proud* of being racist. What is so peculiar about many evolutionary psychologists is that they are explicitly *pleased* with—and completely unapologetic about—their gender profiling tendencies. While they have gotten more careful about making overtly racist claims (though such claims are by no means absent from their theories, as will become clear shortly), their sexism remains largely unchecked, and collectively speaking, we seem remarkably complacent about it. This is what my book is meant to change. I would like us to ask ourselves what makes gender profiling so acceptable in a society that has otherwise become increasingly aware of the damage done by other forms of stereotypical thinking. Does this have to do with the fact that women—who usually bear the brunt of gender profiling—have been too meek to complain? Or is it because gender profiling is so endemic in our society that we no longer recognize it as a form of prejudice?

I don't want to give the impression that I think that only women suffer from gender profiling. Quite the contrary, my aim is to show that it hurts both men and women. But it would be hard to deny that it still hurts women more, which is why I tend to argue from a specifically feminist perspective. And if I talk primarily about straight relationships, it's because this is overwhelmingly the focus of the theories I'll be analyzing (precisely because, as I noted above, they regard homosexuality as an evolutionary glitch). Moreover, because gay, lesbian, queer, and other non-normative sexualities have been maligned in our society, those living with the stigma of such sexualities have had to be robustly inventive about how they think about both gender and sexuality, with the result that they have often liberated themselves from the traditionalist discourse promoted by our evolutionary psychologists. The straight world, in contrast, is lagging pathetically behind this inventiveness in part because it seems to find this discourse perversely compelling even as it struggles to move beyond it. One of my objectives in this book is to show just how oppressive this discourse really is— what a straightjacket the gender stereotypes of the straight world really are.

I'm of course well aware that my reporting on how evolutionary psychologists talk about gender and sexuality is selective, that like them, I'm motivated by an ideological agenda. But the difference is that I'm in no way claiming to be presenting an objective argument. I make no secret of the fact that, as a progressive critical theorist, I'm invested in demolishing suffocating gender paradigms so that we can all breathe more easily and live our lives more adventurously. I don't deny that at the heart of my argument resides my personal conviction that all of us—men and women, straights and queers, alike—would benefit from discarding stereotypical thinking. In contrast, the authors I have cited—and will keep citing throughout my discussion—work overtime to convince readers of the *impartial* truthfulness of their assertions. *This*, in my view, is the main problem. In a country with free speech, one is at liberty to say the most offensive things conceivable without being persecuted. As a result, if an author wants to glorify a sexual culture based on male aggression and female coyness, so be it. Please just don't tell me that this glorification is *scientifically* justified.

One of my goals is to show that the very decision to focus on gender differences is already a deeply ideological one. Anyone with even the most rudimentary understanding of how knowledge production works is aware that the hypotheses one arrives at are conditioned by how one frames one's subject matter and interprets one's research results. And a great deal depends on what one deems worth studying to begin with. This is as true of evolutionary psychology as it is of other areas of knowledge production. In her *Anatomy of Love*, Fisher readily admits—as did most of the other authors I reviewed—that variations *within* each gender are frequently greater than *between* the genders. That is, Fisher concedes that men differ from each other more than men as a group differ from women as a group.[19] If this is the case, why place so much emphasis on the differences between men and women in the first place? What is at stake, ideologically speaking, in focusing on what makes men and women different from each other when it would be equally possible to talk about the various ways in which they are fundamentally quite similar? What cultural assumptions is the rhetoric of difference meant to sustain? What does it hide? And what lies behind the valorization of statistical averages over the distinctiveness—the undeniable specificity—of individuals?

The chapters that follow will treat these questions in greater detail. But let me state, as a preliminary point of departure, that the evolutionary psychological decision to highlight gender differences aligns itself with an almost frightening ease with conservative Christian rhetoric—that is, the very rhetoric that Darwinism was supposed to enable us to oppose. I have already called attention to two such points of correspondence, namely the belief that sex is a matter of producing babies and the emphasis on the importance of female coyness (or chastity) as something that is not only unquestionably "natural" but also unquestionably desirable. I will have a lot more to say about these views in the course of this book. For now, suffice it to note that when "scientific" Darwinians and fundamentalist Christians start to sound alike, there is some real cause for concern, not only for self-identified feminists such as myself but for everyone who has any investment in the separation of science and religion.

6

Because I've chosen to focus on evolutionary theories of romantic conduct specifically, much of my analysis revolves around what in the field is known as "the standard narrative" of human mating behavior. As I've already started to suggest, this narrative relies on the imagery of promiscuous men in their prime seeking to impregnate blushing young women in order to ensure the survival of their genes. Given this rather outdated premise, one might expect the narrative to have been discredited a long time ago—but it hasn't. As Christopher Ryan and Cacilda Jethá illustrate in their 2011 *Sex at Dawn: The Prehistoric Origins of Human Sexuality*, it has held sway until our time.[20] Its main components can be found in virtually every evolutionary tome I could find, including recent titles such as Miller and Kanazawa's 2008 *Why Beautiful People Have More Daughters*, Jena Pincott's 2009 *Do Gentlemen Really Prefer Blondes?*, Roy Baumeister's 2010 *Is There Anything Good About Men?*, and Larry Young and Brian Alexander's 2012 *The Chemistry Between Us*.[21] Indeed, the fact that many of the latest texts in evolutionary psychology reference elements of the standard narrative—such as the idea that men are inherently more promiscuous and interested in sexual variety than women—in passing, as one of the field's "givens," only highlights the extent to which it has solidified into a taken-for-granted creed. And there are advocates of evolutionary psychology who will defend it with the perseverance of a terrier holding on to a teddy-bear.

I discovered this when I was invited to blog for *Psychology Today*. One of my first posts was a humorous piece on the so-called cougar phenomenon: older women dating, and sometimes even marrying, younger men. In the post I made fun of the evolutionary psychological argument that older women who opt to sleep with younger guys do so because they are desperate about their waning reproductive potential and want to give it one last hurrah before resigning themselves to encroaching menopause. I pointed out that I could imagine a number of alternative reasons for why older women might want to shack up with younger guys, not the least of which is that many younger men have been socialized into an egalitarian gender culture, with the consequence that they don't smother women with archaic ideals of femininity. By this I didn't mean that there aren't older men who are similarly broadminded. It's just that the younger ones—particularly unattached ones—are easier to find, due to the rapid changes that have in recent years taken place in how men and women relate to each other. And I also suggested that some older women might want sex for the simple reason that they *like* sex—that producing a baby might not be the objective of an older woman bedding a hard-bodied younger chap.

My depiction of cougars mating with younger guys for the sheer pleasure of it struck a nerve among the devotees of the standard narrative because it suggested that some women might prefer sex that has no reproductive utility, and that—even more audaciously—some of them might finally have enough power to reverse the age-old custom of older men sleeping with younger women. My post received a deluge of hate-mail.[22] It was clear that many of the respondents simply just detested the idea that women might like sex for its own sake, that some women might be more interested in multiple orgasms than in multiple offspring. And some of the respondents seemed genuinely disturbed by my conviction that many modern men are actually quite decent—that the idea that the patriarchal alpha male is women's only option is a cultural myth. Many of the respondents were so furious that they resorted to personal insults, ridiculing everything from my credentials to my romantic life (neither of which they knew anything about). Here is one representative response:

> You're a professor of English—why are you writing here? Your utter lack of scientific qualifications is painfully obvious. Ranting about reality is not going to change it. Six million years of evolution will not suddenly vanish because you are insecure about men cheating on you. You cannot harangue humanity into becoming the world you want it to be. *Umpteen scientific studies have revealed and explained the true nature of human mating behavior, including infidelity, monogamy, status dynamics in a relationship, etc. etc.* Your nonsensical statement about "decent guys" may refer to characters in a Jennifer Aniston movie, but in reality there are just male homo sapiens. *And they are biologically programmed to mate with as many females as they can. Because they can.* This may disturb you and fuel your sense of insecurity. Tough luck. Or should I say good luck finding the man who is not a 'jerk'. Outside of Hollywood Romcoms, he doesn't exist. Deal with it. (emphasis added)

Three things are worth commenting on here. First, this respondent is confident that science—evolutionary psychology—reveals "the true nature of human mating behavior" in all of its aspects, so that the matter has been decided for the rest of eternity; there is no possibility of revising the existing theories. And no one else—least of all (female) professors of English—can have anything meaningful to say about the topic. Second, the respondent is certain that men are *natural* jerks, so that my faith in the possibility of finding a decent guy is drastically misguided. Indeed, the respondent seems to believe that if I were less insecure as a woman, I would instantly realize that *all* men are philandering bastards. Third, the respondent wants me to believe that if men philander, it's because they are *biologically* programmed to spread their seed. Never mind that most straight men I know are quite careful about making sure they don't accidentally impregnate the women they sleep with. The overall message is that, as a woman, I have no choice but to learn to tolerate men's indiscretions along with my own inferior social status—a theme I will return to in Chapter 5.

Generally speaking, the utterly irrational, foaming-from-the-mouth tenor of some of the responses I received hardly increased my faith in the scientificity of the science they were defending. Wading through the hate-soaked prose, I kept thinking that I no longer knew which was worse: the conservative creationists who insist that evolution didn't happen (and that Darwin is the devil) or those who insist that evolutionary psychology can explain *every* facet of human behavior (so that it's those interested in complex sociocultural explanations who are the devil). I tried to shake off the experience as an example of the nasty things that happen on the internet when people get to hide behind anonymity. But several things kept nagging me. The first was the smug misogyny of many of the respondents, who seemed to think that it was okay to say spiteful things about women in the name of scientific inquiry. The second was that, not too long after my brawl with these folks, one of my fellow bloggers, Satoshi Kanazawa—co-author of the aforementioned *Why Beautiful People Have More Daughters*— posted a piece about how evolutionary psychology "proves" that black women are less attractive than other women. *Psychology Today* pulled the post,[23] but I was still flabbergasted by how far a "scientist" could go on a quasi-academic internet site before getting in trouble. Third, I could tell from the aggressive tone of my critics that this was not the first time they felt attacked, that they were defending a story of some kind—a story about what made men men and women women. It was obvious that I had stepped on some very sore toes, and I wanted to find out why. And, fourth, I realized that these were people who were used to bullying others into silence; they were hurling sexist slogans and personal insults at me in an effort to intimidate me into swallowing my objections. This book is my response to that effort. If its tone is a little biting, it's because I don't like to be bullied.

7

In Chapters 3 and 4 of this book, I'll demonstrate that the standard narrative is increasingly under fire from the more progressive representatives of evolutionary psychology. Yet the defenders of the status quo endorse this narrative with the same degree of vehemence as the respondents to my blog post, frequently accusing its critics of giving into political correctness, social sensitivities, or feminist humbug. The implication is that the defenders of the standard narrative are doing hard, objective science whereas those scientists who deviate from it are caving in under the egalitarian demands of our cultural environment. The defenders of the standard narrative seem uninterested in the possibility that the evolutionary thinkers revising it might actually be presenting more rigorous and convincing arguments. This is a situation where the willingness to go against cultural trends—in this case the trend toward greater gender parity—is confused with objectivity. I don't deny that the ability to resist social pressures is often the precondition of impartiality in knowledge production. But the problem is that, in this particular case, this "impartiality" cannot be scientifically defended, so that the attempt to obscure the problematic nature of the "science" in question by recourse to the image of scientific heroism—the image of bravery in the face of collective disapproval—merely accentuates the overall insidiousness of the enterprise. We are not here dealing with Galileo fighting unjust persecution; we are dealing with a bunch of socially conservative thinkers who choose to define "objectivity" as a matter of being free to say sexist (and racist) things under the auspices of science.

In the first two chapters of this book, I outline the classic version of the standard narrative by focusing on some of the main arguments of Wright and Buss. I selected these two authors because they have been immensely influential not merely among their scientific peers but also among non-specialist readers; they have been instrumental in introducing the standard narrative to the general public and in popularizing the evolutionary rhetoric of gender and sexuality that currently dominates our cultural imagination. One indicator of the standard narrative's persistence is that Buss's 2011 *Dangerous Passion* relies on more or less the same arguments as his earlier *The Evolution of Desire* (a text originally published in 1995 and reissued in 2003).[24] I've chosen to focus on the updated 2003 edition of the earlier text because it remains among the most respected and frequently cited in the field while also offering a strong example of the kind of gender-bifurcated reasoning I would like to examine. If one wants to know how Buss thinks men and women differ from each other, *The Evolution of Desire* is still the best place to find out. Chapters 3 and 4—which focus on Miller's *The Mating Mind* and Ryan and Jethá's *Sex at Dawn*, respectively—shift the tone somewhat by going into some detail about the modifications to the standard narrative that have started to surface, but that, in my view, still do not sufficiently address the narrative's fundamental problems.

I've chosen to proceed through a fairly close rhetorical analysis of this select group of texts because this makes it possible for me to illustrate, in a concrete manner, how cultural ideology gets woven into scientific analysis. In a way, I felt that some of the arguments of evolutionary psychology were so preposterous that outlining them in the abstract—without providing detailed textual evidence—might lead those outside the field to assume that I was setting up a straw man; readers needed to see it to believe it, as it were. I admit that my decision to limit the number of texts I discuss in depth to the four I have named is also due to my having quickly reached my saturation point for seeing the same sexist arguments, such as the attempt to reduce women to their ovaries, repeated in text after text, usually with no other "scientific" grounding than that others in the field had made them before. In addition, I tried to be somewhat evenhanded in my selection in the sense that two of the four texts that made the final cut—*The Mating Mind* and *Sex at Dawn*—are ones I actually like quite a bit. Much of the evolutionary literature, like the respondents to my blog posts, made me feel terrorized by its insistence that it *alone* had the capacity (and the right) to define what a man or a woman is. *The Mating Mind* and *Sex at Dawn* stood out from the lot for being smart and well reasoned, even if they still sometimes lapse when it comes to women specifically.

I began my research with a fairly open mind, optimistically assuming that if I read enough, I would eventually find evolutionary psychological texts that I could relate to—that treated gender and sexuality in complex, productive ways. To my dismay, this turned out to be an unfounded assumption. An early critic of the manuscript of this book told me that she wished that I could have provided "an image of a science that would reflect and support the positive changes we see in the current social world around intimate gender relations, rather than regressively deny and undermine them." In response I can only say that I also wish that I could have provided such an image. Unfortunately, I found little support for this undertaking in the field of evolutionary psychology. There may be excellent science being done on gender and sexuality in related fields—such as evolutionary biology—but the popular evolutionary psychology I read in preparation for writing this book seemed to be on an overt mission to "regressively deny and undermine" the positive changes taking place in today's intimate gender relations. Ryan and Jethá's *Sex at Dawn* is an exception to this, which is why I have devoted an entire chapter to it.

I should also specify that I did not want to write a book about the interface between biology and culture in the production of our gendered and sexual realities, for I think that there are others—Anne Fausto-Sterling jumps to mind—who are better qualified for such a project (and who have, indeed, already done this work).[25] Instead, I wanted to look at how evolutionary psychology is being used to reinforce dominant social ideologies about gender and sexuality. I do not mean to imply that evolutionary psychology single-handedly generates these ideologies, or that it alone is responsible for perpetuating them, but merely that, in a society that views science as the epitome of "truth," it plays a disproportionately powerful role. And it asserts this role with a relentlessness that is hard to counter without losing one's temper. Indeed, if my own rhetoric in this book becomes relentless at points—if I keep circling back to the same arguments—it is because I am trying to illustrate the doggedness with which the field advances its retrograde pronouncements about gender and sexuality. One of my points is that when readers encounter such pronouncements time after time, they eventually take on the status of uncontested facts even if they in reality are nothing but cultural mythologies that have now—miraculously—acquired the prestigious patina of "science." It is this insidious translation of myths into "facts" that most interests me in this book, for such "facts" shape our social world in ways that in turn have a tremendous impact on how we choose to live our lives.

This is why I end this book—in Chapter 5—by considering the larger cultural implications of gender profiling, proposing that evolutionary arguments about mating behavior serve to buttress a conservative social agenda of traditional marriage and reproductive heterosexuality. It is clear that the more people are opting out of conventional heteronormative arrangements—as large segments of our society are doing right now—the greater the pressure on the social establishment to prove the "naturalness" of these arrangements. That evolutionary psychology participates in this process of naturalization is beyond question, though there are some dissenting voices, such as Ryan and Jethá's. On the most basic level, the core arguments of evolutionary psychology strive to set the clock back on women's liberation, return us to the gender norms of the 1950s, and arrest the cultural shift toward a more fluid understanding of both gender and sexuality. This is one reason it's important for critics such as myself—for gender and sexuality scholars in the humanities—to resist the temptation to dismiss evolutionary theories for the kinds of reasons I've already mentioned: they are simplistic, reductive, suffocating, and terrorizing. I confess that my most consistent reaction to the evolutionary psychological arguments I was studying was an incredulous, "How can *anyone* take this seriously?" The field's tendency for crude oversimplifications made me hesitant about providing counterarguments because it felt that in so doing I was merely validating what really didn't deserve anyone's attention. But the trouble is that in a highly pragmatic society such as modern America, simplicity sells. If evolutionary theories of gender and sexuality have had a much bigger impact in the mainstream realm than the more intricate deconstructive theories produced in the humanities, it's in part because they promise easy, clear-cut answers to life's myriad dilemmas. I wrote this book in part because I've realized how dangerous it is to do nothing while faux-scientific theories of gender differentiation are literally taking over the world.

1

The Myopia of Men vs Women

Darwin conceived his theory in a society that glamorized a colonial military and assigned dutiful, sexually passive roles to proper wives. In modern times, a desire to advertise sexual prowess, justify a roving eye, and disregard the female perspective has propelled some scientists to continue championing sexual selection theory despite criticisms of its accuracy.

JOAN ROUGHGARDEN

1

When it comes to human relationality, evolutionary psychology has a standard narrative—one that has been repeated faithfully since Darwin. According to this narrative, romantic relationships amount to producing as many children as possible. Love, intimacy, and other details of emotional behavior are entirely secondary to the cold economics of reproduction. Gays and lesbians are evolutionary anomalies because their attempts to pass their genes onto the next generation are indirect at best.[1] Straight men and women, in turn, are defined by their conflicting reproductive strategies. Forget about your family background, personal history, education, socialization, and unique existential dilemmas. If you're a heterosexual man, your entire life—including your personality, goals, aspirations, and achievements—is determined by your need to spread your seed as far and wide as possible. And if you're a straight woman, it all comes down to your ovaries, so you might as well stop worrying about having a personality, goals, aspirations, or achievements. Not only is your sole purpose in life to give birth to and take care of babies but you're destined to become obsolete by the age of fifty. Indeed, by your mid-thirties, you might as well slip into your bathtub and slit your wrists because you're nearing the end of your shelf-life.

This way of summing things up may seem extreme, but I trust that by the end of this chapter, the reader will understand why it does not violate—even if it, admittedly, mocks—the core beliefs of evolutionary psychology. Let's begin with the basics. According to the standard narrative of sexual selection, "men court, women choose," which means that just like a peahen chooses a mate from among the peacocks that display their decorated tails for her pleasure, and just like a female gorilla chooses from among the males who seek to impress her with their physical prowess, the human female chooses from among the eligible bachelors who devise ever-flashier ways to parade their investment portfolios, seaside villas, and sports cars in front of her. And the ability to play football, hockey, or other rough sports also helps (tennis and figure skating not so much, except perhaps insofar as they may make you rich). Some evolutionary theorists recognize that even poetry and humor might work on some women—that some women might prefer wit to hundred dollar bills. But the overall point of the standard narrative is that money (and high status) is what works on women.

Given that there may be some women who agree with this view, it's important to be explicit about just how problematic the evolutionary line of reasoning really is: you see, because women merely choose from among the men who compete for their attention, there really is no need for women themselves to develop any of the characteristics that make a person romantically (or otherwise) appealing. In this sense, women are an evolutionary afterthought, a bit like Eve was God's afterthought. Simply put, if you don't have as much intellect, ambition, creativity, imagination, and general competence as men do, it's because you don't need these characteristics to fulfill your reproductive duty. After all, you won't be the one supporting your family (or composing poetry, for that matter). As long as you're young, pretty, and fertile, you're golden. If anything, some of the more complicated human traits might actually get in the way of your evolutionary mission, which—let us recall—is to produce as many of those "good rapists" as your body can handle.

According to this ideology of eager males and choosy females, men will court a porcupine while women will defend their virtue at all costs. We are told that biology is destiny in the sense that more or less every aspect of gender differentiation arises from the simple fact that men have an endless supply of sperm whereas women have a finite number of eggs. This is why men are randy whereas women are coy, why men can't get enough whereas women—unwilling to squander their precious eggs on just anyone—are the careful and chaste sex. The rhetoric of masculine randiness frequently reaches a hyperbolic pitch, as when Geoffrey Miller writes: "Typically, males of most species like sex regardless of their fitness and attractiveness to the females, so they tend to treat female senses as security systems to be cracked. This is why male pigeons strut for hours in front of female pigeon eyes, and why male humans buy fake pheromones and booklets on how to seduce women from the ads of certain magazines."[2] Is this what men in our society "typically" do? Good to know.

And women? When it comes to women, evolutionary psychology hasn't come very far from 1857, when Lord Acton—a famous Victorian physician—declared that "the majority of women (happily for them) are not very much troubled with sexual feelings of any kind. What men are habitually, women are only exceptionally ... there can be no doubt that sexual feeling in the female is in the majority of cases in abeyance ... and even if roused (which in many instances it never can be) is very moderate compared with that of the male ... the best mothers, wives, and managers of households know little or nothing of sexual indulgences. Love of home, children, and domestic duties, are the only passion they feel": "As a general rule, a modest woman seldom desires any sexual gratification for herself. She submits to her husband, but only to please him."[3]

2

Robert Wright begins his discussion of the differences between men and women in *The Moral Animal* by quoting most of Acton's statement. He also seems to agree with Donald Symons who, back in the 1970s, expressed the matter as follows: "among all peoples sexual intercourse is understood to be a service that females render to males."[4] Wright admits that some modern women might hold a slightly different view on sex. But then comes his evolutionary punch line: "Still, the idea that there are *some* differences between the typical male and female sexual appetite, and that the male appetite is less finicky, draws much support from the new Darwinian paradigm."[5] This conviction about the divergent sexual appetites of men and women is repeated from one male-authored evolutionary tome to the next even as some female researchers, such as Sarah Hrdy,[6] have worked overtime to show that it has no basis in the evolutionary record, including in the sexual behavior of our closest primate cousins. Men's sexual urges, we are told again and again, are robust, irrepressible, indiscriminate, and ever-present; women, in contrast, don't have a sexual bone in their bodies. For Wright this explains everything from the sexual double standard to the Madonna-whore complex (more on these below), and it also explains why, as he puts it, there isn't a single culture in which women with unrestrained sexual appetites aren't "regarded as more aberrant than comparably libidinous men" (45). Needless to say, he makes this assessment without any attention to cultural or religious ideology, or without being able to explain why women's sexuality has been so strongly constrained throughout history. If there's nothing to curtail—if women really are the asexual creatures that Wright and his colleagues portray them as—why bother placing so many restrictions on their sexuality?

Surveying the evolutionary literature on human sexuality, I repeatedly had the vision of a bunch of male scientists sitting around a camp fire and taking immense satisfaction in the idea that men are hypersexual studs who will screw pretty much anything that moves whereas women need to be persuaded with lavish dinners and pricey engagement rings (or, if all else fails, physical force). Acton might be forgiven for viewing women as pure creatures who weren't bothered by sexual feelings of any kind. Likewise, Darwin might be exonerated for having bemoaned during one of his expeditions that he had "almost forgotten" what an English lady was—"something very angelic and good."[7] After all, we are all limited by our cultural contexts. But one has to wonder about the persistence of such archaic notions about female sexuality until the beginning of the twenty-first century. In their scathing critique of this aspect of evolutionary theory, Christopher Ryan and Cacilda Jethá point out that it's clear that evolutionary thinkers from Darwin on have been projecting the sexual norms of their cultures—as well as their own personal ideals about proper gendered sexual behavior—onto the evolutionary past, so that "the standard narrative is about as scientifically valid as the story of Adam and Eve ... It hides the truth of human sexuality behind a fig leaf of anachronistic Victorian discretion repackaged as science."[8]

Joan Roughgarden sums up the problem astutely when she states, "Contemporary sexual selection theory predicts that the baseline outcome of social evolution is horny, handsome, healthy warriors paired with discreetly discerning damsels. Deviations from this norm must then be explained away using some special argument."[9] Roughgarden's book, *Evolution's Rainbow*, not only catalogues the immense diversity of gender expressions and sexual practices found in the animal world but also outlines a variety of reasons for why Darwin's theory of sexual selection—the theory that produces the archetypes of the ardent male and the coy female—is scientifically inaccurate even if his general theory of natural selection still holds. One of these reasons is that human mating, like animal mating, is not always primarily undertaken for the purposes of sperm transfer but rather to create and sustain relationships.[10] That is, non-procreative sex did not, as Roughgarden puts it, await "the invention of condoms" (173). Moreover, females of many animal species, like human females, often initiate sex, and sometimes males are known to refuse. In addition, females do not invariably select males for their genetic quality. And there is plenty of evidence for female promiscuity. Finally, same-sex sexuality is common among animals as well as humans. "The sheer number of difficulties with sexual selection theory precludes plugging all the leaks," Roughgarden reasons: "An occasional leak might be fixable, but this many leaks make repair impossible. The theory of sexual selection was taking on water long before evidence was found of widespread homosexuality, but homosexuality is the final torpedo" (171).

When a scientific theory "says something's wrong with so many people, perhaps the theory is wrong, not the people" (1), Roughgarden notes. By now the sexual selection theory has to account for so many exceptions, so many counterexamples, that one has to wonder why it is still the dominant narrative both in college textbooks and evolutionary treatises aimed at the general public. Roughgarden explains that one reason is that evolutionary theory finds it difficult to account for diversity, which it tends to consider irrational. A second reason is that some evolutionary psychologists are invested in perpetuating "ethically dubious gender stereotypes that demean women and anyone else who doesn't identify as a gender-normative heterosexual male" (172). A third reason, in Roughgarden's blunt assessment, is "male hubris": "According to today's version, males are supposed to be more promiscuous than females because sperm are cheap, and hence males are continually roaming around looking for females to fertilize... . A male is naturally entitled to overpower a female's reluctance lest reproduction cease, extinguishing the species" (167–8). If I quote Roughgarden extensively on these points—points that are obvious to anyone who surveys the evolutionary literature with any degree of critical aptitude—it is because I wish to show that we are not here dealing just with a battle between the humanities and the sciences but also with a battle between the defenders of (an obviously inaccurate) scientific status quo and other scientists who believe that scientific hypotheses need to fit the data rather than merely the ideological wishes of those promoting them; we are dealing with the need to think beyond normative social codes and on a level higher than a bedbug.

3

What is equally disturbing about the standard narrative is its conviction that men and women are destined to pursue mutually antagonistic genetic agendas, so that they won't think twice about betraying each other. As Roughgarden observes, "The second contemporary mistake is elevating deceit into an evolutionary principle" (168). Ryan and Jethá in turn state, "Permeating the standard narrative of human sexual evolution is the depressing claim that men and women always have been and always will be locked in erotic conflict. The War Between the Sexes is said to be built into our evolved sexuality: men want lots of no-strings lovers, while women want just a few partners, with as many strings as possible. If a man agrees to be roped into a relationship, the narrative tells us, he'll be hell-bent on making sure his mate isn't risking his genetic investment by accepting *deposits* from other men" (269). This is an accurate synopsis of the field's customary arguments, which consistently pit men and women against each other in a vicious reproductive conflict that can only end in mutual disappointment. The idea that men and women might have common interests—and that they might well prefer to couple up with those who share their values, goals, and basic life approach— seems completely foreign to many evolutionary psychologists, who appear strangely invested in proving that men and women are each other's "natural" enemies. I find this especially bizarre given that the males and females of other species are not invariably portrayed as each other's adversaries. If male and female bonobos generally seem to get along so splendidly, why are human men and women "naturally" so hostile to each other?

Because evolutionary psychology reduces intimate relationships to reproduction, its theories are as unromantic as they are inappropriate for modern, postindustrial contexts. Men, we are told, care primarily about the quantity of children whereas women—due to the fact that they are the ones who get pregnant, give birth to children, and usually also raise them—care about quality. Personally, I would like to meet the twenty-first-century American man who is dying to bring a thousand children into the world. Anecdotal evidence implies that he would be much more likely to want to prevent pregnancy than to knock up every woman he sleeps with. But, according to evolutionary reasoning, this doesn't matter. What matters is that, regardless of what a guy consciously seems to want, he is driven by the same evolutionary imperatives that governed his ancestors millions of years ago; underneath the intricacies of modern romance pulse the same raw reproductive instincts that allowed his ancestors to survive and reproduce. As Wright asserts, the Darwinian view shows that "men (consciously or unconsciously) want as many sex-providing and child-making machines as they can comfortably afford, and women (consciously or unconsciously) want to maximize the resources available to their children" (96).

Wright admits that men's affection for their children somewhat complicates the picture. But even the high MPI (male parental investment) found in human societies doesn't, according to him, change the fact that the "basic underlying dynamic between men and women is mutual exploitation" (58). If men are driven to treat women as sexual and reproductive ATMs, women, the standard narrative informs us, strive to marry a meek, faithful sop with a hefty bank account while constantly looking for an opportunity to cheat with an aggressive alpha male with superior genes. The premise here seems to be that the tasty prospect of superior genes can tempt even the most reticent females to momentarily drop their coy ways. And they are especially likely to stray during ovulation when their chances of getting pregnant are the highest (note to self: if you're going to cheat on your boyfriend, make sure to puncture the condom). That's when they slip into a slinky outfit, spray on a gallon of perfume, paint their nails fire-engine red, put on six-inch heels, false eyelashes, and push-up bras, and head to the nearest country-music joint for a cowboy quickie in the filthy bathroom. When they get pregnant, they let their trusting hubby think that the godly child they're about to give birth to is his, using his money to buy the most expensive baby-carriage they can find. After all, evolutionary psychology assures us that, outside the occasional steamy fling, female sexuality amounts to barely disguised prostitution: women exchange their sexual services for access to men's wealth, status, and other material benefits. As Ryan and Jethá succinctly put it, "Darwin says your mother's a whore. Simple as that" (50).

Women, then, only deign to have sex with their husbands—preferably as seldom and virtuously as humanly possible—because they want to secure a safe haven for their children. Men, in turn, aren't genetically meant to settle down, buy a house, and mow the lawn on a regular basis no matter how much they try to convince themselves that they are capable of love. As Wright boldly announces, masculine feelings of love are a "finely crafted self-delusion" (66). Evolution, in turns out, is so cunning that it allows men to *think* that they are in love when in fact they are merely looking to exploit women. "Human brains evolved not to insulate us from the mandate to survive and reproduce, but to follow it more effectively," Wright writes, so that "as we evolve from a species whose males forcibly abduct females into a species whose males whisper sweet nothings, the whispering will be governed by the same logic as the abduction—it is a means of manipulating females to male ends, and it serves this function" (53–4). That is, the "good rapist" and the guy who whispers sweet nothings to you during intimate moments are ultimately both after the same thing: they want to use you as a vessel for their genes. And males in high MPI human societies are the worst because they are capable of even greater treachery than males in low MPI species. In Wright's view, "Even if long-term investment is their main aim, seduction and abandonment can make genetic sense," so that men are "ever alert for opportunistic sex." The result of all of this—of men's affinity for exploiting women and of women's understandable aversion to being exploited—is, Wright cheerfully tells us, "an evolutionary arms race." "Natural selection," he concludes, "may favor males that are good at deceiving females about their future devotion and favor females that are good at spotting deception; and the better one side gets, the better the other side gets. It's a vicious spiral of treachery and wariness" (61).

Talk about the battle of the sexes! All men are dogs who are only interested in "getting some." And, women, though idiotically prone to romantic swoons that occasionally cloud their judgment, are genetically wired to make sure they don't. And let's not forget that men suffer (oh, how they suffer!) from monogamy whereas women—especially poor ones, the ones who need to be supported by a male breadwinner—would benefit from polygamy, so that we might as well turn modern America into a polygamous society. The anthropological record, Wright declares, reveals that if polygamy were legalized, "the market" would immediately "right itself" so that wealthy, high-status men would have multiple wives (96). I suppose I might buy this if Wright were able to show that the majority of American male lawyers, doctors, and business moguls would like to have three wives to come home to every night. Don't get me wrong. I understand that many men like sexual variety—as do many women. I just don't think that this is the only thing that interests modern men. The ones I've had the privilege to know have been fairly strongly invested in building a high-quality relationship with a woman they feel emotionally connected to. Cheating is common. But so is love, fidelity, and mutual respect. If some women keep saying that "men are basically pigs" (140), as Wright proclaims, perhaps it's in part because evolutionary psychologists, not to mention the self-help authors, magazine columnists, and other cultural authorities who feed on the opinions of these psychologists, are so keen to prove to us that this is what men truly are. For my part, I think we might get a lot further if we admitted that many men—not all, but many—are quite decent and that, like women, they sometimes make mistakes.

4

I don't have a problem with the idea that humans are promiscuous rather than monogamous, though I think this depends on the person. But I do have a problem with Wright's assertion that only men are promiscuous,[11] whereas women won't mind sharing a husband because this—you guessed it—releases them from the tedium of frequent sex! Wright admits that women might sometimes be resistant to sharing a man. "But, typically," he claims, "they would rather do that than live in poverty with the undivided attention of a ne'er-do-well" (95). Here we go again. *Typically?* I recommend conducting a survey in America's poor neighborhoods to find out how women actually feel about this.[12] And, as a "strategy" for reducing American poverty, this one seems particularly bizarre. What, exactly, makes polygamy a more desirable solution than giving poor women greater educational opportunities, jobs that pay a reasonable salary, and affordable health care? The answer seems to have something to do with Wright's explicit affinity for a conservative social agenda that vilifies single-parent households, teen pregnancy, divorce, and female promiscuity—particularly the promiscuity of poor women. It turns out that he would prefer a genuinely polygamous society—one where men get to have multiple wives while women's sexuality is strongly restrained—over our present system of "serial monogamy" because the latter lets poor women have the kind of sex that leads to children being born outside of wedlock. Whenever marital institutions "are allowed to dissolve," Wright earnestly proclaims, "so that divorce and unwed motherhood are rampant, and many children no longer live with both natural parents, there will ensue a massive waste of the most precious evolutionary resource: love. Whatever the relative merits of monogamy and polygyny, what we have now—serial monogamy … is, in an important sense, the worst of all worlds" (104).

For Wright, as for many other social conservatives, serial monogamy is problematic because it lets people disband marriages, which in turn—so the story goes—leads to a host of collective troubles that fray the fabric of American society. Yet Wright admits that polygamy also has its problems because it lets a small number of powerful men steal women "from the jaws" (101) of less fortunate men (the rhetoric of aggression here is somewhat startling but certainly consistent with the "good rapist" ideal). The problem with polygamy, in other words, is not that it forces women to share a husband but that it allows some men to hoard all the women so that weaker men are left out of the mating game. This, in turn, *also* leads to an array of social problems, such as homelessness, alcoholism, violence, and theft, by generating a pool of single men who are not the beneficiaries of women's tempering influence (100). This is why Wright concludes that traditional monogamy—not the serial monogamy of contemporary society but a more strictly Victorian version of monogamy—might be an even better response to our social evils than polygamy. Indeed, like many thinkers of Darwin's England, Wright believes that the role of women is to save men from their risk-seeking, self-destructive behavior. This is why his final solution to our social problems is a return to a pre-1960s social climate which "distributed female resources" (101) more equitably by ensuring that most men had a wife. Never mind that women prior to the 1960s had few educational or professional opportunities. What matters is that every man got to have his own angel of the house.

Let me recap. Polygamy is good for women because it rescues them from poverty (not to mention from the dreariness of regular sex), but it's bad for those men who can't secure mates. Serial monogamy, in turn, is terrible because it leads to the erosion of family values that is at the root of the disintegration of American society. The only solution, then, is a return to *real* monogamy—the kind that makes divorce difficult no matter how much you despise (or even fear) your spouse. As a matter of fact, much of *The Moral Animal* reads like a treatise commissioned by President Bush. And if we dig deeply enough, we discover that the real problem with serial monogamy, for Wright, is that it allows *both* men and women to have multiple sexual partners. The problem, in short, is *female* sexual freedom. Actual polygamy is still palatable to Wright because he likes the idea that men might want multiple partners. The problem with serial monogamy is that it lets women out of the cage so that promiscuity is no longer an exclusive male right. In both polygamy and strictly traditional monogamy, women's sexuality is constrained whereas men are relatively free. While traditional monogamy certainly places constraints on male sexuality as well, the sexual double standard of societies organized around it ensures that men have a degree of leeway for straying. Wright in fact comments approvingly on the countless brothels of Victorian England, for these provided an invaluable service in releasing men from the burden of monogamy while simultaneously ensuring that the virtue of bourgeois wives remained intact (143). Wright is thus quite at peace with the idea that men will always sleep around, even in societies that pretend to be strictly monogamous. But what really frightens him is our current paradigm of serial monogamy where women also get to have sex with more than one guy during their lifetimes.

Objective science? Not a chance.

5

Lest you think I'm exaggerating, let us, once again, turn to Wright's story about what differentiates women from men—a story that consistently uses Victorian England as the gold standard for gender relations. "The Victorians were very clear about their division of aesthetic labor," Wright writes, "and it was consistent with evolutionary psychology: good financial prospects made for an attractive husband, and good looks made for an attractive wife" (109). There you have it, plain and simple: the gender arrangements of Victorian England *fulfilled the scientific predictions of evolutionary psychology*. In this society, Wright notes approvingly, men were gauged by their ability to provide materially for women whereas women were seen "as providing a pleasant visual and auditory environment for a man" (109). That women weren't allowed to vote, inherit, or claim many earning options hardly mattered. What did was that they were "charming" until they married, and that, after marriage, they fulfilled their preordained role of producing a large number of children, as did Darwin's wife, Emma Wedgwood (the couple had seven children). And they of course also faithfully fulfilled their role as the "redeemer" of men, for they were "innocence and purity incarnate." They "could tame the animal in a man" while also rescuing "his spirit from the deadening world of work." But they could "only do this in a domestic context, under the blessing of marriage, and after a long, chaste courtship" (123). Best of all, Victorian England invented the perfect antidote to the natural promiscuity of men: sexual repression and strict divorce laws. "Its particular inhibitions were strikingly well-tailored to the task at hand," Wright explains: "Perhaps the greatest threat to lasting marriage—the temptation of aging, affluent, or high-status men to desert their wives for a younger model—was met with great social firepower" (142–3).

But the English were not stupid. As I mentioned above, London's many brothels—not to mention the country's disempowered house-maids—ensured that men still had an outlet for their uncontrollable sexual urges. This, Wright specifies, was an excellent arrangement because male infidelity doesn't "threaten a marriage so long as it doesn't lead to desertion." After all, "women, more easily than men, can reconcile themselves to living with a mate who has cheated," and "one way to ensure that male infidelity doesn't lead to desertion is to confine it to, well, whores" (143). Those Victorians sure were clever! They figured out what evolutionary psychology was later to prove, namely that women are better off being married to unfaithful husbands than divorced, and that women really don't even mind it that much when their husbands sleep around. That women might have tolerated the double standard and stayed in bad marriages primarily because they had no other place to go, no other way to support themselves or their children, never occurs to Wright, who proclaims, "The double standard may not be fair, but it does have a kind of rationale. Adultery per se is a greater threat to monogamy when the wife commits it (Again: the average man will have much more trouble than the average woman continuing a marriage with a mate known to have been unfaithful)" (144). How convenient for men. They can rest assured that when they cheat on their wives, these wives won't be genuinely upset (even if they dare to complain a little) whereas they themselves get to rant and rave when their wives cheat on them; after all, evolutionary psychology proves that it is "natural" for men to suffer from sexual betrayal more than it is for women.

I would say that this is patriarchy having its cake and eating it too. Wright qualifies himself by specifying that this "is *not* an argument on behalf of the double standard, or any other particular aspect of Victorian morality" (144). Well, what is it then? What could possibly justify these kinds of "scientific" generalizations about men and women? Wright is not here ironically describing a long-lost era. The thrust of his argument is that, in evolutionary psychological terms, we would do well to reinstate some of the moral arrangements of Victorian England. After all, the rampant sexual freedom of our era has not only led to skyrocketing divorce rates and all the ensuing social problems I have already mentioned but also—and I'm not sure whether to laugh, cry, or throw frying pans—*a lack of respect for women* (135). You see, back in Victorian England, women may have been sexually repressed and socioeconomically disempowered, but at least they were *respected*. The lax divorce laws of our time, not to mention confused, misguided feminists, are to blame for our current situation where men can't be forced to marry the women they sleep with. And the feminists are especially culpable: "They preached the innate symmetry of the sexes in all major arenas, including sex," with the unfortunate result that many young women thought that they "could follow their sexual attractions and disregard any vague visceral wariness" (135–6). That is, feminists brainwashed young women with their ideology of sexual freedom, which explains why women in our society are no longer respected.

Let's get this right: Victorian patriarchy = respect for women; feminism = disrespect for women. So it's really *feminism* that is oppressive for women! The reason Wright upholds this absurd view is that he seems to genuinely believe that sleeping with a guy who has no intention of marrying her is the worst thing any woman could ever do. He seems to think that such a woman will forever suffer from the disgrace and emotional turmoil of this careless act. Would someone please tell this dinosaur that times have changed and that many women don't actually in any way suffer from sex, even from extramarital sex? Would someone please tell him that many women these days are not in the least bit interested in getting a marriage proposal from every guy who shares their bed? And would someone please tell him that the fact that a man doesn't want to marry a woman he sleeps with doesn't automatically mean that he *disrespects* her. Indeed, in countries where a large number of people never marry (yet have a lot of sex), such as the Scandinavian nations, respect for women is a social given. In other words, there is absolutely no correlation between sexual freedom and disrespect for women. If a vestige of this correlation is still discernible in the United States, it is because the United States remains closer to Victorian morality and religious ideology than Scandinavia. That is, Victorian morality is hardly the solution to women being disrespected; rather, it is a big part of the problem in the first place in the sense that only a culture that thinks that sexually liberated women are sluts can make women feel badly about sex.

The reason Wright can't understand why feminists would want sexual freedom for women—and why he thinks that "a woman voting for divorce is like a turkey voting for Christmas" (134)—is that he is so stuck on the archaic ideal of the coy female that he assumes that a premarital orgasm will make a woman feel dirty, disgraced, and disrespected, that sex out of wedlock somehow scars a woman for life. He assumes this because he believes that the gender roles of Victorian England reflect the *innate* natures of men and women, so that women somehow made a mistake when they chose to follow the feminist doctrine of sexual symmetry. Contraception and other social changes are also a factor, of course. But Wright takes special delight in the idea that feminists have actively "aided" in the exploitation of women (137). And he also blames feminism for the difficulty of having "an honest discussion" about the essential differences between the sexes, for it's the wrath of feminists that has historically kept upright scientists from advancing their Darwinian views (137). Even now, Wright bemoans, the "truth sometimes gets sugarcoated": "It is often tempting, for example, to downplay differences between men and women. Regarding the more polygamous nature of men, politically sensitive Darwinian social scientists may say things like ... . 'Remember, behavior is influenced by the local environment and conscious choice. Men don't *have* to philander.' True—and crucially important. But many of our impulses are, by design, very strong, so any force that is to stifle them may have to be pretty harsh" (150–1). Feminists, then, are to blame for the fact that, as a society, we don't simply just admit that men's philandering nature can't be changed, and that consequently, the only thing to be done (short of legalizing polygamy) is to return to Victorian sexual norms.

Wright approvingly quotes Lawrence Stone, who wrote in 1977: "It is an ironic thought that just at the moment when some thinkers are heralding the advent of the perfect marriage based on full satisfaction of the sexual, emotional, and creative needs of both husband and wife, the proportion of marital breakdowns, as measured by the divorce rate, is rising rapidly" (142). Wright never considers the possibility that the rising divorce rate might be a small price to pay for more rewarding, more libidinous, and more egalitarian marriages; he never considers the possibility that people are getting divorced precisely because they expect more of their marriages. He in fact appears to assume that an unhappy marriage is invariably a superior option to divorce. In this, as in so many other things, he seems to agree with the Pope: "If we are really serious about restoring the institution of monogamy, *combat*, it seems, will ... be the operative word. In 1966, one American scholar, looking back at the sense of shame surrounding the sexual impulse among Victorian men, discerned 'a pitiable alienation on the part of a whole class of men from their own sexuality.' He's certainly right about the alienation. But the 'pitiable' part is another question. At the other end of the spectrum from 'alienation' is 'indulgence'—obedience to our sexual impulses as if they were the voice of the Noble Savage" (145). I take back the comparison to the Pope. Even the Pope wouldn't have thrown in the line about the Noble Savage. But let's complete the thought, just so we know what we are dealing with: "A quarter-century of indulging these impulses has helped bring a world featuring, among other things: lots of fatherless children; lots of embittered women; lots of complaints about date rape and sexual harassment; and the frequent sight of lonely men renting X-rated videotapes while lonely women abound. It seems harder these days to declare the Victorian war against male lust 'pitiable'" (145).

6

Pay attention, fellas! If you thought evolutionary psychology was safe for you, think again. For the more moralistic of its representatives, there is a straight, if somewhat torturous, line of logic that leads from the randy male to the sexually shackled Victorian husband, the reasoning being that the only way to tame the naturally wild male libido—and therefore to guarantee the survival of civilized society—is to subject it to an almost unbearable degree of repression. As for women, Wright's abiding faith in the dichotomy between the randy male and the coy female leads him to advise playing hard to get, for in so doing women supposedly capitalize on their chastity:

> Consider the sexual double standard. The most obvious Darwinian explanation is that men were designed, on the one hand, to be sexually loose themselves yet, on the other, to relegate sexually loose women ("whores") to a low moral status—even, remarkably, as those same men encourage those same women to be sexually loose. Thus, to the extent that men shape the moral code, it may include a double standard. Yet on closer inspection, this quintessentially male judgment is seen to draw *natural* support from other circles: the parents of young, pretty girls, who encourage their daughters to save their favors for Mr. Right (that is, to remain attractive targets for male parental investment), and who tell their daughters it's "wrong" to do otherwise; the daughters themselves, who, while saving their virtue for a high bidder, self-servingly and moralistically disparage the competing, low-rent alternatives ... There is a virtual *genetic conspiracy to depict sexually loose women as evil*. (146; emphasis added)

The double standard's condemnation of female promiscuity, then, is not a result of patriarchy but merely *nature's* crafty way of ensuring that women end up married so that they can produce the well-adjusted children they desire (148). In Wright's words, its "harsh treatment of female promiscuity may be a natural by-product of human nature" (147). That is, when well-meaning parents advise their daughters to wait for Mr. Right, they do so for natural rather than cultural reasons. Even better, the moral judgment that loose women are "evil" hides a *genetic* imperative to guide women into monogamous sexual arrangements; it may seem unfair, but it has an evolutionary rationale. Wright claims that he is not placing a moralistic judgment on women who choose to have sex out of wedlock (something I find hard to believe at this point in the argument) but merely suggesting that it makes no evolutionary sense for them to do so. As he puts it, he is offering "self-help, not moral philosophy" (147). And like many actual self-help authors, he seems to think that because men desperately want sex, and because women could well live without it, women might as well barter with it to ensure that men don't think of them as sluts; he seems to think that women should invariably withhold sex in the early stages of courtship to ensure that men make a commitment to them rather than merely bedding them for pleasure. Indeed, like many self-help authors, Wright is convinced that sleeping with a man too soon will guarantee that a woman will get miserable rather than married—the assumption being (needless to say) that every woman is dying to get married.

In building his ever-so-enlightened argument, Wright starts from the premise that evolutionary psychology lends strong support to the so-called Madonna-whore dichotomy whereby men do not marry the women they like to have sex with (another important note to self: the guy who doesn't like to have sex with me is husband-material). "The Madonna-whore distinction has the earmarks of an efficient adaptation," Wright explains, for it "leads men to shower worshipful devotion on the sexually reserved women they want to invest in—exactly the sort of devotion these women will demand before allowing sex. And it lets men guiltlessly exploit the women they don't want to invest in, by consigning them to a category that merits contempt. This general category—the category of reduced, sometimes almost subhuman, moral status—is ... *a favorite tool of natural selection*" (73–4; emphasis added). That is, natural selection—rather than, say, cultural norms—is what dictates that sexually loose women ("whores") are reduced to an "almost subhuman" category. As a result, the last thing any sane woman would want to do would be to let slip that she actually likes sex. In contrast, "If a Madonna-whore switch is indeed built into the male brain, then a woman's early reticence can lastingly affect a man's view of her. He is more likely to respect her in the morning—and perhaps for many years to come—if she doesn't weaken under his advances. He may *say* 'I love you' to various women he yearns for, and he may mean it; but he may be more likely to keep meaning it if he doesn't get them right away. There may have been a bit of wisdom in the Victorian disapproval of premarital sex" (123).

Wright sure loves those Victorians! He informs us that the great punishment awaiting a sexually adventurous Victorian woman was "permanent consignment" to the whore side of the Madonna-whore divide (29). Likewise, the hard "evolutionary" reality of today's society is that men continue to recognize the difference between a wife and a slut: "The fact is that many men still speak openly about 'sluts' and their proper use: great for recreation, but not for marriage" (30). Even worse, women's willingness to make themselves available leads to "what the Victorians would have called ongoing moral decline": "A proliferation of low-cut dresses and come-hither looks might send the visual cues that discourage male commitment; and as men, thus discouraged, grow less deferential toward women, and more overtly sexual, low-cut dresses might further proliferate" (141). So low-cut dresses result from men's disrespect for women? And here I thought that they came from Donna Karan. But let's not miss Wright's main point, namely that any active display of female sexual desire results in her being disrespected, even deemed "contemptible," so ladies, once again, you have a clear-cut choice: sex or respect. The possibility of the two coexisting never occurs to Wright, who seems most interested in reversing the moral decrepitude of modern times by a motto that runs through much of evolutionary psychological theorizing on gender relations: "The more Madonnaish the women, the more daddish and less caddish the men, and thus the more Madonnaish the women" (141).

If you've ever wondered where our self-help authors and magazine columnists get the idea that women should play hard to get, now you know: from evolutionary psychologists enamored of Victorian morality. This venerable source believes that the tactical value of women's sexuality lies in the fact men can't live without sex, and that women can therefore get what they want—*which, apparently, is never sex*—by rationing it. A man's passion is fanned to the pitch of everlasting love when it is not immediately quenched because, as Wright posits, a chaste courtship "helps move a woman into the 'Madonna' part of his mind" (124). A smart woman's plan therefore runs as follows: "if you want to hear vows of eternal devotion ... don't sleep with your man until the honeymoon" (139). Wright labels this "the Emma strategy," after Darwin's wife, for Emma Wedgwood, like the rest of Victorian women, knew that—and note how seamlessly "science" meets social cliché—"a man won't buy the cow if he can get the milk for free" (139). Wright acknowledges that some modern women might find the Emma strategy beneath their dignity or even a bit reactionary. But all in all, he has faith that evolutionary psychology will help women recognize the "harsh truths" about human nature, particularly male nature, so that they will come to understand that it's in their self-interest to move toward greater sexual "austerity" (140).

Evolutionary psychology thus helps modern women become as virtuous as Emma Wedgwood. In contrast, Wright concedes that giving "men marriage tips is a little like offering Vikings a free booklet titled 'How Not to Pillage'" (139). That is, red-blooded men will flee from marriage like from the plague. While brides might also have jitters, "their doubt seems more often to be whether their choice of a lifelong mate is the right one." For men, in contrast, "the panic isn't essentially related to any particular prospective mate; it is the *concept* of a lifelong mate that is at some level frightening" (114). Men, it comes as no surprise to anyone, are afraid of entrapment; they fear commitment. And when they hit middle age, they start to yearn for their freedom, for "the interests of husband and wife may diverge as time goes by. The older the children ... and the older the wife, the less support a man's devotion gets from his evolutionary heritage. More and more of the harvest has been reaped; the ground is less and less fertile; it may be time to move on" (126). I may have sounded a bit harsh in the introduction to this book when I said that I found some of the evolutionary psychological arguments childish. But it's impossible to avoid this impression when faced with pronouncements such as the ones I have here foregrounded. What kind of science *is* this? It appears to be primarily concerned with elevating the most worn-out of our social platitudes to a scientific status so as to ensure that such platitudes retain their power. Why? To keep all those confused, misguided feminists from achieving the more egalitarian ethos of gender relations they are after? To keep women from enjoying the lustful sexuality that is their birthright? Or to keep men from recognizing that the more social freedom women enjoy, the better their own relationships, including their sex lives, are likely to be?

7

One of the peculiarities of Wright's argument is that though he readily admits that monogamy is not natural—"and emphatically not for men" (130)—he wants all of us to end up in enduring monogamous marriages (in the understanding that the double standard gives men the option of straying). In this manner, he joins the chorus of social voices telling us that even a marriage that feels like a life-sentence to the Russian gulag is better than not being married. The ardor of new love, Wright warns us, is sure to fade, "and the marriage will then live or die on respect, practical compatibility, simple affection, and (these days, especially) determination" (131). We are all familiar with this line of reasoning, for it is a common pearl of wisdom distributed to those about to get married in our society. Many of us in fact accept without argument Wright's conclusion, namely that this kind of love—love based on hard work—is "more impressive" than love based on passion (131). Yet if we pause to give the matter a moment's thought, this is actually quite a strange assertion. Why, exactly, is a relationship based on tremendous effort more impressive, or more noble, than a passionate but fleeting love affair? Why is a durable but ultimately unrewarding (or even deadening) relationship better than an alliance that may not last but that both parties experience as satisfying and deeply transformative? Given that so many children suffer in unhappy marriages, and that there is even a lot of child abuse going on in the folds of married life, there isn't even much foundation for the belief that marriage invariably benefits children. Why, then, see it as a tragedy, as Wright does, that the American divorce rate has doubled since the social upheavals of the 1960s?

I don't have anything against those who choose marriage as a way of organizing their lives, for obviously there are many fulfilling marriages in the world. But it may be worth asking why—as a society—we place so much faith in the idea that marriage is the best way to go about intimate relationships. I'll return to this question in Chapter 5. In the present context, let me merely note that Wright makes no secret that his valorization of marriage arises primarily from his belief that stable marriages lead to a more stable social organization. Like many other social conservatives, he understands that married people are more predictable, and therefore more easy to manipulate, than those whose relational lives are more inconsistent. That is, *unlike* most of his colleagues in evolutionary psychology—who (falsely) insist that their theories have no direct moral, social, or political implications—Wright readily admits that his interpretation of evolutionary psychology has an ideological agenda. In other words, while he defends the "objectivity" of his science, and while he pays lip service to the idea that we are not obliged to adopt the values of natural selection as our own (31), he simultaneously suggests that in many instances it would be smart for us to do so. This is why his book reads more like a family values primer than a scientific discussion—one that relies on the holy trinity of the nuclear family, reproductive sexuality, and the chaste, all-suffering wife who agrees to tolerate the fact that her husband consorts with sexy (but filthy) "whores."

To his credit, Wright also concedes what many of his colleagues do not, namely that one can't first say that men are genetically wired to cheat and then berate (some) men for using this statement as a justification for cheating; he concedes that claiming that something is "natural" is akin to saying that "the impulse runs so deep as to be practically irresistible" (345). In other words, he admits that it's impossible to keep people from sliding from "it's natural" to "I can't help it." In this sense, evolutionary psychology can't dodge ethical concerns no matter how much it tries to present itself as value-neutral science divorced from the social world; it can't deny that its arguments can be used to excuse dubious behavior. As Wright concludes, "The truth depends on what we say the truth is. If men are told that the impulse to philander is deeply 'natural,' essentially irrepressible, then the impulse—for those men, at least—may indeed be so" (358).[13] One of the virtues of Victorian morality, in Wright's view, was precisely that it gave men the opposite message: it gave them a strict moral code that emphasized the power of culture over nature. The Victorians, Wright posits, were "products of their environment, of a time and place where belief in the possibility of self-control was in the air— as were (therefore) stiff moral sanctions against those who failed at the task" (358). As we have seen, this, for Wright, represents a strong argument for trying to reinstitute some of the lost tenets of Victorian morality, including the prohibitions that discouraged men from cheating on their wives (even if some slippage was admissible); it represents an argument for returning to the gentle-manly manners and chaste feminine airs of Victorian England.

I find it interesting that a thinker who, in all earnestness, claims that modern American men and women can't transcend the basic sexual impulses that governed the behavior of their ancestors millions of years ago *also* claims that Victorian men were (for the most part) held in check by their social environment. On the one hand, Wright is saying that the Victorian social ethos had such an immense impact on men that it managed to overpower their genetic impulses. On the other, he implies that modern social organization has not made any kind of a difference in how men and women function, so that, as we have discovered, men are still driven by the evolutionary imperative to exploit women while women are still coyly protecting their precious eggs. That is, Victorian morality was all-powerful but the new romantic culture of our era—a culture that, among other things, values the equality of men and women—supposedly hasn't made any difference in how men and women act.

I find it extraordinary that Wright believes that the social organization of modern America hasn't in any way altered the underlying genetic natures of men and women but that reverting to Victorian morality would immediately do so. Perhaps this is because, as I showed above, he believes that Victorian morality captured much of the intrinsic natures of men and women, so that the only thing that remained to be fixed was the excessive randiness of men. But I'm inclined to believe that the contradiction is better explained by the fact that Wright is utterly resistant to social explanations of human behavior when they do not suit his ideological agenda but quite amenable to them the minute they support this agenda. It's because he is not in the least bit interested in seeing a gender-egalitarian social ethos win the day that he refuses to acknowledge that this ethos might have some power against the inequalitarian legacies of our evolutionary past (legacies that Wright takes for granted but that, as we'll see later, are by no means a scientific given). In contrast, because he would be perfectly happy with a conservative moral order that replicates the social mores of Victorian England, he is willing to grant Victorian culture a tremendous degree of influence. The same author who has spent an entire book arguing that modern men and women are trapped in their evolutionary heritage—that it's useless to pretend that things have really changed since men forcefully abducted women and relegated them to the status of "sex-providing and child-making machines"—is suddenly, in the context of Victorian morality, eager to declare that "the fact that some people's sexual impulses get diverted from typical channels is just another tribute to the malleability of the human mind. Given a particular set of environmental influences, it may do any number of things" (385). Adapting to a more egalitarian environment of gender parity apparently isn't one of these things.

8

As we'll see in the next chapter, it's common for evolutionary psychologists to resort to cultural explanations whenever this suits them yet completely discount such explanations when it doesn't. But what interests me here is Wright's admission that evolutionary psychology will affect "moral and political discourse for decades to come" (363), for this is—as I've already started to suggest—an atypical admission. E. O. Wilson, the father of modern socio-biology, was still fairly open about the ideological commitments of his new "science." But after the scorching critiques of the 1970s, which accused sociobiology of being a racist, right-wing ideology, most of the field's practitioners have been keen to pepper their theories with frequent disclaimers about social implications. These usually take the following form: "Saying that X is true isn't the same thing as saying that it's socially desirable." That is, we are supposed to believe that a choir of evolutionary psychologists chanting that women are naturally coy isn't the same thing as them arguing that women *should* be coy. Call me a cynic, but I just don't buy it, particularly as there is little scientific evidence to suggest that women in fact *are* "naturally" coy, so that this claim is an ideological fabrication to begin with. As far as I can tell, the scientific "method" used to validate it consists of repeating it so often that it starts to sound true. This is exactly how ideology functions: the more frequently we hear something, the more likely we are to think it's valid. What begins as a particular way of looking at the world congeals into an apparently incontestable belief. After a while, we forget how this belief came into being and come to view it as how things naturally just "are." This, I would argue, is precisely what has happened with the trope of female coyness.

I'll come back to female coyness in Chapter 4. For now, let's stick to Wright's unusual confession that evolutionary psychology *does* have clear social ramifications. He for instance concedes that evolutionary psychology hugely erodes the notion of free will. Darwin "got the basic idea," Wright explains, namely that "free will is an illusion, brought to us by evolution. All the things we are commonly blamed or praised for—ranging from murder to theft to Darwin's eminently Victorian politeness—are the result not of choices made by some immaterial 'I' but of physical necessity" (350). Moreover, Darwin recognized that this degree of biological determinism might threaten the moral fiber of his society by weakening the ideal of ethical accountability. But he wasn't overly concerned because he understood that as long as this knowledge was "confined to a few English gentlemen," and didn't infect the masses, everything would be fine (351). The trouble right now, according to Wright, is that the masses are "getting infected" (351). In modern times, one doesn't have to be a gentleman to keep up with the advances of science, to realize that scientists are, for example, linking crime to low levels of serotonin. And let's not forget about the so-called "Twinkie defense": the idea that a junk-food diet can leave a person with a diminished capacity to think clearly, so that if he murders someone, he can't be charged with premeditation; he can't be held fully responsible for his crime (352).

Wright's rhetoric of gentlemen versus the masses accentuates the elitist (white masculinist) tone of evolutionary psychology. But otherwise he is for once saying something that I can actually agree with, namely that it's useless for evolutionary psychologists to pretend that their science doesn't have social effects. Indeed, he warns us, "The landslide of news about the biology of behavior is just beginning. People, by and large, haven't succumbed to it and concluded that we're all mere machines. So the notion of free will lives on. But it shows signs of shrinking. Every time a behavior is found to rest on chemistry, someone tries to remove it from the realm of volition" (351–2). Wright goes on to envision a world in which women resort to the premenstrual syndrome, men to high levels of testosterone, and rapists to their need for an endorphin high as ways to insulate themselves from criminal charges. And these defenses might actually work because, as Wright acknowledges, biochemistry is "what really gets a jury's attention" (352). Already, he specifies, an expert witness has traced something called an "action-addict syndrome"—a dependency on the thrill of danger—to "endorphins, which the criminal desperately craves, and obtains via crime" (352). "If defense lawyers get their way and we persist in removing biochemically mediated actions from the realm of free will," Wright concludes, "then within decades that realm will be infinitesimal" (352–3).

9

I agree with Wright that this doesn't mean that scientists shouldn't study evolution or build scientific hypotheses. But I would want evolutionary psychologists to be a great deal more careful about what counts as science. Wright declares that self-criticism "is not an essential part of science" (149). This is a startling claim for any academic to make.[14] And it seems particularly problematic in a society that views science as a source of truth. Take the kinds of gender stereotypes that Wright so blithely endorses: the more such stereotypes are perpetuated in the name of science, the more social legitimacy they gain, sometimes even producing the very behaviors that they are supposed to "explain." That is, if a given man or a given woman buys the evolutionary line about gender, that man or woman might work quite hard to make sure that he or she lives up to the image that the stereotype paints. No one, after all, likes to think of him- or herself as a freak of nature. Against this backdrop, it's genuinely disturbing that Wright proclaims to be doing science at the same time as he admits, for instance, that to call his theory of the Madonna-whore divide "speculative would almost be an understatement" (141). As a theorist, I understand that speculation is an important part of knowledge production. But speculation needs some critical distance from dominant social ideologies: it can't be a matter of translating cultural norms into scientific paradigms. And it certainly can't be a matter of positing that these paradigms capture the "truth" about men and women, as Wright repeatedly does (recall, for example, his argument about "truth" being sugarcoated because of feminist wrath).

Generally speaking, in a field where theories routinely get overturned by new ones within the span of a decade, it's hardly reasonable to grant one's current argument the status of a scientific "fact." I found it striking that most of the authors I studied acknowledge that earlier theories in evolutionary biology were somewhat biased, particularly in relation to gender. Author after author admits that Darwin was mistaken about many of his pronouncements about female behavior, and that the early thinkers who followed in his footsteps were similarly corrupted by their social context.[15] Yet each author proceeds to advance many of the same ideas that Darwin and his followers held, and they do so seemingly without any awareness of the obvious inconsistency of their reasoning. They are relatively good at pointing out the biases of previous thinkers but largely oblivious to their own. Wright, for instance, maintains that sociobiological discussions of the 1970s were somewhat questionable in depicting "men as wild, libidinous creatures who roamed the landscape looking for women to dupe and exploit." Women, in turn, were portrayed "as dupes and exploitees" (86). If so, what could possibly justify recycling these very same representations a quarter of a century later, as Wright himself does? This is why I cannot but agree with Ryan and Jethá who remark that, despite their years of training, "even scientific types slip into thinking they are observing something when in fact they are simply projecting their biases and ignorance" (20). And unfortunately, when it comes to the standard narrative, we are dealing with "contemporary moralistic bias packaged to look like science and then projected upon the distant screen of prehistory, rationalizing the present while obscuring the past. Yabba dabba doo" (149).

All theories have the power to impact our behavior and belief systems, but I'm inclined to agree with Wright that genetic theories are particularly authoritative. Our culture tends to assume that the natural order of things is the rightful order of things. This is why it is important to remain vigilant about how one portrays this order. As the philosopher Philip Kitcher argued already in the 1980s, evolutionary psychology—at that time still usually called sociobiology—should be very careful about the kinds of assertions it makes, for there is a good chance that these assertions will govern not only cultural beliefs but also social policy.[16] Many other scientific endeavors don't have such a direct bearing on our cultural organization, so that a faulty hypothesis about worm holes hardly impacts the way we live our lives. But a faulty evolutionary hypothesis does have such a bearing. And while the same thing could be said about social scientific hypotheses, the matter is not as grave because the social sciences do not carry the same cultural weight as do the "actual" sciences (which evolutionary psychology stubbornly insists on being): a claim about gender made by a sociologist won't have the same influence as one made by a scientist for the simple reason that our society has the kind of faith in scientific inquiry that it does not have in other types of inquiry. Readers are much more likely to think that a sociological argument is

relativistic and influenced by the researcher's agenda than they are
to think the same about evolutionary arguments. This is why it's
so dangerous for this science to be wrong; it's why I would urge its
practitioners to exercise some caution, and perhaps even some of
that "self-criticism" that Wright thinks is so unnecessary in scientific research.

Evolutionary psychologists may try to uphold the difference
between description (how things are) and prescription (how they
should be). In other words, they may try to avoid the so-called
"naturalistic fallacy" of assuming that what (naturally) *is* is what
should be. To return to the example I gave above, they may try
to tell me that saying that women are naturally coy isn't the same
thing as saying that they should be coy. But this line of reasoning
is useless in a culture that thinks that what is biological is more
"real" (and thus more legitimate) than what is merely socially
constructed. But perhaps I'm being unfair? Perhaps I shouldn't
hold scientists responsible for how their theories are appropriated
by the wider cultural environment? However, this doesn't take
care of the deeper problem, namely that—as I've attempted to
illustrate—there is nothing impartial about evolutionary theories
of gender difference to begin with. This is a field where the line
between facts and values is blurry at best, so that the problem is
ultimately not just that its ideas are being distorted by non-scien-
tists but that the ideas themselves are fundamentally distorted.
Indeed, in the case of someone like Wright, I found no evidence
whatsoever of any attempt to resist the lure of the naturalistic
fallacy. This is not a thinker who is worried about his ideas being
misused by the reading public. Rather, he is someone who has no
qualms about using his "science" as a means of promoting his
particular worldview among that public.

Wright points out that evolutionary psychology has recently
experienced an important shift due to the growing number of
female Darwinians, "who have patiently explained to their male
colleagues how a woman's psyche looks from the inside" (86).
Wright presents this as a sign of progress, but to my mind, it merely
highlights the problem that has plagued the field since Darwin: as
I have already noted, a scientific theory that depends on the gender
of the scientist cannot by definition be objective. To be sure, male
and female scientists might focus on slightly different things. And,
to be sure, the personality of the researcher always enters the

scientific picture in one way or another. But something seems to be drastically amiss when male and female scientists arrive at mutually exclusive hypotheses, so that, for example, the male scientists are saying that women are sexually reticent whereas the female scientists are saying that they are not. Indeed, there is something alarming about the very notion that female scientists need to "explain" to male scientists how a "woman's psyche looks from the inside." This assumes not only that all women have the same psyche but also that this is a science that depends on an "insider" look at things: the idea that only men can understand men and only women can understand women. This has all the absurdity of saying that I can't comprehend the philosophy of Jean-Paul Sartre because he was a guy.

The troubled history of evolutionary psychology has made the field unusually defensive so that while most other academic fields, including some of the sciences, have in recent decades emphasized that knowledge production is rarely entirely unbiased, evolutionary psychology appears to have a strong investment in asserting that its findings are "hard" science, and therefore entirely neutral and devoid of ideological lapses. Yet this is a science that is light-years from being to able to declare this, for it is filled with unproven hypotheses, unfounded conjectures, and careless analytic thinking. And what is perhaps most disconcerting is that many of its claims are so crude that I can honestly say that my nineteen-year-old humanities undergraduates have a more sophisticated understanding of gender and sexuality than some of the most famous proponents of evolutionary psychology. Unlike my undergraduates, who work very hard to question dogmatic cultural assumptions, much of evolutionary psychology trades in clichés, caricatures, and juvenile stereotypes. Unlike real science, which understands that "findings" that merely duplicate social prejudices are a mockery of science, this so-called science is often—not invariably, but often—the very antithesis of real science. It's stuck in a state of arrested development, unable to embrace intellectual complexity or even tolerate the idea of it. If anything, it seems to perceive any request for complexity as a direct threat to its sacrosanct territory. In this sense, the problem is not just that much of it is ideological drivel masquerading as science but that the more we, as a society, get seduced by its one-dimensional claims, the more bankrupt our thinking about gender and sexuality becomes.

2

The Ideology of Gender Difference

Men want sex objects; women want status objects.
HELEN FISHER

1

Fisher writes these words in the context of summarizing David Buss's argument about human mating behavior in *The Evolution of Desire*. It's an accurate summary. Though Buss's rhetoric is less hyperbolic, less moralistic, than that of Wright, and though he shies away from the explicitly misogynistic tone of the latter, his argument follows the main outlines of the standard narrative I have delineated. Most importantly for our purposes, he makes the by now familiar claim about women trading their sexuality for men's material resources. Buss bases his observations on an international study—conducted by a team of researchers overseen by him—of the mating preferences of 10,047 people in thirty-seven countries.[1] This may seem genuinely impressive, unless one realizes that large sample sizes tend to produce statistically significant differences—in this instance, gender differences—more or less automatically, that it is in the nature of large sample sizes to generate the very variation that one is looking for. In other words, the methodology chosen for the task was, in this case, designed to yield the desired result, namely the "proof" that men and women differ significantly in their mate choice preferences. In addition, in social scientific research that relies on statistics, the temptation to use relatively minor statistical variations to back up major hypotheses is ever-present, for it is clearly sexier to be able to assert a positive finding than it is to admit that one's data doesn't yield such a finding.[2] This is one reason that complexity often gets lost in such research.

I would like to use Buss's data to illustrate that the very decision to focus on gender differences is an ideological one—that, given his data, he could have just as easily written a book that tells us that men and women are essentially quite similar in their approaches to love, romance, marriage, and relationships. That Buss chose to highlight differences rather than similarities tells us quite a bit about the clandestine commitments of evolutionary psychology, including its stubborn adherence to the idea that gender differences arise primarily from the conflicting reproductive strategies employed by men and women—that they are primarily biological rather than cultural. Among other things, Buss's book showcases how easy it is to present data selectively in order to lend credibility to the scenario one wishes to promote—how easy it is, say, to over-accentuate some aspects of the data while downplaying or even omitting other aspects in order to advance the preferred interpretation. Buss's statistical results may be formidable, but so are his efforts to force them into a rigidly dichotomous account of what men and women, respectively, want from their partners. Indeed, his entire argument hinges on two early chapters—entitled "What Women Want" and "Men Want Something Else"—that set the stage for the notion that the desires of men and women are inherently at odds with each other. And he goes to inordinate lengths to ensure that his interpretation of the data supports this (rather predictable) organizational choice. Worst of all, since Buss assures us that he is presenting us with "the *universal* preferences that men and women display for particular characteristics in a mate" (8; emphasis added), we are asked to accept the idea that *all* men and women fall tidily into his binary structure.

Buss's assertions about gender differences in *The Evolution of Desire* are based on studies conducted prior to 1990, and this includes the international study undertaken by his team that I already alluded to. The revised 2003 version of the book that I'm using includes some later materials, but the datedness of Buss's main references might still raise questions about the continued relevance of his arguments. It may be useful, then, to recall that—as I already mentioned in the introduction to this book—Buss's principal claims about men and women's mate preferences remain largely unchanged in his 2011 *Dangerous Passion*. Indeed, in this later text he continues to rely on the same international study that jolted him into prominence in the 1990s. I suppose this shouldn't surprise us, given his insistence on the universality of his findings, for with the expectation of universality almost inevitably comes the expectation of longevity in the sense that we tend to think that what is universally valid is valid for all times to come.

What, then, does Buss think women (universally) want in a man? Quite a few things, it turns out: wealth, social status, mature age, ambition and industriousness, dependability and stability, intelligence, compatibility, physical size and strength, good health, as well as love and commitment. At first glance, this doesn't seem too unreasonable. But the same can't be said of men's wants, for these are rather rudimentary: youth, beauty, and a 0.70 waist-to-hip ratio. So important are these traits to men, in fact, that "physical beauty," "body shape," and "physical appearance" merit three separate sections in the chapter on what men want. And these three sections, along with "chastity and fidelity," sum up the entirety of men's desires. Stripped to its bare bones, Buss's argument, as he himself summarizes it, is that "at this point in history, we can no longer doubt that men and women differ in their preferences for a mate: primarily for youth and physical attractiveness in one case, and for status, maturity, and economic resources in the other" (211). In the course of his discussion, he occasionally admits that his emphasis on differences obscures similarities between men and women.[3] And he also acknowledges at points that evolutionary psychology alone cannot explain everything about gendered behavior. But the overall thrust of his book is that, when it comes to mate selection, men and women have next to nothing in common and that the differences between them are genetic.

2

The Evolution of Desire is aimed at a lay audience, which made me skeptical about some of its easy generalizations. The book's binary structure seemed so drastically simplified that I decided to veer off my focus on mainstream evolutionary psychology and to consult some of Buss's academic articles on the same topic. These articles—published by Buss and his associates in *Behavior and Brain Sciences* and *Journal of Cross-Cultural Psychology*—rely on the same data as his mainstream tome. But, as I suspected, they present a very different picture.[4] When talking to his fellow scientists, Buss is relatively cautious about the conclusions that can be drawn from his data. To begin with, he admits that gender differences accounted for very little of the variation in mate preferences: "In general, *the effects of sex on mate preferences were small compared with those of culture. Across the 31 mate characteristics, sex accounted for an average of only 2.4% of the total variance in preference*" (1990, 44; emphasis added). Why, then, does his book—which, as I noted, is aimed at non-specialist readers very unlikely to dig up his articles—suggest that this 2.4 percent is the only thing that matters? What besides a social agenda about what men and women *should* be like can possibly account for translating 2.4 percent into a rhetoric of *universal* gender differences? Likewise, one might wonder about the fact that one of the articles admits (after having once again affirmed that "the effects for sex are substantially lower than those for culture") that "there may be *more similarity between men and women from the same culture than between men and men or women and women from different cultures*" (1990, 17; emphasis added). If this is the case—if men and women in a given culture tend to differ from each other *less* than men from different cultures and women from different cultures—what is the point of arguing that the only thing that matters are the differences between men and women, and that these differences are, moreover, biological rather than cultural?

The finding that men and women in a given culture tend to be more similar to each other than men from different cultures and women from different cultures seems to immediately discredit the notion that biology and genetics have more power than cultural ideals and socialization. But this is not all. Buss's scholarly articles reveal that, in a cross-cultural survey of eighteen desired characteristics, both men and women ranked "mutual attraction—love," "dependable character," "emotional stability and maturity," and "pleasing disposition" as the top four characteristics (and men and women ranked them in the same order). "Education and intelligence" was ranked #5 by women and #6 by men. This introduces a slight gender variance, but the general picture (of men and women agreeing on the top four characteristics) is one of immense similarity. A more restricted survey of thirteen variables, in turn, shows that men and women rated "kind and understanding," "intelligent," "exciting personality," and "healthy" as the top four characteristics (again in the same order). Why, then, did most of these characteristics (with slightly different wording) end up in the chapter on what *women* want in Buss's mainstream book? If both surveys clearly indicate that they were equally valued by men and women, what, besides the wish to sell the non-academic reader a very particular story about gender could explain their migration to the female side?

Because of Buss's investment in the standard narrative, which dictates that women should look for men with money and status and that men should look for women with youth and beauty, his target variables of desirability are money (for women) and good looks (for men). In the eighteen-variable study women ranked "good financial prospects" at #12 and men at #13. There is a strong statistically significant difference, but in the larger scheme of eighteen variables, these rankings hardly support Buss's argument that women value money *above all other things* (whereas men place little value on it). If there are eleven other variables that women value more, it doesn't seem reasonable to say that money is women's number one priority. Along similar lines, in the thirteen-variable study, "physically attractive" was rated #5 by men and #7 by women. Again, there is a strong statistically significant variation, but this hardly erases the larger picture of gender agreement, and this is particularly the case given that women in this study rate "physically attractive" *above* "good earning capacity." Buss's book relies on the idea that women want money (and status) above everything else whereas men want youth (and beauty) above everything else. What happens to that argument when we realize that women actually value "physical attractiveness" *more* than "good earning capacity"?

In his chapter on women's desires, Buss admits that his study shows that "mutual attraction or love" is the most highly valued characteristic for both sexes, being rated 2.87 by women and 2.81 by men (where 3.00 signifies indispensable). In other words, there is no statistically significant difference between men and women. Likewise, Buss concedes that in thirty-two of the thirty-seven countries surveyed, the "sexes are *identical* in valuing kindness as one of the three most important qualities out of a possible thirteen in a mate" (44; emphasis added). Yet Buss ends the relevant section of the chapter by positing that "requiring love and kindness helps *women* to solve the critical adaptive mating problem of securing the commitment of resources from a man that can aid in the survival and reproduction of her offspring" (45; emphasis added). How, I want to ask, do we get from the surveys that reveal that men and women value love and kindness equally to the idea that these characteristics are particularly important to women?

When it comes to dependability, Buss in turn specifies that in twenty-one of thirty-seven cultures, men and women have the same preference, and that averaged across all thirty-seven cultures, women rate dependable character at 2.69, and men rate it nearly as important, with an average of 2.50. In the case of emotional stability or maturity, women (averaging across all cultures) give this quality 2.68 whereas men rate it at 2.47. Yet the concluding sentence of the paragraph reads: "*In all cultures*, in effect, *women* place a tremendous value on these characteristics" (32; emphasis added). It is brazenly contradictory to acknowledge that men and women in many cultures value the characteristics in question more or less equally at the same time as one asserts that it is *women* specifically ("in all cultures") who value them. Yet this twisted line of logic is precisely what Buss seems to want to feed his non-academic readers, for in each of the examples I have given, his rhetoric shifts from admitting that men and women don't vary that much in their preferences to emphasizing that women, in particular, value the traits under consideration and that they do so for evolutionary reasons.

It's this kind of slapdash reasoning that frustrates me as an intellectual, and frankly, as a woman. Buss stresses that his eighteen-variable study found that women rate education and intelligence fifth out of the desirable characteristics. He fails to mention that men rate it sixth. And although he admits that in twenty-seven of thirty-seven cultures, men and women rate intelligence equally highly, he concludes by stating, "Ancestral *women* who preferred intelligent mates would have raised their odds of securing social, material, and economic resources for themselves and for their children ... . Modern *women* across all cultures display these preferences" (35; emphasis added). This gender-specific argument (regarding women "across all cultures") hardly makes sense when almost three-quarters of the samples show that men and women rate this quality equally. Sure, women want intelligent mates. But, according to Buss's own data, so do men in many corners of the world. His overall interpretation of the numbers reveals a fantasy at play that desperately wants to produce a differentiated result even when it clearly doesn't exist.

The power of this fantasy is tremendous, so that even though Buss's thirteen-variable study reveals that men and women rate "health" at #5 (2.31) and #7 (2.28), respectively—meaning that men rate health as being more important than women do—he draws the following inference: "The premium that *women* place on a man's health ensures that husbands will be capable of providing these [financial] benefits over the long haul ... . These multiple facets of current *women*'s mating preferences thus correspond perfectly with the multiple facets of adaptive problems that were faced by our *women* ancestors thousands of years ago" (48; emphasis added). From this, Buss goes directly to stating that ancestral men "were confronted with a different set of adaptive problems" (48). Yet there is little about his data—and certainly not the negligible difference between 2.31 and 2.28—that justifies this type of false dichotomization, particularly as the lower figure here belongs to women.

3

As I've already suggested, given his own data, Buss could easily have written a book arguing that, when it comes to choosing a mate, men and women are looking for more or less the same things. At the very least, he should have supplemented his chapters on women's wants and the (supposedly) entirely different things men want with a chapter on "what all of us want." Instead, he opts to build a starkly binaristic model that implies that men and women are so completely different from each other that they might as well be from Mars and Venus. He does admit at various points during his discussion that when men and women are choosing a long-term mate (rather than a casual partner), their desires tend to converge. But the bulk of his argument is an insistent tirade on the contrasting wants of men and women. Why? The obvious answer is that Buss—like many of his colleagues—is for some reason deeply invested in downplaying the similarities between men and women. He seems anxious to prove that Robert Trivers was right when he, back in 1972, stated, "One can, in effect, treat the sexes as if they were different species, the opposite sex being a resource relevant to producing maximum surviving offspring."[5] In addition, the fact that attributes such as love, commitment, and intelligence end up on the female side of desired mate characteristics shows an (unacknowledged) ideological commitment to the notion that women *should* want these things more than men. In other words, this is a "science" that erects its hypotheses on cultural assumptions about gender and is willing to manipulate evidence to prove the accuracy of these hypotheses. This, by most accounts, is the opposite of genuine science.

One also has to wonder what might be the advantage of reducing something as complex as how men and women relate to each other to such an overly stylized depiction that it loses all resemblance to lived reality (and therefore all of its explanatory power). Let's take a moment to follow Buss's gender caricature to its logical conclusion: I'm Joe Standard, living in Columbus, Ohio. I'm thirty-six, the oldest of three siblings. My mother is a nurse. My father is a car salesman. One of my sisters has a law degree from Georgetown and practices family law in Atlanta. My other sister is a stay-at-home mom with a college degree and a plan to become a real estate agent when her kids are older. I'm a fairly well-paid accountant in an insurance agency. One day I meet Ms. Perfect. I don't care about how smart she is, or whether she is passionate, compassionate, or in any way compatible with me. Her sense of humor is irrelevant, as is the degree of our shared interests. And I sure don't give a damn about how she feels about me. What makes her *perfect* for me is that she's a looker, has a 0.70 waist-to-hip ratio, and has never had a boyfriend. Best of all, she's only nineteen!

Or let's say I'm Ann Average, living in Boston, Massachusetts. I'm twenty-eight. My father is a mild-mannered school teacher and my mother works as a personal assistant to a high-powered venture capitalist. When I visit her at work one day, I meet a fifty-eight-year-old business executive called Chris who makes a ton of money, sits on the board of the Metropolitan museum, has an apartment in Manhattan, a summer house in the Hamptons, and a luxury pad in Paris. I start dating him but quickly realize that he's demeaning, aggressive, arrogant, and controlling. On top of all this, he drinks too much and has bad breath. After a few months, I meet Alex, a struggling fiction writer: he's drop-dead gorgeous, sweet as sugar, kind and attentive, egalitarian, cooks like an angel, and thinks that I'm the best thing that ever happened to him. But I *still* marry Chris because he has more money and power.

Show me a man or a woman who makes these choices and you will have shown me a complete idiot! Surely there is something borderline insane about the idea that modern gender relations follow (or should follow) this type of reductive logic. There is such a high level of absurdity to some of the evolutionary psychological arguments about the centrality of the reproductive imperative that it's difficult to take the rest of the field's assertions seriously. For instance, Wright, in striving to prove that passing our genes onto the next generation is what truly matters to all of us, proposes that adoptive and step parents "will generally tend to care less profoundly for children than natural parents."[6] I trust that some adoptive and step parents might object, but it gets worse. As a means of validating his claim, Wright tells us that "in a Canadian city in the 1980s, a child two years of age or younger was seventy times more likely to be killed by a parent if living with a stepparent and natural parent than if living with two natural parents" (103). Seventy times more likely? That *is* an impressive figure, until one remembers the relatively low murder rate of Canadian cities, particularly in the 1980s: exactly how many children two years of age or younger were killed in the average Canadian city by parents of any kind (biological, adoptive, or step)? Are we talking about a sample size of three? To cite such a figure as scientific proof only shows the inordinate lengths to which this science is willing to go to substantiate its shaky hypotheses. And how many adoptive or step parents would agree with Wright when he claims that "a young stepchild is an obstacle to fitness, a drain on resources" (104). How reductive do we need to get before we realize that there is more to human emotions than genetic, reproductive logic?

4

Buss is guilty of some comparably reckless feats of logic. In an attempt to prove his hypothesis about the specifically male predilection for good looks, he explains that a study of personal ads reveals that only 41.5 percent of lesbians list physical attributes among their assets. This contrasts with 64 percent of straight women, 74 percent of gay men, and 71.5 percent of straight men. Buss concludes: "It is clear that homosexual men are similar to heterosexual men in the premium they place on physical appearance. Lesbians are more like heterosexual women in their desires, but where they differ, they place even less value on physical qualities" (62). Presumably, Buss's point here is that, in the same way that gay men and straight men share a penchant for good looks by virtue of being men, lesbians and straight women don't care as much about physical appearance because of their female genes. Yet whose appearance we are even talking about remains somewhat ambiguous: if more straight men (71.5 percent) than straight women (64 percent) offer physical "assets" in their personal ads, does this mean that they want attractive women or that they are invested in their own looks? I assume that Buss's evolutionary logic dictates that people in their ads highlight what they assume their objects of desire value. But in that case, why do women advertise their attractiveness less frequently than men? And how does the 22.5 percent difference between lesbians (42.5 percent) and straight women (64 percent) prove that lesbians and straight women are *alike*, while the 7.5 percent difference between straight men (71.5 percent) and women (64 percent) proves that men and women are entirely *different* from each other?

Buss's argument is further undermined by the fact that anyone with even the slightest familiarity with lesbian communities knows that there may be specific subcultural reasons for why lesbians might not want to participate in our society's habitual objectification of women by highlighting their physical "assets." If lesbians don't advertise their attractiveness as often as the rest of the country's population, it may be because a history of feminism and anti-patriarchal thinking has taught them to focus on other qualities. Particularly among older lesbians, who came of age in the 1960s and 1970s atmosphere of radical feminism, there has often been an explicit attempt to challenge social norms of attractiveness that reduce women to objects of male visual consumption. To read the weak emphasis that lesbians place on attractiveness through a purely evolutionary lens is to overlook some very obvious sociohistorical factors.

Furthermore, if we return to the idea that, in writing personal ads, straight men and women seek to accentuate traits they assume the "opposite" sex values, doesn't the fact that more straight men than straight women in this study play up their physical assets imply that men recognize that many straight women actually pay a lot of attention to how men look? Indeed, why not admit that there is, generally speaking, little evidence in contemporary America for the idea that women don't care about men's appearance? A quick survey of our billboards, magazines, movies, and television shows reveals the tremendous appeal of the fit, shirtless man with a six-pack (think of David Beckham in a Calvin Klein ad). This may not be cultural progress per se. But it certainly puts into question the notion that men are genetically "wired" to obsess about attractiveness whereas women aren't. As a matter of fact, I've always wondered how evolutionary psychology arrived at this conclusion in the first place, given that Darwin already stressed that females in many animal species select male mates primarily by aesthetic criteria, such as the peacock's tail. How do we get from this to the idea that human females are willing to marry any frog that hops on their path as long as this frog has a hefty bank account? Buss himself admits that "people suspect that a homely man must have high status if he can interest a stunning woman" (59). But if women don't care about male attractiveness, why should this be the case?

But let's not split hairs. Let's showcase yet another hopeless attempt to prove that evolutionary theory applies to modern American women. As "proof" of the fact that women don't like casual sex, many authors, including Buss, cite the following 1989 study. An attractive college student was commissioned to approach members of the opposite sex at Florida State University with the following statement: "Hi, I've been noticing you around town lately, and I find you very attractive. Would you go to bed with me tonight?" The study reports that seventy-five percent of the men who were approached in this manner said yes while *none* of the women did. Now there may be several explanations for this, including the pitifully unsexy nature of the pick-up line, which gives one the impression that one is being approached by a guy who possesses the social graces of a robot. But what is sure is that even in 1989 the study didn't prove anything about women's libido or attitudes about casual sex. I would be willing to bet that most sane women—even ones with unusually vigorous sex drives—would say no for the simple reason that it's hard to tell the next Jeffrey Dahmer from your average mommy's boy. Most women don't like the prospect of being raped, mutilated, or murdered by a guy who turns out to be a homicidal maniac. And please don't try to sell me a clean-cut college guy. Isn't he usually the prime suspect?

If you gave the same women the following scenario, the results might be quite different. Let's make it 6 p.m. at your local bar in Echo Park, Los Angeles. Your best friend shows up with a cute guy she has known since she was seven. He's a law student visiting from Pittsburgh. The two of you hit it off, so you keep chatting over a glass of wine even when your friend has to run off to meet her girlfriend for dinner. When he gives you a meaningful look at 10 p.m., you might say yes even though you know that you're unlikely to see him again (since he's scheduled to fly off in the morning). You'll know that the sex will be casual. But you'll also know that the guy is most likely not a serial killer, or even a rapist, so you don't hesitate. Anyone who has actually *talked* to women rather than just devised arm-chair theories about them knows that this is not an unlikely scenario. And anyone who has any sense of the hookup culture of contemporary American college life knows that casual sex is a reality of life for many young women these days. Women have historically held out because they have been told all their lives—by the likes of Robert Wright—that they're whores if they don't, because their religious beliefs teach them that it's the right thing to do, or because they're afraid of being physically violated. But it's highly unlikely that it's because they are naturally less sexual than men. To add insult to injury, Buss argues that women who are not desirable might resort to casual sex because they know they can't attract a husband (94). So, in the same way that gay men are second-rate men, women who have casual sex are second-rate women? But we learned that in the previous chapter already, didn't we?

5

I already mentioned that Buss is quite careful about drawing inferences from his data when he is talking to his fellow scientists—that his scholarly articles don't display the same degree of reductive reasoning about gender as *The Evolution of Desire*. Even so, many of the peer commentaries (commentaries written by scientists in his own field and in related fields) that follow his article in *Behavioral and Brain Sciences* are fairly scornful: one respondent after another attacks him on the validity of his generalizations, on the fact that many of his findings could be explained by socialization rather than biology, and even on his interpretation of his statistical data. Here it suffices to mention some of the highlights: neo-Darwinian ideas are not terribly applicable to modern societies because of the small average number of children people have in such societies; Buss's evolutionary predictions are oversimplifying and coarse-grained; Buss exaggerates the magnitude of sex differences and downplays individual differences; Buss exploits the fact that very large sample sizes (such as his sample of 10,047 respondents) produce statistically significant results even when the differences between groups are very small; Buss uses large aggregate numbers to wash away human diversity, with the result that he "takes us further away from, rather than closer to, the nature of human nature" (1989, 19)[7]; there are many potential causes for statistical variation and there is no way to dissociate evolutionary (genetic) hypotheses from non-evolutionary (sociocultural) ones; people tend to respond to statistical surveys with the answers that they know are culturally expected of them (so that if women know that they are expected to want money and status from men, this is what they will report wanting regardless of what they actually want); the statements people make about their mate preferences in surveys are not necessarily a good predictor of how they will actually behave in choosing a mate; in real life, we are not attracted to a potential mate as a list of characteristics, but as a complex nexus of values, history, personality, and idiosyncratic passions.

Let's start a new paragraph: Buss assumes that human reproductive behavior is a set of static responses when in fact even evolutionary logic dictates that people adapt to their environments; modern societies are not anything like the ancient environment of our prehistoric ancestors or even tribal hunter-gatherer societies; Buss is mistaken in taking it for granted that men always have greater access to material resources than women; evolutionary predictions may not hold much sway in societies where women earn their own living; it's possible that men choose women who are erotically stimulating rather than merely fertile; older men do not necessarily prefer women in their teens and twenties to women in their thirties and forties; some older men might find older women more mature, intriguing, and engaging; even when men show a preference for younger women, it's not necessarily because of an evolutionary imperative but because social ideals—which command that men should be older than their wives—predispose them to do so; what people report in surveys are the cultural norms they have internalized rather than their biological makeup; alpha males may not be the most attractive mates for women because they tend to be aggressive, possessive, and philandering; young and beautiful women do not automatically make good mothers. And so on and so forth.

A couple of the major criticisms are worth fleshing out in greater detail. First, by far the most consistent criticism of Buss is that there is no way to prove that his survey findings reflect genetic, biological differences rather than sociocultural conditioning. When people respond to sociological surveys, they tell us a lot about their socialization and about the cultural ideals that surround them, and there is no way to accurately dissociate these factors from their genetic predilections. Even behaviors that show a lot of cross-cultural uniformity cannot be assumed to have a biological foundation. David Rowe, one of Buss's critics, offers the following counterexample: "The use of business suits is now nearly a cross-cultural universal, at least in cities, yet one finds little evidence of a strong genetic compulsion to adopt this dress code" (1989, 30). In other words, the fact that something is found in a large number of cultures doesn't automatically prove that it's biologically based. As Linnda Caporael, another one of Buss's detractors, succinctly notes, "There is no way to distinguish evolved sex differences from the multitude of gender differences that have no basis in biological evolutionary processes." Men and women may have "identical preferences, but social structural arrangements produce gender differences" (1989, 17). I couldn't agree more. And it seems to me that when there is no way to disentangle biology from cultural and sociohistorical forces, making claims about biology is highly problematic because it implies the kind of immutability that cultural and sociohistorical conditioning does not. While biology certainly also evolves, this doesn't usually happen quickly enough to change things within a given generation, so that arguing that the differences between men and women are genetic amounts to saying that they can't be changed during our life times.

Even if Buss were able to show that women universally rate men's financial resources higher than any other desirable characteristics—which he can't—he would not be able to prove that this is the case because of a genetic variation rather than because women in most societies do not have the same economic resources as men do. When women are barred from financial opportunities, it makes sense that they look to men for basic security. At one point in his book, Buss cites an American study from the 1950s which illustrates that women "far more often than men desire mates who enjoy their work, show career orientation, demonstrate industriousness, and display ambition" (31). But even a nine-year-old could tell you that this is because in the 1950s, few American women worked, so that they were dependent on their husbands (or fathers) for their survival. Indeed, the tremendous changes that have taken place in women's work habits—and related displays of ambition—in the decades since the 1950s are an easy way to counter the evolutionary argument, for it is not possible for our genetic makeup to have evolved so rapidly since the time of Elvis and Marilyn that it could explain these changes. That many American women these days place a great deal of emphasis on their own career goals is a cultural and sociohistorical phenomenon—one that implies that a huge array of gendered behavior is better explained by these forces than by genetics. Factors such as women's access to education, jobs, and financial independence, along with the availability of birth control, changing sexual norms, the rise of the non-patriarchal, "gender-egalitarian" man, and most recently, the increased fluidity of how people experience their gender, sexuality, and relationships account for modern romantic choices much more accurately than genetic gender differences ever could.

Take Buss's argument that even though many women in our society are highly successful professionally, they still want successful husbands with money and ambition. This may well be true, but there is no way to prove that this desire is genetically based. It may be a mental relic of a time when wanting a successful husband made economic sense; it may be a sign that it takes time to reverse the effects of gender socialization. Even though sociocultural changes are more rapid than genetic ones, they can still take a while to sink in on the psychological level, so that the persistence of some remnants of earlier eras does not necessarily prove that such remnants are biologically based. Furthermore, if I prefer an ambitious man to a less ambitious one—as I happen to do—it's not because I'm expecting to prey on his resources but because I like ambitious people. I'm ambitious myself, and it makes sense that I would prefer to be coupled up with someone who has the same basic values as I do. That is, if women who are themselves successful want successful men, it may be quite simply because they are looking for someone like themselves. This applies to men as well, so that successful men might well want successful women because they want mates who share important characteristics with them. Fisher in fact reports that recent studies have found that we tend to be attracted to those like ourselves, so that "similar personality traits, shared habits, parallel interests, common values, joint leisure activities, and mutual friends were the best predictors of marital stability."[8] This is not a matter of reproductive fitness in some straightforwardly evolutionary sense but of shared goals, aspirations, and lifestyles.

6

The second criticism of Buss that merits closer attention is that his sample of cultures includes some deeply traditional societies that make his generalizations hugely questionable in the context of modern Western societies. It's hardly a secret that more traditional cultures—cultures where men and women are socially, politically, and economically unequal—also show greater gender dichotomies. Buss himself admits, in one of his scholarly articles, that "more traditional societies showed more sexual dimorphism than modern societies": "In general, the Asian and African samples showed the most sexual dimorphism; the Western European samples showed the least sexual dimorphism; and North and South American samples showed intermediate degrees of dimorphism" (1990, 44).

Moreover, within Western Europe, Greece, Spain, and Ireland—that is, the more religious societies—showed less similarity between the sexes than their neighbors (1990, 44). Buss thus concludes, "The most pervasive difference between cultures appears to be a traditional versus modern orientation toward mating, with the former placing great value on chastity, home and children, domestic skills, and resource provisioning, and the latter devaluing these traditional attributes" (1990, 45). Additionally, Buss notes that it is "intriguing" that "two of the countries with the highest degree of sexual dimorphism, Nigeria and Zambia, are also the two that practice polygyny" (1990, 37).

This doesn't seem too intriguing to me. Isn't it absolutely obvious that countries with the most traditional gender arrangements would also show the greatest gender dimorphism? And isn't it equally obvious that, as Norval Glenn, one of Buss's critics, states, socioeconomic development "tends to diminish some of the male-female differences predicted by evolutionary theories" (1989, 23)? Given how incredibly obvious these things really are, I—in my turn—find it "intriguing" that there is no mention of them in Buss's mainstream book. I find it "intriguing" that such an important qualification is left out of the picture, with the result that, unbeknownst to non-specialist readers, Buss is approaching them—trying to convince them of the continued relevance of evolutionary arguments to their modern American lives—armed with data that includes statistics gathered from some of the most traditional societies in the world. In other words, he willfully omits the key fact that when the numbers yielded by his international study are averaged, the gender differences are greater than they would be if he had focused exclusively on postindustrial societies where sexual dimorphism is lower. Why does he do this? The answer, once again, can only be an ideological investment in the idea of clear-cut gender differences.

Glenn reanalyzed Buss's data by adjusting for four major indicators of economic development: projected birth rate; per capita gross national product; life expectancy at birth; and less versus more developed countries. Of these, the projected birth rate is a negative indicator of development, so that the higher the birth rate, the less developed the country's economy. The other three indicators are positive indicators of development, so that the higher the per capita gross national product, the life expectancy of children, and the overall development of a country, the more developed its economy. Glenn sums up his findings as follows: "Except for the importance of good looks, all four indicators of development are inversely and significantly related to Buss's measures for each sex. According to the data, in the more developed societies as compared with less developed ones, both males and females prefer smaller age differences between self and spouse, and both sexes place less importance on financial prospects, industriousness and ambition, and chastity of spouse" (1989, 23). That is, the more developed the country's economy, the less likely men and women are to differ in their preferences for age, wealth, ambition, and chastity of their spouse, the implication being that in more developed countries, men and women are more similar to each other than in less developed ones—a finding that, as I already indicated, hardly comes as a surprise. And, as Glenn asserts, this finding lends strong support for structural and social explanations rather than evolutionary ones; it points to cultural rather than genetic reasons for gender dimorphism (1989, 21–3).

7

Consider the variable measuring chastity—the lack of previous sexual experience. In his book, Buss argues that female chastity is *universally* important to men because they want to be sure that their children are their own. Yet in his scholarly articles, he admits that cultures differ in how much emphasis they place on the issue. In his own words, "Cultures in this study vary tremendously in the value placed on this mate characteristic. The samples from China, India, Indonesia, Iran, Taiwan, and Israel (Palestinian Arabs only) attach high value to chastity in a potential mate. At the opposite extreme, samples from Sweden, Norway, Finland, the Netherlands, West Germany, and France indicate that prior sexual experience is *irrelevant or unimportant* in a potential mate. A few subjects even indicated in writing that chastity was *undesirable* in a potential mate. The Irish sample departs from the other Western European samples in placing moderate emphasis on chastity" (1989, 11–12; emphasis added). By Buss's own admission, people in many Western European countries indicate that chastity is not a relevant factor in mate selection (and in some instances may even be *undesirable*). Moreover, Buss specifies that in many of the more modern cultures, there was no gender difference in the valuation of chastity, so that it was just as important (or unimportant) to women as it was to men. Buss does mention this latter finding in his book, conceding that in societies where women have economic parity, such as Sweden, men don't usually expect a lack of prior sexual experience from their mates. But the qualification is given merely a brief mention whereas the idea that *all* men (universally) expect chastity from women is given its own prominent subsection in the chapter on what men want in a potential mate.

Oddly enough, Buss tries to dismiss the "anomalous" results from Sweden (which actually aren't that anomalous, given that many Western European countries, and particularly the other Nordic ones, follow the same pattern) by implying that people in Sweden don't place much value on chastity because they grow up in the context of "harsh, rejecting, and inconsistent child-rearing practices, erratically provided resources, and marital discord" (217). His comparison case is China where people value chastity a great deal. But why exactly do people in Sweden—a social welfare state with a slew of social services and little poverty—grow up in "harsh, rejecting, and inconsistent" circumstances or lack basic resources more than people in China? Buss assumes that this is because in Sweden, "many children are born out of wedlock, divorce is common, and fewer fathers invest consistently over time" (217). But it seems to me that Buss is here going out of his way to dismiss two basic factors about Swedish society—factors that have a readily observable impact on social norms, such as the valuation of chastity: 1) the relative lack of religious influence, and 2) the relative equality between men and women. If neither men nor women in Sweden place a premium on chastity, it's because the country is secular and gender-egalitarian, not because its children grow up in cruel conditions or lack resources. As a matter of fact, underneath the latter (fairly preposterous) claim, one hears the familiar American dread of single-mother households, which Sweden has an abundance of. Buss appears to presume, like Wright does, that the absence of a husband automatically results in a harsh, rejecting, and inconsistent childhood experience. Yet this may not be at all the case in a country like Sweden, which provides affordable day care and other social services to single mothers.

The fact that people in Sweden don't require their mates to be virgins of course doesn't mean that they don't get jealous when their mates cheat on them. Buss seems to conflate the two issues, as if chastity and fidelity were always the same thing. He in fact believes that chastity—the lack of prior sexual experience—*predicts* future marital fidelity. Yet this logic seems completely out of touch with the sexual realities of modern Western societies where neither men nor women wait until marriage to have sex (unless they happen to be unusually religious). A man might sleep around quite a bit prior to making a commitment to a specific woman yet never cheat on her once this commitment is made (and vice versa). Likewise, a woman might sleep with a man on the first date not because she is promiscuous—she might have rejected a whole host of guys in the years leading up to this moment—but because the man in question truly excites her. To conclude that her lack of "chastity" in this instance prophesies her future infidelity would be to completely misread the situation.

Like other supporters of the standard narrative, Buss also speaks as if the expectation of fidelity (or chastity) was essential to men but not to women. After all, as we have seen, the narrative dictates that women's infidelity is deadly to men because it places their paternity in question whereas women aren't too bothered about men's infidelity as long as it doesn't lead to a loss of resources (desertion). But this component of the argument—as so much else about the standard narrative—seems like a fantasy designed to justify the sexual double standard; it seems like a convenient way to explain why men get to philander without punishment while women are vilified for doing the same. In Chapter 4, I'll go into detail about some recent studies that reveal that women get just as jealous about sexual infidelity as men do. Here it suffices to state that Walter Lonner—who is otherwise sympathetic to Buss's arguments—found, in replicating Buss's study about chastity among Western Washington University students, that it was actually women "who appear to want more 'chaste' males" (1989, 27). Likewise, an alternative study of a thousand British couples indicates that both men and women dislike partners who are sexually unfaithful, and that women are in fact more put off by unfaithful husbands than husbands are by unfaithful wives (1989, 32–3). And in any case, surely it doesn't take a scientific study to know that modern women often want faithfulness just as much as men, and that this is particularly the case in relationships where they themselves are expected to be faithful (open or casual relationships are another matter for both genders). To reduce something as thorny as jealousy over infidelity to the idea that men want to guarantee their paternity is, once again, to oversimplify human psychology to a fairly ludicrous degree.

One of Buss's critics, Brian Gladue, suggests that it's a massive blow to the evolutionary argument that the variable measuring previous experience in sexual intercourse (chastity)—the variable that is the closest to reproduction and thus to evolutionary reasoning—is the one that also shows the greatest *cultural* diversity, thereby demolishing the idea that it has a purely genetic, biological base. Faced with this result—one that doesn't fit his evolutionary prediction—Buss is in fact forced to concede that there might be cultural factors at play. This prompts Gladue to state, "One of these days, sociobiological theorists will *not* use cultural or mating system differences to excuse findings they don't like, while ignoring those same cultural differences as explanations for findings they *do* like. The schema and model must be consistent. If bioevolutionary explanations don't fit nicely with the chastity data, why should they account for the findings regarding 'good financial prospects' or 'ambition and industriousness'? Buss can't have it both ways" (1989, 21). *Exactly.* To ignore cultural explanations as long as one's findings support the evolutionary model but to resort to them whenever one's data no longer aligns with this model is to be inconsistent (that is, unscientific). And it also reduces culture to a wholly secondary or supplementary status despite the fact that human beings are immensely cultural creatures. Culture is not just incidental to human life; it's what human life is made of. By this I don't mean that biology doesn't matter, for obviously it does. But I don't see any reason to assert that it plays a bigger part than culture does. And, as I have argued, there is no way to separate it from culture in the first place, so that explanations of human behavior that ignore cultural factors are not very convincing to those of us who recognize the immense role played by culture in the organization of human life.

Though Buss's rhetoric is less overtly conservative than Wright's, ultimately he seems to have the same aim: to convince us of the naturalness (and therefore of the desirability) of traditional gender norms. Both thinkers valorize social arrangements that maximize gender differentiation, conveniently ignoring the fact that societies with pronounced gender dimorphism tend also to be the least egalitarian, the least likely to grant women the same economic, educational, and professional opportunities as men. While it may be impossible to find a society where men and women are completely equal, it's hard to refute that those where gender differentiation is not a priority tend to come the closest. Buss would of course object by claiming that he is merely describing the realities of our evolutionary heritage—that he is not advocating a specific kind of gendered world. As he asserts, "Evolutionary psychology strives to illuminate men's and women's evolved mating behavior, not to prescribe what the sexes could be or should be. Nor does it offer prescriptions for appropriate sex roles. It has no political agenda" (18). Perhaps he genuinely believes this. But the claim is pure rubbish. If it were actually true, he would have used his data differently: he would have not written a book that meticulously sidesteps all the ways in which men and women converge in their dating behavior, that remains largely silent about the significant cultural differences revealed by his international study, and that translates minor statistical differences into a rigidly dichotomized male-female paradigm that leaves little space for more egalitarian relations. It's one thing to endorse antifeminist views. But it's even worse to deny that this is what one is doing, as Buss does when he states that he wishes for "equality among all persons regardless of sex" (18). In this sense, Rush Limbaugh is easier to deal with than some of our evolutionary psychologists.

8

What is perhaps least forgivable about the political agenda of thinkers such as Wright and Buss—who claim the status of public *intellectuals*—is that this agenda leads them to completely anti-intellectual modalities of reasoning. As we saw in the previous chapter, Wright's political need to condemn divorce and single-mother households leads him to argue that polygamy might be a reasonable solution to the social problems of modern America (and if that fails, let's reinstitute the sexual double standard of Victorian England). Brilliant! Likewise, we have here seen that Buss's political need to attack divorce and single-mother households in Sweden leads him to overlook the two most obvious reasons for the country's lack of emphasis on chastity—secularism and gender equality—in favor of a farcical argument about how Swedish children grow up in inhospitable environments and lack basic resources. More generally speaking, the evolutionary psychological need to uphold the gender bifurcated world of the standard narrative, and therefore to equate human mating behavior with the needs of reproduction, routinely leads thinkers in the field to ignore important psychosocial complexities. Among other things, its reductive logic renders sex, love, and romance purely "strategic," as Buss does in the opening pages of his book when he maintains: "Our mating is strategic, and our strategies are designed to solve particular problems for successful mating. Understanding how people solve those problems requires an analysis of sexual strategies. Strategies are essential for survival on the mating battlefield" (5).

Yet it's simply not the case that people make mating choices based on reproductive strategy alone. Indeed, there is often very little that is strategic about human desire. To begin with, we frequently desire people who are not particularly good for us— who hurt, demean, or disappoint us in various ways—and we tend to do this repeatedly, time after time, as if we were incapable of learning from past experience. When it comes to other areas of life, we are usually quite good at making sure that we don't repeat the mistakes of the past. But when it comes to desire, we are much more likely to repeat mistakes than to get things "right": we are experts at reproducing our own misery by getting into relational scenarios that wound us. If anything, many of us spend our lives trapped in patterns of relating that we would like to overcome but for some reason can't. And sometimes it's precisely when we think that we have finally broken a torturous pattern that it takes us by surprise so that we, once again, find ourselves caught up in its tentacles. This is of course not true of everyone. But it is true of many of us, which is why intimate relationships are just as likely to bring us suffering as they are to lead to harmonious unions that are optimally designed to help us rear our children. And even those of us who eventually end up in such unions often have to go through a whole array of problematic ones to get there. And, once there, there is absolutely no guarantee that the union will endure until our children are old enough to survive on their own.

What evolutionary advantage could this possibly have? How do wounding relationship patterns aid our reproductive aims? One of the things that evolutionary psychology cannot explain is why humans often make such bad relationship decisions. And it also cannot account for the utter specificity of human desire. Evolutionary psychologists tend to talk as if our desire were akin to the reproductive instinct of other animals. But this is a misrepresentation, for most of us are not willing to sleep with another person just because he or she might give us a reproductive advantage. Even when the person in front of us is a genetic jackpot, we can't force ourselves to feel desire for him or her if he or she doesn't fulfill the always idiosyncratic requirements of our desire. Some of us are less selective than others, but what is really striking about human desire is how discriminating it tends to be. I might meet hundreds of men in my life who fulfill all the necessities of reproductive fitness, but I might only be attracted to a few dozen of these. Likewise, a given man might find a particular woman attractive for reasons that he cannot name, desiring her over a whole host of others who are younger and prettier, even though evolutionary psychology dictates that the latter qualities are what should most appeal to him. As a matter of fact, the detail that draws our attention in another person is frequently astonishingly small. We can be captivated by the tone of someone's voice, by a connotation we catch in his or her eyes, by the shape of his or her nose, chin, eyebrows, or fingernails, or by his or her manner of picking up a coffee cup. The way in which a person talks or moves can have a tremendous impact on us. A hint of vulnerability—of past heartache—in a man's demeanor can go a long way in arousing the desire of some women. Others speak of a man's "aura" to describe the enigmatic quality that entices them without necessarily having any concrete sense of what they are referring to.

Most of us routinely reject a large number of people who would be perfectly appropriate in reproductive terms. And we often look high and low for someone who resonates on the precise frequency of our desire. This specificity of desire is in fact the cause of a lot of suffering in our lives in the sense that when the person we have fixated on doesn't return our desire, we feel rejected and forlorn. And when we lose a beloved person—through death or abandonment, for instance—our mourning can seem endless. We experience such a person as inimitable, which is why it is difficult for us to shift our desire to a new person, no matter how good a reproductive "catch" this new person might be. It can take us a long time to even begin to fathom the possibility of finding a suitable substitute for the lover we have lost, which is why during times of deep mourning our desire may seem dead or dormant. We, in short, experience specific people, specific mates, as utterly irreplaceable in a way that evolutionary psychology cannot account for.[9] This is as true of men as it is of women. When in love, men can be utterly devoted, and when they lose a woman they love, they often mourn with the kind of heart-wrenching intensity that keeps them from wanting to have sex with anyone else until they have completed the mourning process. Modern American men have been socialized for emotional intimacy, love and companionship, and a mass of other factors that have no direct bearing on reproduction. The idea that none of this matters, that the male psyche can be summed up by the urge to produce as many babies as possible, ignores all the ways in which human lives diverge from the lives of other animals.

I have no intention of denying that humans are animals or that we are closely related to primates such as bonobos and chimps. Indeed, as I've already implied, I believe that evolutionary psychologists would benefit from a more honest look at how much human sexuality has in common with the promiscuous sexuality of bonobos and chimps. Yet I also think that it would be foolish to disregard the enormous differences that exist between humans and our primate relatives. The intricacies of human language alone bring the kinds of complications that make it impossible to equate human behavior with bonobo or chimp behavior. Think, for instance, of the various ways in which humans routinely hurt each other through language. Insults large and small characterize our daily lives, and we often spend considerable energy mulling over something that someone said to us. When it comes to traumatizing pronouncements, our memories are long, so that we sometimes recall slights from years, even decades, ago. Presumably, this is not something bonobos and chimps waste their time on.

They probably also do not make relationship choices based on their painful family histories or prior romantic disillusionments. Human desire is motivated by unconscious currents that drive us toward specific individuals for very specific reasons. And we are haunted by existential dilemmas—such as the quest for self-completion or emotional security—that cannot be easily resolved, and that other animals do not seem to be terribly bothered by. This is why, when it comes to our desire, a man is never just a man, and a woman is never just a woman, but each object of our desire speaks to something unique in our ongoing struggle to live the kind of life that feels meaningful and worth living. Buss, in responding to the critics of his article on mate selection quotes Darwin's 1871 assessment of gender differences: "No one disputes that the bull differs in disposition from the cow, the wild boar from the sow, the stallion from the mare ... . Woman seems to differ from man in mental disposition." But does the bull have self-consciousness? Does it feel pity, grief, remorse, or elation over a job well done? Does it mourn the loss of love and lament the passage of time? Does it feel nostalgic when confronted by the bittersweet evanescence of life? Does it repeatedly fall into excruciating romantic patterns? Does it sit around with its buddies complaining about how its past family traumas guide it to make disappointing relationship choices? If not, what makes it a suitable comparison point for modern American men?

9

As far as I'm concerned, saying that men are like bulls and women like cows is akin to saying that green-eyed people are sinners and blue-eyed ones saints. It's no more convincing—and a lot less entertaining—than a Hans Christian Andersen fairytale. Likewise, I find evolutionary arguments about the "incompatible" desires of men and women wholly unpersuasive. We have seen that the evolutionary psychological world is one of cheating men and gold-digging women. Both genders are portrayed as selfish con-artists who are always on the lookout for ways to deceive their mates. Because evolutionary psychology cannot admit that men and women might have a great deal in common, that their shared quest for personal fulfillment might, for instance, create a high level of empathy and understanding between them, it also cannot admit that they might have relational capacities other than the war of the sexes; it cannot admit that men and women might relate to each other on a human level that is deeper than the superficialities of gendered identity.

Buss confidently declares that "men and women often cannot simultaneously reach their goals without coming into conflict" (143). But one could say the same about any two people, regardless of gender. One could in fact argue that whenever two people bring their different histories and backgrounds, different dreams and priorities, and different unconscious fantasies and motivations into an intimate encounter, some tension is bound to arise. Indeed, unless we can prove that gay, lesbian, and queer couples never experience relationship troubles, it's hard to attribute such troubles to gender differences specifically. Yet Buss is convinced that relationship conflicts are a gendered predicament: "A man who seeks sex without investing in his partner short circuits a mating goal of many women, who want greater emotional commitment and bigger maternal investment. This kind of interference runs both ways. A woman who requires a long courtship and heavy investment interferes with a man's sexual strategy, which involves acquiring sex with a minimum of obligation" (143). We are once again asked to worship the icons of the sex-crazed male and the coy, careful female who can't envision the possibility of sex without long-term commitment (or the prospect of motherhood). But imagine what would happen if we quite simply just rejected Buss's paradigm, if we noted that men and women frequently have similar sexual objectives (pleasure being one of these). The bottom of the conflict model would immediately fall out.

The notion that men and women are inherently hostile to each other only holds *if one starts from the premise that they are fundamentally different*. The minute one recognizes their shared struggles and headaches, sorrows and hardships, goals and ambitions, romantic anxieties and delights, the expectation of hostility becomes unnecessary. Personally, I would like to avoid approaching every man as a potential enemy. Buss, however, would like me to stay focused on how to trick men into giving me what I want—which, predictably, is marriage. Equally predictably, like Wright, Buss assumes that men are most likely to marry women who frustrate them by withholding sex: "By withholding sex, women increase its value. They render it a scarce resource. Scarcity bumps up the price that men are willing to pay for it. If the only way men can gain sexual access is by heavy investment, then they will make that investment" (147). "Sexual withholding," Buss continues, "may encourage a man to evaluate a woman as a permanent rather than a temporary mate. Granting sexual access early often causes a man to see a woman as a casual mate. He may perceive her as too promiscuous and too sexually available, characteristics that men avoid in committed mates" (147). We are back at the Madonna-whore dichotomy. And we are also on the terrain of dime-a-dozen self-help guides: men only marry when it's their only way of getting sex. Does this mean that the vast majority of American men getting married haven't slept with their future wives? I hugely doubt this. Or maybe the point is that by withholding sex during the initial stages of courtship, women rope men into a mindset that eventually causes them to propose marriage? Again, I hugely doubt this, for I'm willing to bet that the emotional effects of pining for sex will dissipate during the two or three years that couples routinely have sex before they get anywhere near the proposal stage.

Buss of course takes it for granted that men suffer when women withhold sex but that women don't experience any feelings of deprivation. Like many of his colleagues, and like many self-help gurus, he assumes that women really aren't that interested in sex, so that withholding it is no hardship to them. Yet there is absolutely nothing to warrant this assumption. But it gets worse, for Buss states, "It is often in women's best interest ... to have a man so devoted to her that all of his energies are channeled to her and her children. It is often in a man's best interest, however, to allocate only a portion of his resources to one woman, reserving the rest for additional adaptive problems, such as seeking additional mating opportunities or achieving higher social status. Hence, the sexes are often at odds over each other's commitments" (148). So ... the *natural* arrangement is one where women sit at home taking care of kids while men sleep around the neighborhood and pursue high-status careers? Buss goes on to explain that one reason men fail to express their emotions is that being less emotionally invested in one woman "frees up resources that can be channeled toward other women or other goals" (149). In other words, when your husband remains quiet at the dinner table, it's because he is (consciously or unconsciously) saving up resources for his mistresses and his stock options. But why would you want to be married to this guy in the first place? Who, exactly, benefits from this kind of reasoning? I can only think of one person: the patriarchal guy who thinks it's his birthright to treat women badly. I guess now this guy has his very own "science" to justify his caveman ways.

Astonishingly, Buss argues that his goal in foregrounding the differences between men and women is to help us build *better* relationships. He appears to believe that his dichotomous model can help men and women relate to each other more successfully. As he writes, "Although conflict between the sexes is pervasive, it is not inevitable. There are conditions that minimize conflict and produce harmony between the sexes. Knowledge of our evolved sexual strategies gives us tremendous power to better our own lives by choosing actions and contexts that activate some strategies and deactivate others. Indeed, understanding sexual strategies, including the cues that trigger them, is one step toward the reduction of conflict between men and women. This book explores the nature of conflict and offers some solutions for fostering harmony between the sexes" (13–14). What is so sad about this is that Buss doesn't realize that it's precisely the kind of binary thinking that he advocates that creates the conflict between the sexes to begin with. In other words, his "solution" is the root of the problem in the sense that as long as we believe that men and women are utterly different, we are doomed to perpetuate the gender antagonism that this mentality fans. To get confirmation of this, one only needs to take a quick look at what happens in self-help literature that relies on evolutionary insights such as Buss's: book after book tells women that they need to learn to "outwit" men, to beat men at their game, to manipulate men, to make sure they come out on top even if this means resorting to deception and dishonesty. The discourse of war permeates this literature, pitting men and women against each other, as if romance were primarily a matter of defeating one's opponent.

Many people are seduced by the evolutionary discourse of difference because it seems to have the backing of science. What I have tried to illustrate is that this backing is rickety at best and reactionary at worst. It's a backing that aims to uphold deeply patriarchal gender arrangements, as well as to convince women that such arrangements are their only option because, after all, one can't beat "nature" (or nature's intention). Buss writes, "Although some worry that inquiries into the existence and evolutionary origins of sex differences will lead to justification for the status quo, it is hard to believe that attempts to change the status quo can be very effective if we remain ignorant of the sex differences that actually exist, the causal forces that gave rise to them, and the contexts in which they are expressed. Knowledge is power."[10] I would like to see just one example of how the evolutionary psychological obsession with gender differences has helped bring about change in the patriarchal status quo. Indeed, it's hard to take Buss seriously here, given that much of his book reads like an apology for traditional patriarchy: "Fulfilling each other's evolved desires is the key to harmony between a man and woman. A woman's happiness increases when the man brings more economic resources to the union and shows kindness, affection, and commitment. A man's happiness increases when the women is more physically attractive than he is, and when she shows kindness, affection, and commitment" (221). I'm all for kindness, affection, and commitment. But isn't the rest of this description more or less a feminist nightmare—one where men are assessed by their financial worth and women are assessed by their beauty, as if they had nothing else to make them interesting as human beings? For the record, personally I'm super-happy when I make a ton more money than my drop-dead gorgeous boyfriend. But if there's something that makes me super-*un*happy, it's male "scientists" telling me what my happiness should consist of.

3

The Arrogance of the Backlash

The relationship between sexuality and reproduction has never been much more than a theological fantasy.
JUDITH HALBERSTAM

1

What's so alarming about the standard narrative of evolutionary psychology is that it is doing its best to reinstate—and lend scientific validity to—gender stereotypes that the rest of us have spent decades dismantling. It promotes an inequalitarian outlook on gender at a time when large segments of our society are doing their best to move onto more egalitarian ground. It fans people's anxieties about the rapid changes that have taken place in gender relations, offering a false sense of certainty to those who find it hard to tolerate ambiguity about what it means to be a man or a woman. It reasserts the status quo of gender without openly acknowledging that this status quo is relentlessly patriarchal. And it insists on a rhetoric of difference at a cultural moment when the everyday lives of men and women are becoming increasingly similar. In the rare instances that it references feminism, it reveals its utter ignorance, assuming that feminism is an attempt to elevate women over men when in fact contemporary feminism—at least in its deconstructive, academic forms—is largely a matter of dismantling the walls that have historically kept the two genders separate (and often at odds with each other); it's a matter of creating a society where everyone, regardless of gender, has the capacity to pursue his or her idiosyncratic priorities and passions.

If evolutionary psychology strives to reify existing gender dichotomies, third wave feminism strives to move beyond them. I'm not saying that feminists have forgotten about the realities of patriarchy and the historical oppression of women. The equality of men and women is obviously still a major goal. But we have long known that the stakes are even higher than this, that ultimately, we want to live in a world where people are not categorized—or treated differently—on the basis of identity markers of any kind. These include not only gender but sexual orientation, race, ethnicity, religion, social class, and other indicators of differentiated status. As long as evolutionary psychology doesn't understand this basic fact about feminism—that it's not about pitting women against men in some sort of a battle of the sexes but about liberating both men and women—it will continue to misjudge why it is that feminists are so exasperated with its pronouncements. The misogyny of evolutionary psychology is merely a part of the problem, though it certainly *is* a problem, as this chapter will continue to illustrate. The bigger problem is its insistence on a practice of gender profiling that contemporary feminists view as both antiquated and tyrannical.

And one doesn't even have to be a feminist to feel this way. Modern societies have migrated to a place where there is absolutely no advantage—evolutionary or otherwise—to extreme gender differentiation. There is no adaptive benefit to modern women in spending all their time having and taking care of children. There is no adaptive benefit to modern men in spending all their time devising ways to bed women. Indeed, it might be highly adaptive to create egalitarian alliances that liberate us from the stifling, gender-differentiated relationships of the past—relationships where both partners had a relatively restricted (and inflexible) role to play. This is even economically adaptive, given that the countries where men and women are the most similar (and equal) are often also the most affluent. Furthermore, these countries also have the lowest infant mortality rates, so if the goal is to produce viable children, then gender equality seems to have a great deal going for it. And, contrary to the fears that both Wright and Buss express about the social corruption that might result from extramarital sex, the most sexually tolerant places seem also to be the ones with the lowest crime rates. Scandinavia, the Netherlands, and Canada are notoriously safer than many other places in the world. And guess what? Both men and women in these countries have a lot of sex outside of marriage.

Greater gender equality, as well as our increased understanding of what men and women share with each other, has freed all of us, men and women alike, in countless different ways. It has freed us to express a greater range of our human potential. And in the romantic realm, it has freed us to choose mates according to criteria other than reproductive fitness. What baffles me is that evolutionary psychologists seem so *bothered* by the idea that times have changed and that modern men and women are no longer constrained by the reproductive imperatives of yesteryear. Isn't it *great* that women's increased economic independence has liberated them to select men based on reasons other than the traditional ones of money and status; isn't it *wonderful* that it has liberated them to pay attention to the kindness, generosity, and wittiness of men, among other things? Likewise, isn't it *marvelous* that now that men's social status is no longer measured by the number of their children, they are free to select women (or men, for that matter) based on reasons other than fertility? Isn't it a cause for celebration that men can these days look for things like emotional maturity or career ambition in the women they date? What makes evolutionary psychology such a hard sell to someone like me is that it insists on fetishizing the very icons of masculinity and femininity (wealthy, powerful, and philandering men; young, pretty, and asexual women) that have poisoned the gender dynamics of the past.

Why are evolutionary psychologists trying to tell us that we have somehow taken the wrong turn when in fact we have gotten away from our enslavement to reproduction? And why are they propping up the ideal of the alpha male precisely when so many men are striving to move beyond this ideal, not only because they don't feel that it captures their lived experience but also because it doesn't present a particularly appealing picture? The ideal shuns men who are emotionally savvy, sensitive, and non-aggressive, implying that "real" men are the ones who dominate women. Consequently, those who valorize this ideal automatically shore up a very particular, enormously outdated model of masculinity—one that seems to bring comfort to those men who have the most to lose from the erosion of patriarchy.

Along related lines, evolutionary psychologists talk as if the increased wisdom of old age had nothing to contribute to women's lives. This is particularly disturbing given that it's often older women—like older men—who make the greatest contributions to our social, cultural, and political life. Young men and women are alluring for a variety of reasons—physical attractiveness being the most obvious among these—but older men and women have their own significance. They possess a store-house of experience that lends their characters a special kind of weightiness. Often, they are competent, insightful, multifaceted, and interesting. They may have access to frequencies of human emotion that remain closed to those who haven't yet lived through as many of life's pleasures and periods of suffering. And when they are lucky, they have gained the ability to critically sift through the morass of existential dilemmas to separate what truly matters in life from what doesn't. To ignore all of this by reducing women to the lifespan of their ovaries is to rob them—all of us—of too much.

2

Many of us experience the greater fluidity of gender and sexuality that characterizes contemporary society as enlivening. We have realized that living outside (or beyond) stereotypes makes our lives—including our romantic lives—a great deal more satisfying. We are not willing to go back into the suffocating gender boxes of earlier epochs because we are hugely enjoying our new freedom. We like the dexterous renegotiating of gender relations that is going on in our society. Isn't it precisely because so many of us, men and women, straights and queers, have recognized that traditional, patriarchal gender arrangements don't serve us very well that the defenders of the status quo—be they fundamentalist Christians or socially conservative evolutionary psychologists—are so desperate to convince us that they are the only *natural* way of organizing human sexuality? Surely there is something almost pathetic about the struggle to promote the notion of female coyness and the sanctity of heterosexual reproductive coupling at a time when many women are choosing to act in ways that are far from coy and when many people are more and more open about the fact that their sexual behavior has little to do with reproductive aims. Add to this the increasing cultural visibility and legitimacy of gays and lesbians, as well as the dramatic rise in the number of straight people who opt out of the more repressive forms of heterosexuality, who prefer to stay single, and who (intentionally or unintentionally) have children out of wedlock, and it becomes obvious that a science that advocates the "naturalness" of traditional relational configurations is doing something besides advancing a purely scientific platform; it's exactly because outdated notions of family, domesticity, and reproduction are under siege that there is such a "scientific" urgency to persuade us of their inevitability. And the more traditional forms of marriage get destabilized, the more frenzied, even manic, the effort to renaturalize them becomes.

It's thus not a coincidence that much of evolutionary psychology reads like a last-ditch effort to counter the tide of gender equality that is finding its way to the various levels of our social world. And it's definitely not an accident that evolutionary psychology's insistence on archaic gender models coincides with the considerable victories of feminism and the loosening of gender binaries in our society. This is a backlash phenomenon frantically trying to set the clock back. Let's be clear: to the extent that evolutionary psychologists still adhere to the idea that our ancestors lived in hierarchical, patriarchal societies populated by randy males and coy females—and in the next chapter we'll discover that not all evolutionary psychologists hold this view—every argument *for* the continued relevance of evolutionary gender models is an argument *against* gender equality, and particularly against the achievements of feminism. Whether its advocates admit this or not, the overall thrust of the standard narrative is to thwart women's liberation. Sure, it pays some lip service to the idea that "different doesn't mean unequal." But, as I mentioned in the last chapter, when one looks at the history of gender relations, it's clear that the emphasis on difference tends to promote inequality. The empirical evidence is fairly incontestable on this: as Buss's own data clearly reveals, where men and women are thought to be most different is also where they are most unequal.

While many of us are striving to create new, imaginative stories about desire, relating, and the increasingly unpredictable relationships between men and women, evolutionary psychology seems invested in making sure that such stories don't get past the opening paragraph. For instance, even as researchers such as Roughgarden have compiled overwhelming evidence about the diversity of sexual expression in the animal world, the supporters of the standard narrative have fixated on heterosexual reproduction to such an extent that the nonreproductive sexual activity of many species—such as the bonobos—has been sidelined. Predictably, this attempt to equate sexuality with reproduction spills over to mainstream culture. Queer theorist Judith Halberstam uses the 2005 blockbuster documentary, *The March of the Penguins*, to illustrate this point. This film was seen by millions of average Americans. Some churches even organized special screenings for their congregations. Why? Well, the film, as Halberstam notes, shows "little heroic families striving to complete their natural and pregiven need to reproduce."[1] Besides stigmatizing the nonreproductive penguins, the film conveniently sidesteps the fact that penguins are only monogamous for the duration of one reproductive cycle—that serial monogamy rather than life-long monogamy is the norm of their relational arrangements.[2] And for all its talk about the dignity of penguins, it presents them through a thoroughly anthropomorphic lens—one that faithfully reproduces the heteronormative narratives that govern our society. That is, it not only imposes on penguins behavioral patterns borrowed from humans but chooses the most conservative patterns conceivable; it produces a very specific account of animal sexuality in order to, as Halberstam observes, "locate heterosexuality in its supposedly natural setting" (36). And, worst of all, it does this while pretending to give us a documentary-style "truth" about penguins.

3

The standard narrative implies that the "truth" about men and women lies deeper than our current egalitarian cultural climate: in biology. At the same time, as I have demonstrated, its biggest flaw is precisely its tendency to reduce all of human life to biology. This is why it keeps equating sexuality with the reproductive instinct. As we have seen, everything follows from this reduction: the idea that men are inherently polygamous (driven to spread their seed) while women are inherently monogamous (driven to guard their eggs); the idea that men actively pursue mates while women merely choose from among the qualified candidates; and the idea that women trade their fidelity for men's resources and protection while men are motivated solely by youth, beauty, and the correct waist-to-hip ratio. Sex, in this picture, is understood as a matter of fertilization (or the attempt to fertilize). Yet we all know that human sexual behavior is much more complicated than this. Humans have sex for all kinds of reasons, for instance, to experience pleasure, to cultivate intimacy, to release tension, to resolve conflict, or to entertain themselves and their partners. Many of us work quite hard to make sure sex doesn't lead to reproduction. And even those who organize their lives around their children routinely have more sex than is, strictly speaking, required for the task. Women who are past the childbearing age often continue to have plenty of sex. And a lot of people have sex with members of the same gender, so that there is absolutely no way to explain their sexuality by the urge to produce babies. In short, reproduction is hardly the only reason people have sex, crave romance, or pursue relationships.

The versatility of human sexual expression is so obvious that it is fairly astonishing that evolutionary psychology has been able to advance its standard narrative for as long as it has. Indeed, only a deliberate dismissal of empirical evidence can account for the discrepancy between the standard narrative and the realities of human sexuality, including the fact that the minute birth control became widely available, large numbers of people started to relish the idea that they could have sex without the fear of inadvertently bringing a child into the world. To be sure, there are still some societies where sex beyond the reproductive imperative is frowned upon, but the reasons for this are invariably religious or cultural; it's impossible to name a human society where nonreproductive sex is shunned for "natural" reasons, for reasons that have nothing to do with sociohistorical concerns. If anything, many societies work overtime to impose restrictions on sexuality—particularly on female sexuality—precisely because it is common knowledge that human libidinal impulses far exceed the demands of reproduction. This makes it all the more striking that Western science has been so interested in convincing us that sex, in the final analysis, is a matter of reproduction. Our societies may not stone adulterous women to death, but our science surely is doing its best to impress upon women the idea that sexuality beyond the chaste borders of the marital bed renders them unnatural, unfeminine, and even somehow polluted (let's not forget about Wright's Madonna-whore dichotomy). And it's also trying to impress upon men the notion that the only women worth loving are those who display an appropriate reticence about sex.

Back in the early 2000s, when I was teaching gender and sexuality studies to Harvard undergraduates, I occasionally had a student who was also enrolled in the sociobiology course on human sexuality that E. O. Wilson taught just a couple streets over. I learned to anticipate the moment when this student realized that sexuality, in my course, wasn't synonymous with reproduction. "So are you saying that sex isn't the same thing as reproduction?" he or she would ask. I always responded with some questions of my own: "Well, when you're having your 3 a.m. hookup at Winthrop House, are you trying to produce a baby?" "Why do you think so many American women spend much of their lives on the pill, despite the unpleasant side-effects?" "You don't seriously think that two gay men getting it on are hoping that a child will follow, do you?"

I rest my case.

The larger point I'm making is that the standard narrative's unwillingness to admit that, in the context of human sexuality, there is no such thing as biology divorced from its social context repeatedly leads its proponents down a path that cannot be rationally defended. As a matter of fact, one of Darwin's basic insights was that biology adapts to its environment, which is one reason that evolutionary development is possible in the first place. This being the case, it's hard not to be stunned by evolutionary psychological accounts of gender differences that insist that these differences are stable in being genetically based, as if our cultural setting had no impact whatsoever. Many of the advocates of the standard narrative explicitly deny the importance of culture, no doubt because they are feeling defensive in relation to the numerous social scientists (sociologists, anthropologists, and psychologists) who have challenged them on this issue. But this defensiveness produces the kind of myopia that is hard to justify in scientific (or any) terms, for neglecting a huge part of human experience (culture and socialization) immediately makes it impossible to understand the first thing about human life. Even the neck-ache I often feel has a social cause: the stresses of living in a fast-paced modern society. How could it, then, possibly be that something as fundamental as my experience of myself as a woman could be fully divorced from social influences? And how could it possibly be that something as culturally intricate as human romantic behavior could be summed up by the biological urge to have children?

4

Talking about the ways in which biology and culture are intertwined, psychoanalyst Stephen Mitchell states, "We do not begin as sexual creatures who encounter social constraints. We begin as bodily/social creatures, and our sexuality is as profoundly, deeply cultural as it is physical. Human sexuality emerges within relational and linguistic contexts. Behaviorally, sexual acts can take place with or without other people. But psychologically, the meanings of sexuality derive from social structures, interpersonal forms of relatedness, and linguistic categories."[3] Human sexuality, in short, draws its various valences from its cultural setting. More generally speaking, Mitchell notes that we are increasingly realizing that the bodily and the social, the biological and the cultural, interpenetrate: "they bring each other to life and also constrain each other. There is no sexuality or aggression or any other bodily experience that is unmediated by social and linguistic shaping. And conversely, we experience all social and linguistic influence as embodied creatures" (68).

Mitchell goes on to explain that the old distinction between nature and nurture has been challenged by recent advances in neurophysiology, which have revealed that, far from being "a complete package at birth," the newborn presents herself as a surface for the formative influences of culture: "It turns out that much of the wiring that will *become* the biology, the very constitution, of the adult is *not* present at birth, but is laid down in the first few years of life, in the social, linguistic, familial, interpersonal, nurturing context that the infant requires for survival." The brain of the newborn, for example, is only partially developed, which means that its nerve cells and neural pathways are shaped by the infant's interactions with the surrounding world, including other people: "Patterns of arousal and quiescence, thresholds of excitation and relaxation, diurnal rhythms—many features of what used to be understood as purely inborn temperament or constitution—are now understood to be partly shaped in early interactions with caregivers" (70).[4] This suggests that culture is pleated into our biological structure from the get-go, so that it doesn't make sense to talk about humans as purely biological creatures. Mitchell asks us to imagine the convergence of two streams in a whirlpool: "Before they meet, it is possible to isolate and describe the waters of each separately. After they meet, their drops are interfused. It is no longer possible to dip a cup into the whirlpool and separate what has come from each stream. Nature and nurture operate in a similar fashion" (74). Biologists such as Anne Fausto-Sterling agree, and have taken pains to elucidate the various ways in which the social enters the bodily.[5] This makes it all the more noteworthy that the supporters of the standard narrative go to inordinate lengths to downplay the importance of culture in human life. It's as if they were afraid that any admission of social influences might automatically undermine the idea that humans are animals.

Yet there is no reason to think this way. It's possible to acknowledge that humans are animals at the same time as one emphasizes the myriad ways in which they differ from other animals. Humans are witty, funny, smart, chatty, articulate, and hugely imaginative. They have multifaceted emotional lives. They fall madly in love and they get scorched by it. They feel not only pain, fear, and grief but also anxiety, nostalgia, disappointment, and disillusionment. They can sometimes even tell the difference between disillusionment and disenchantment. In addition, they have constructed an incredibly complex cultural edifice—one that consists of art, music, science, politics, economics, educational systems, bookstores, nightclubs, websites, and television shows (among other things). This edifice has a tremendous impact on human lives. As a consequence, when evolutionary psychologists talk as if biology were the only thing that matters in human romantic behavior, one has to seriously wonder about the blinders they are putting on.

I have no doubt that human culture has evolutionary origins— that it didn't materialize out of thin air or by an act of God. But I think it would be useless to deny that once this culture—some form of this culture—was in place, it in turn influenced the future evolution of human beings. That is, culture may have biological origins, but once it emerged, there was no longer any way to dissociate it from biology; it became a part of the environment that dictated the course of evolution. This is why it seems intellectually irresponsible to keep asserting an evolutionary arrow from biology to culture without also considering the reverse. When it comes to gender specifically, there is absolutely no hope of ever distinguishing our bodily (including sexual) experiences from the cultural norms of gender that predate our entrance to the scene. In the United States, parents often paint their child's room blue or pink (depending on gender) before the child is even born, usually also adorning the room with gender-appropriate toys. In this sense, gender socialization begins before the child even exits the womb, so that when he or she starts to act like a boy or a girl at the age of two, it's hardly possible to say that this is because of biology rather than socialization. As a friend of mine (a mother) recently said, "I hear a lot of mothers say, 'You can't keep a boy from playing with guns.' But you can. All you need to do is to take away the gun and tell the boy that he can't play with guns. It's as simple as that." It's just that many mothers don't do this because they have been taught to think that boys can't be prevented from playing with guns. And they have also been taught to think that boys are more aggressive than girls, so that when their son acts out, they tolerate it more than they would if the outburst came from their daughter. They are trapped in a vicious cycle: because they believe that they can't keep their son from playing with guns, they in fact can't keep him from doing so. If they believed the opposite, they would have no trouble stopping the behavior.

I emphasize the cultural rather than biological origins of gendered behavior in part because I believe that culture is the more influential of the two (which is not to say that biology plays no role). But in part I do so because cultural conditioning is easier to alter than genetic makeup. This doesn't mean that biology can't be tampered with. We do so increasingly not only with surgical and genetic interventions but also with medications from painkillers to anti-depressants. People even change their gender through a combination of surgery and hormone treatments. But this is quite different from the idea that we could change gendered patterns of behavior simply by intervening on the level of biology. Moreover, in a culture that is much more likely to remedy inequalities that have social causes than ones that are presumed to result from biological differences, the biological argument is a slippery slope. It basically gives us license to ignore inequalities that could be addressed by social adjustments. As long as we can resort to the idea that women are inherently less skilled at X than men, we don't feel obliged to modify anything. But if we think that women keep failing at X (say, running a company or being a politician) because of unfair social structures and belief systems, we may feel motivated to revise these structures and systems.[6] Social explanations, in sum, give us more leverage for adjusting things than do most biological arguments. In the realm of gender in particular, they open up the possibility that formerly oppressive gendered realities can be rectified by new cultural arrangements and patterns of socialization.

5

One way in which evolutionary psychology keeps refuting the centrality of culture is by insisting that we are "just like" our early ancestors, that even when we think that we're living modern, egalitarian lives, our genetic makeup forces us to lapse back into basic evolutionary patterns. When it comes to the notorious model of "men court, women choose," for instance, most of the authors admit that in modern, postindustrial societies things are usually not this straightforward, that men sometimes choose and women sometimes court. But these concessions tend to be overshadowed by the notion—repeated with an almost religious fervor—that even if our environment is very different from the ancestral environment that shaped human evolution, the ancient model of "men court, women choose" still runs our evolutionary brains without our knowledge. Buss, for example, asserts, "Whereas modern conditions of mating differ from ancestral conditions, the same sexual strategies operate with unbridled force. Our evolved psychology of mating remains. It is the only mating psychology we have; it just gets played out in a modern environment."[7]

The *only* mating psychology? How is it possible that the lengthy history of human evolution allows for only *one* mating psychology? And given the enormous role of culture in shaping human behavior, how could our altered environment not matter?[8] Fortunately, some of the more nuanced evolutionary thinkers admit that it might. In *The Mating Mind*, Geoffrey Miller, for

instance, acknowledges (in the context of talking about reproductive fitness) that "an organism that shows high fitness in an
ancestrally normal environment will not necessarily show high
fitness in a novel environment" (107). Miller further speculates that
the extraordinary creativity of humans may be "the culmination of
a long trend toward ever more sophisticated brain mechanisms that
produce ever less predictable behaviors" (417). That is, humans are
not only able to deal with unpredictable circumstances but are also
able to act unpredictably, in ways that don't have a clear precedent.
Miller notes that this is why psychology is "maddeningly difficult
as a predictive science" (417).[9] But it's also why humans have such
an immense ability to adjust to novel settings. Furthermore, this
adaptive ability is not only something we display in relation to
the larger material or social world that surrounds us but even in
relation to individual people, particularly ones we choose to know
intimately. This is why Miller proposes that it might help us to
view human sexual behavior as a romantic comedy, for in so doing
"we might understand not only creative capacities for producing
witty novelties, but also our ability to reinvent ourselves with each
new sexual relationship. People act differently when they're in love
with different people ... . In courtship, we work our way into roles
that we think will prove attractive" (419).

Miller makes this argument in the context of trying to explain
why humans are so different from other animals; why we, for
example, possess a much greater degree of creative intelligence and
linguistic capacity than other primates—why we are, as he puts it,
"the first articulately conscious species on Earth" (78). The survival
of the fittest can't explain the matter because we don't need to
be articulately conscious in order to survive. This leads Miller to
propose that high levels of articulacy—along with other distinc-
tively human characteristics, such as strong cognitive and rational
abilities—might have helped our ancestors to attract desirable
lovers. In other words, Miller hypothesizes that the intricacies of
human cultural, emotional, and psychological life originally came
into being because humans developed mating strategies that are
very different from those of other animals. More specifically, if
classical evolutionary theory tells us that male and female animals
in various species respond to visual reproductive fitness indicators,
or ornaments, so that those with the most attractive adornments
get chosen for mating, Miller posits that, somewhere along the

line, human mental traits such as creative intelligence and linguistic capacity became a means to secure sexual partners for both genders. To put the matter simply, humans are not only magnetized by physical indicators of sexual fitness (such as shiny hair) but also respond to mental attributes.

Miller conjectures that within early human communities, individuals with the best brains—with the wittiest courtship displays, the best storytelling, the most enticing music, the most pleasing artistic practices, the most interesting ideas, the most dexterous problem-solving skills, the most advanced social graces, the deepest capacity for empathy and kindness, not to mention the funniest jokes—became the most desirable partners.[10] This, in turn, explains why human brains developed so much faster than the brains of other primates; it explains why human societies have been capable of the kinds of achievements—as well as of the kind of destructiveness—that no other animal society has been able to approximate. This doesn't make us better than other animals; it just makes us different.

One of Miller's examples of how human mating strategies might have developed in a direction different from those of other animals is the emphasis that many humans place on sexual faithfulness. If our earliest ancestors were anything like bonobos and chimps, fidelity was probably not high on the agenda of either men or women. Yet, as Miller correctly observes, fidelity is these days quite attractive to many people. Even if other primates rarely show signs of sexual commitment to a particular mate, humans tend to value loyalty and, in Miller's words, we "have the capacity to inhibit our own courtship and copulation behavior, even in the face of awesome temptation" (333). That is, even if monogamy is not "natural," many of us—men as well as women—favor it in our romantic lives. In the next chapter, we'll see that Ryan and Jethá deem this emphasis on monogamy as a useless battle against our basic nature. But Miller sees it as a useful evolutionary adjustment, one that may be "perfectly adapted to a Pleistocene world in which the highest reproductive success went to those who were almost always faithful" (334). Miller further notes, "Our ancestors favored kind, fair, brave, well-mannered individuals who had the ability and generosity to help their sexual partners, children, stepchildren, and other members of their tribe. They were sexually unattracted to cheats, cowards, liars, and psychopaths." This is why altruism, in Miller's view, is not "an evolutionary paradox" but "a sexual ornament" (339).

I'm not sure how we can know any of this, but it's still refreshing to find an evolutionary psychologist who is willing to entertain the possibility that the sexual strategies of humans have *evolved* over time. What's so frustrating about the proponents of the standard narrative is that they insist on static models of sexuality in the evolutionary context—a context that is *by definition* a matter of understanding how humans have *changed* over time. If their reasoning doesn't make sense, it's in part because they contend that our sexual strategies are exactly like those of our earliest ancestors at the same time as they admit that more or less everything else about our lives has altered.

6

Until now, I have criticized the standard narrative in two ways. First, I have pointed out that it overlooks the behavior of our closest primate cousins in order to construct a story about human sexuality that fits the mold of Victorian morality (the assumption being that there is something about this morality that reflects the "true" natures of men and women). Second, I have argued that the lives of modern men and women are nothing like the lives of our evolutionary ancestors, so that it's unrealistic to think that our sexual behavior follows the template of the standard narrative. Miller's theory supports the second of these critiques, but it shifts the orientation somewhat by focusing on how it is that we came to be the way we now are. His analysis is still somewhat unidirectional in the sense that he is more interested in how biology has impacted culture than in how culture might have impacted biology, but at least he is capable of giving a reasonable explanation for why modern humans appreciate fitness indicators other than money and status or youth and beauty. While the advocates of the standard narrative worship the frozen icons of the randy male and coy female, Miller is able to account for the development of a whole host of human predilections, including mating preferences, that are readily observable in contemporary societies and that the standard narrative can't even begin to explain. According to Miller, if our current sexual choices are so intricate, it's in part because our ancestors already developed, somewhere along the course of evolutionary history, a preference for a complex mix of characteristics: "They selected instincts to provide for the common good even at high personal risk. They selected principled moral leadership capable of keeping peace, resolving conflict, and punishing crime. They selected unprecedented levels of sexual fidelity, good parenting, fair play, and charitable generosity. They helped to shape the human capacity for sympathy. They helped to make us reasonably agreeable, sincere, and socially responsive" (340).

For me, what is perhaps most interesting about Miller's theory is that it opens up the possibility that gender equality might be an efficient evolutionary adaptation. As we'll learn in the next chapter, Ryan and Jethá maintain that such equality was a normal feature of human societies prior to the invention of agriculture. This seems possible. But even if we—for the sake of argument—chose to see it as a recent cultural invention, there is no reason to think that it is antithetical to evolutionary logic. The supporters of the standard narrative speak as if gender equality somehow violated the basic principles of evolution. But wouldn't it be just as possible to assert that it merely represents the latest step in evolutionary development? If it's conceivable—as Miller maintains—that a degree of altruism at some point became a desirable trait in a potential mate, then it seems to me that it's equally conceivable that an egalitarian mindset, in today's society, is one of the strongest indicators of reproductive fitness. Miller himself appears to deny this when he claims that "women's ongoing liberation from the nightmare of patriarchy has been due to cultural changes, not genetic evolution" (83). I agree. But if I were to adopt the evolutionary frame of mind for a moment, I would argue that an egalitarian attitude is these days one of the best ways for men to make sure that they get laid on a regular basis.

I would propose that a lot of straight American women are, in the twenty-first century, likely to choose a man who treats them as his equal over one who doesn't. Speaking for myself only, I can honestly say that I'm much less interested in a man's bank account than I am in his gender politics: the kind of caveman that the standard narrative is promoting would have absolutely no chance. The alpha male holds no attraction for me, and a quick survey of our mass entertainment confirms that many other women feel the same way. Our movies and television shows are full of emotionally available, sincere, considerate, and even a tad vulnerable men. As we saw in the introduction to this book, one of my critics on *Psychology Today* mockingly asked me if I liked Jennifer Aniston's movies because of all the sensitive guys found in these movies. Well ... *why wouldn't I*? While I don't have any particular preference for Aniston's movies, I know that their portrayals of modern masculinity are a great deal more appealing than those of evolutionary psychology. And fortunately for me, they are not always wholly unrealistic depictions of the kinds of men I happen to know in real life.

On the flipside, our movies and television shows present female characters who are driven and ambitious, intelligent and sassy, sexually assertive and not in the least bit embarrassed about their sexual urges. These are not just fantasies that have no basis in our society. Many men and women relate to such models because these models mirror the values they themselves live by. Clearly, many screen-writers, producers, and directors have figured out what so many of our evolutionary psychologists (and self-help gurus) haven't, namely that modern men and women tend to like enlightened gender models. If Hollywood movies sell, it's in part because they often (not always, but often) break gender stereotypes in ways that speak to audiences a lot better than the obsolete "man-the-hunter" paradigm that the supporters of the standard narrative insist on advancing. I don't doubt that some such hunters still roam the bars and streets of our society. But they are by no means the only model of masculinity available today. Modern men and women identify with egalitarian role models because this is how they experience their gendered lives, or at the very least would *like* to experience them. That is, the fantasy aspect of movies and television echoes a real desire in modern viewers: a desire for fairness, decency, and emotional openness in their own relationships.

This is of course not to deny that many movies and television shows contribute to the idealistic story-book expectations that some women have of men (and vice versa). Obviously, what we get on the screen are impossibly gorgeous men who make it harder for us to get excited about the flawed guys who populate the real world. But even this may not be *all* bad, for at least now it's both men and women who are being objectified, so that the male supporters of patriarchy are forced to swallow some of their own medicine (the proponents of the standard narrative would do well to watch one season of *The Vampire Diaries*, *White Collar*, *Covert Affairs*, or the remake of *90210* to get a sense of what I'm talking about). And, as I've started to suggest, the male ideal these days often includes a lot of admirable attributes, such as emotional competence and respect for women: it's not enough to have great abs but you must also be kind and thoughtful. While it's certainly possible to find movies and television shows that denigrate women at the expense of men, these are becoming more and more rare, and this is because the entertainment industry understands that many viewers are turned off by them.

One of the major shortcomings of the standard narrative—and perhaps of much of evolutionary reasoning overall—is that it doesn't allow sufficient room for psychological changes resulting from social changes. It remains fixated on the idea that genes determine our psychology when clearly we are dealing with a combination of genes, social forces, and unconscious motivations. And, as I have emphasized, social changes can lead to very rapid psychological changes, which is exactly why gender relations have altered so quickly not only on the level of social arrangements but also of psychological realities. I admitted in the previous chapter that the latter often lag behind social changes—that it can take more than one generation for psychological realities to begin to match social realities. But there is hardly any doubt that the greater gender equality of our time has given rise to psychological processes that are very different from those in effect just a few decades ago. This reality is what the standard narrative, inexplicably, tries to deny, which is why it keeps insisting that even though our social environment has altered, our psyches are still pretty much the same as those of our ancestors. Yet given how obvious it is that there are many men and women in the world who want nothing to do with traditional gender models, it's hard to remain sympathetic to those who continue to tout their timeless validity. If the standard narrative in no way corresponds to the actualities of modern life, then what, besides the perpetuation of sexism, could possibly be the reason for upholding it?

7

This sexism is so ingrained within evolutionary psychology that even its most female-friendly thinkers, such as Miller, can't seem to avoid slipping once in a while. Miller starts off promisingly enough, arguing that the standard narrative of sexual selection—the narrative of "men court, women choose" that I have outlined—must be replaced by what he calls a "mutual choice" model: the idea that both men and women choose (as well as court). The latter model has the advantage of capturing something about the reality of modern gender relations. Moreover, it has the added bonus of explaining why women are not total idiots—why men and women are equal in their mental aptitudes. You see, one of the problems with the "men court, women choose" model—the model that Wright and Buss still adhere to without question—is that, as Miller states, it depicts "the female mind as riding along on the evolutionary coattails of the male mind, and female intelligence as an evolutionary side-effect of male intelligence." In this theory, "the males are portrayed as doing all the interesting things: the courtship displays, the storytelling, the music-making, the creative idea-work" (94). Given that evolutionary theory aligns the effort required by such activities with brain development, and given that it has until recently assumed that men were the ones making this effort, the implication is that their brains have been the ones to reap the benefits. To put the matter bluntly, the fact that men have throughout the ages been desperate for sex means that they have had to hone their brains to devise intricate schemes of seducing women. The result? They have better brains than women.

Oops.

It is well known that Darwin, as Helen Fisher observes, "thought men were naturally smarter. This superior male intelligence, he proposed, arose because young men had to fight to win mates. Because ancestral males had to defend their families, hunt for their joint subsistence, attack enemies, and make weapons, males needed higher mental faculties, 'namely, observation, reason, invention or imagination.'" As a result, "intelligence evolved—in men."[11] Fisher further notes that Darwin saw proof of this gender inequality everywhere around himself: "the poets, merchants, politicians, scientists, artists, and philosophers of

Victorian England were overwhelmingly men." Fisher generously concludes that this was "the climate of the times" (190), implying that we are now beyond this.

But are we?

On the one hand, Miller certainly implies that we are. Because his rendering of evolutionary theory—and particularly the notion of "mutual choice"—posits that both men and women engage in elaborate courting rituals, it allows for the idea that male and female brains have developed in tandem. As Miller specifies, "I do not think that female creative intelligence is a genetic side-effect of male creative intelligence, or arose simply as a way of assessing male courtship displays. I think that female creative intelligence evolved through male mate choice as much as male creative intelligence evolved through female mate choice" (98). On the other hand, even Miller cannot entirely banish the traces of the earlier "men court, women choose" paradigm. Even as he defends the validity of "mutual choice," he keeps suggesting that it's still possible that men might be genetically more creative than women because evolutionary sexual selection has forced them to make *greater* sexual displays than women, "to advertise their creative intelligence through trying to produce works of art, music, and literature, amassing wealth, and attaining political status" (82). That is, even within mutual choice, men might have still done more of the courting and women more of the choosing, which implies that men would have had to develop their intellectual capacities more than women.

Miller goes on to argue that in the same way that males of other animals "waste" energy on flamboyant sexual ornaments such as the peacock's tail (ornaments that cost them a great deal because they make them more vulnerable to predators), "male humans waste their time and energy getting graduate degrees, writing books, playing sports, fighting other men, painting pictures, playing jazz, and founding religious cults" (129). In this manner, Miller implies that cultural production is a matter of specifically masculine sexual display, as if women didn't get graduate degrees, write books, fight in wars, play sports, paint pictures, play jazz, or—and this is perhaps nothing to be proud of—become religious fanatics. And he also ignores all the exertions—such as emotional intelligence, the capacity to nurture the young, or the intricate talent demanded by delicious cooking—that women have traditionally been exceptionally good at (by now it should be obvious that I'm not saying they have been good at these things because they are biologically designed for them but because these are the activities that many societies have expected of them). I'm not sure why playing football takes more mental capacity than preparing a Thanksgiving meal for your entire extended family. But because Miller is convinced that men have historically made a greater creative effort, he ends up asking, "Should we reject a theory of mental evolution that successfully predicts an observed sex difference, in favor of some other sex-blind theory that predicts a desired sexual equality in cultural production that has not yet been observed in any human society?" (84). In other words, let's not allow our political correctness to keep us from positing an evolutionary explanation for what is everywhere evident, namely that men are better at cultural production than women.

8

The wastefulness of courtship is, according to Miller, precisely what makes it romantic, what lifts it above the utilitarian concerns of mere survival. As he maintains, "The wasteful dancing, the wasteful gift-giving, the wasteful conversation, the wasteful laughter, the wasteful foreplay, the wasteful adventures. From the viewpoint of 'survival of the fittest,' the waste looks mad and pointless and maladaptive" (128). This is exactly why it's such an effective mating strategy: like an expensive engagement ring, it handicaps the individual who is willing to mount the effort, thereby indicating a strong investment on his or her part. This is an interesting argument. But surely it's problematic to claim that wasteful courtship rituals are a specifically male tendency. The fact that men in our society are the ones who usually buy engagement rings doesn't mean that women don't exert themselves romantically. If anything, many women have been conditioned to think that they are solely responsible for making their relationships last, so that they often work a lot harder than men to make sure that everything unfolds smoothly. The emotional labor women routinely put into their relationships—their endless efforts to communicate, to negotiate their way through rough patches, to be supportive without being smothering, to anticipate the needs of their partners, to prop up men's egos, and to present themselves in just the right light—arguably take a lot more effort (not to mention skill) than a trip to the jewelry store does. It's just that such labor is culturally invisible because it is what women are "naturally" supposed to be good at.

Miller might claim that men have to work extremely hard to afford that engagement ring. But women also have to work quite hard to afford the things that are required for the maintenance of "feminine" desirability in our society (it doesn't help that they pay double for haircuts, clothes, and shoes). And because it's not enough, these days, to be young and pretty, let's not forget about all the factors that have women worrying about everything from their careers to their personalities: trying to be successful; trying to be an interesting person; trying to be emotionally balanced; trying to be good at intimacy; trying to be sexy, and so on. All in all, I would say that modern women, on average, probably "waste" more effort on relationships than most men.

As much as Miller tries to transcend the misogynistic inflections of traditional evolutionary theory, this theory keeps pulling him back to the Stone Age. Take his attempt to explain how it can be that women score higher in tests that assess verbal capacity, given that men's propensity for more flamboyant courtship displays should have caused them to develop stronger verbal skills. Miller's answer is that the enigma disappears when we take into account that standardized tests assess language comprehension rather than language production. In other words, women may be better at verbal tasks that require passive understanding, but men are still better at actively (and creatively) using language. Essentially, men speak (and write) while women merely listen (and read). In the same way that peacocks grow striking tails while peahens are merely skilled at assessing the value of such tails, human males create verbal displays while women merely judge them. Or, in Miller's words, "Sexual selection makes males better display-producers and females better display-discriminators" (375).

Charming: women are merely passive recipients of cultural production while men are its active creators. Given the male inclination for sexual display and the female inclination for choosiness, Miller writes:

We should expect female superiority in language comprehension and male superiority in language production. For example, females should recognize more words, but males should use a larger proportion of their vocabulary ... In this simple picture, more women might understand what 'azure' really means (so they can accurately judge male word use), but more men might actually speak the word 'azure' in conversation (even if they think it means 'Vermilion'). Standard vocabulary tests measure only comprehension of word meaning, not the ability to produce impressive synonyms during courtship. Reading comprehension questions are more common than creative writing tests. Women are faster readers and buy more books, but most books are written by men. (376)

Leaving aside the question of whether it's actually true that men still write more books, or better books, than women in the America of 2015, what is remarkable here is that Miller pays hardly any attention to the sociohistorical (economic, structural, cultural) reasons for why women haven't written as many books as men (he notes the possibility of such reasons but only as a kind of afterthought). Yet Virginia Woolf argued almost a hundred years ago that the reason Shakespeare doesn't have an equally famous sister is that women haven't historically had the financial independence or mental leisure—or even the room of their own—required for artistic production.[12] And, when it comes to the contemporary situation, Miller's reporting is skewed at best. He asserts that male verbal displays can be observed in churches, parliaments, and scientific conferences, but completely disregards female displays that can be observed in other venues, such as humanities conferences or even the parliaments of nations with egalitarian gender relations. It may indeed be the case that men write more books in biology departments, but this is certainly not the case in departments of English.

I've noted that even the best male minds sometimes become obtuse when they start talking about women—that there is something about gender as a topic that dulls otherwise discerning intellects. This seems to happen to Miller. As we have seen, he is careful to take culture into account when assessing the ways in which human life has evolved since ancestral times. Yet the moment he begins to analyze women's creative capacities, he ceases to be able to think through the complex interactions between biology and culture, implying that biology alone—or at least primarily—explains the trouble women have had in reaching intellectual parity with men. This is just plain bad reasoning. Downplaying the sociohistorical obstacles to women's creativity—implying that patriarchal traditions, sexual and religious norms, and the longstanding cultural and economic restrictions on female intellectual display can be cast aside in favor of a purely genetic argument—is ... well, a little stupid.

Ultimately, Miller seems to agree with Darwin's assessment that men dominate cultural production throughout the world for the simple reason that they are genetically better suited for it. This is akin to taking a look around the globe, seeing that white people have more money and power than pretty much anyone else, and saying that this means that white people are "naturally" superior—that if they control much of the world's resources, it's because they are genetically primed to do so. I trust that most of us would protest if a scientist made this claim. Why, then, are we not protesting when he makes it about women?

Furthermore, if we are going to reason along evolutionary lines, I would like to raise the following question: if men are the ones who are constantly seeking sexual novelty, who get bored with monogamy—as evolutionary psychology so persistently tells us—why wouldn't it be women who would have had to develop a highly evolved repertoire of courtship rituals just to hold onto their men? Personally, I don't for one minute think that either gender is inherently more creative than the other. So my point here is not to say that women are more innovative than men. I'm merely noting a blind-spot in the theory: an obvious bias that keeps even a relatively sophisticated thinker such as Miller wedded to fundamentally sexist ideas. If you are going to insist that creativity evolved from sexual displays designed to procure and hold the interest of a mate, then the famous male propensity for straying should, logically, have led women to develop this trait more strongly than men.

I have argued that evolutionary psychology habitually trades in social clichés in the name of science, and Miller is no exception. He argues that it's possible that after a man's verbal courtship efforts have brought him success, he no longer feels driven to be as interesting or self-disclosing: "The man who used to talk like Cyrano now talks like a cave-man. Once he was a poet, now he is prosaic.

His verbal courtship effort has decreased" (382). Frustratingly, women find that the greater a commitment they make, the less their partners speak: "When women *universally* complain about their slothfully mute boyfriends, we learn two things. First, women have a *universal* desire to enjoy receiving high levels of verbal courtship effort. Second, high levels of courtship effort are so costly that men have evolved to produce them only when they are necessary for initiating or reviving sexual relationships" (383; emphasis added). Universally? Again? But this isn't even the end of the banalities. Miller patiently explains that because verbal courtship is mutual, we might assume that men might feel just as frustrated by women's silences as women do by men's silences. But this doesn't happen because women keep talking longer. Women in fact talk so much, so incessantly, that they tire men to the point that the latter start hiding behind their newspapers. Evidently, this is because women are more desperate to hold their man's interest than vice versa. Because ancestral men might have been tempted to abandon a woman after she became pregnant and search for a new partner, ancestral females had to work quite hard to keep their men around. Again, one has to wonder why this didn't lead women to develop greater creative capacities. But never mind. Miller's point is that this is why modern women also work overtime to hang onto their guy. Unfortunately, this doesn't refine their intellect. Rather, their verbal displays become so annoying to men that the latter become even more negligent.

Miller does in the end qualify his arguments (the afterthought I referred to above), admitting that women's lesser achievements in cultural production might also be due to women having, for millennia, been forcefully kept from intellectual, political, and artistic endeavors. And he also acknowledges that things are now changing swiftly, as a result of our more egalitarian values. But it's too late to salvage his theory from the charge of sexism. The damage is done. The seeds of doubt have been planted in the reader's mind. Maybe it really *is* true that women are naturally less creative than men. Maybe their inferior status worldwide really *does* have a genetic basis. Maybe it really has nothing to do with patriarchal social arrangements. Miller in fact seems quite invested in making sure that patriarchy doesn't get blamed for women's inferior status, positing the following: "The ocean of male language that confronts modern women in bookstores, television, newspapers, classrooms, parliaments, and businesses does not necessarily come from a male conspiracy to deny women their voice. It may come from an evolutionary history of sexual selection in which the male motivation to talk was vital to their reproduction" (377). In other words, men just can't help themselves. Their verbal dominance is not a matter of unequal power relationships but of men's genetic impulse to show off so that they can get more sex. Once again, gender inequality is a matter of nature rather than culture. And ultimately, actually, it's women's own fault because they keep rewarding men who flaunt their prowess in this manner.

9

The idea that women themselves might be responsible for patriarchy is not unique to Miller. Buss similarly argues that patriarchy results from the fact that women prefer dominant men with ample resources. That is, if men control resources around the world, it's because women keep choosing such men (212–13). Never mind that in many societies, making a "choice" such as this is still the best way for women to ensure their comfort and well-being. Never mind that in many societies, women can't easily access the highest-paying jobs (and are often paid less than men for the same work). And never mind that in modern America, there are increasing numbers of women who have no patience with dominant men no matter how many yachts these men possess. As I have suggested, one of the greatest things about women's socioeconomic liberation is that it has freed many women to choose men who exhibit characteristics that are the very opposite of the patriarchal macho man. And one of the many things that is so terrible about poverty is that it makes it harder for disadvantaged women to do the same. Being able to be with a gentle man who is more interested in making conversation than in making money is often a privilege of those women who are able to make their own money. And I have no doubt that one reason evolutionary psychologists are so adamant about the dogmas of the field is that the number of such women has increased rapidly in recent decades, not because poverty has decreased but because middle-class women have entered the workforce. This trend is inherently threatening to those who prefer to explain patriarchy in terms of natural rather than social factors. And it is particularly threatening to those who wish to absolve men of all responsibility for patriarchy, who wish to argue, as Miller does, that from the perspective of evolutionary theory, neither sex deserves blame. Apparently, when it comes to men's control over resources, no one—and least of all men—can be held accountable.

How lucky for men. I'm not the kind of feminist who likes to vilify men, for—as I've indicated—I'm much more interested in liberating both men and women from archaic gender roles. But surely there should be a limit to our indulgence. Saying that men can't be blamed for patriarchy is a bit like saying that white people can't be blamed for racism or for the history of racial oppression. Consider Buss's argument that our "evolved sexual strategies" explain why men have historically tried to control female sexuality: "Over the course of human evolutionary history, men who failed to control women's sexuality—for example, by failing to attract a mate, failing to prevent cuckoldry, or failing to keep a mate— experienced lower reproductive success than men who succeeded in controlling women's sexuality. We come from a long and unbroken line of ancestral fathers who succeeded in obtaining mates, preventing their infidelity, and providing enough benefits to keep them from leaving" (213–14). So, basically, men's attempts to control female sexuality are an evolutionary inevitability that has nothing to do with power, politics, or economic arrangements; it's all just a matter of making sure your genes make it to the next round, which means that there is no space for culpability. We are in fact quite close to the arguments about rape I outlined at the beginning of this book: men can't be blamed for doing "whatever it takes" to advance their genetic agenda; they are programmed to be a little forceful about it, so let's cut them some slack.

One of the customary arguments of evolutionary psychology is that science shouldn't shy away from pronouncing the truth even when it's unpleasant or unpalatable. Evolutionary theory, we are told, is heartless and unromantic. This is why, like many of his colleagues, Miller maintains that "sounding sexist is not a good reason to ban a theory" (94). Is the same true of sounding racist? If not, what's the difference? Miller asserts that science "is the one zone of human thought where ideological preferences are not supposed to influence the assessment of ideas and evidence" (94). Science, he continues, dissociates facts from ideology, from "armchair speculation, entertaining narratives, comforting ideas, and memorable anecdotes" (424). I have already acknowledged that I agree that this is what real science tries to do, albeit with variable results. But it's a little hard to accept the claim that this is what evolutionary psychology does when it talks about the inherent superiority of the male mind or waxes poetic about the evolutionary advantages of men controlling female sexuality. It's also a little hard to tolerate the condescension that infiltrates Miller's tone when he, in all seriousness, proposes that *only* science can tell us anything valid about the state of the world, concluding that "the social sciences and humanities would benefit ... from turning to evolutionary psychology as their conceptual basis, rather than Marxism, psychoanalysis, and French philosophy" (427).

Miller appears to believe that only evolutionary psychology can produce useful knowledge about human life, ethics, language, and other central topics. But this is an absurd claim, given that there are many different ways of assessing what constitutes useful knowledge, and given that what is useful in one setting might not be so in another. In fact, one of the points I've been making throughout this book is that standard evolutionary explanations of romantic behavior are more or less useless in the context of modern gendered lives. Miller's claim is also absurd in the sense that the social sciences and humanities seem to possess a great deal more intellectual complexity and capacity for self-criticism than evolutionary psychology. Indeed, in much of the social sciences and humanities—contemporary approaches to Marxism, psychoanalysis, and French philosophy included—there is a clear admission of being biased (in the sense of always theorizing from a specific point of view). And there is a veritable allergy toward reductive models of human life, which makes it unlikely that social scientists and humanists will swap their ideas for those of evolutionary psychology any time soon. The latter would need to reinvent itself more or less completely in order for this to happen. And if you want feminists to come to the table—as Miller declares he does—it might help to stop telling us that men are genetically more creative than women.

Just saying ...

I've been proposing that many of the gendered arguments of evolutionary psychology represent the intellectual arm of a backlash phenomenon that strives to arrest the wave of gender equality. One of the things that is particularly striking about this phenomenon is its unabashed arrogance. It's absolutely mind-boggling that an academic can publish a book at the dawn of the twenty-first century where he casually tells us that if women haven't risen to the same level of cultural accomplishment as men have, it's because they are *genetically* less creative. In the context of a world where Malala Yousafzai gets shot in the head for wanting to go to school, and where other women get acid thrown in their faces for the same reason, this argument has all the obscenity of reactionary propaganda. Moreover, one can only marvel at the arrogance of declaring that only one's *own* field is capable of saying something constructive about human life, art, ethics, morality, language, or any other area of academic inquiry. One can only marvel at the egotism that leads Miller to write: "Given minds shaped by sexual selection for ideological entertainment rather than epistemic accuracy, what hope do we have of discovering truths about the world? History suggests that we had very little hope until the social institutions of science arose. Before science, there is no apparent cumulative progress in the accuracy of human belief systems. After science, everything changed" (424). Everything? So Plato, Aristotle, Sophocles, Homer, Buddhist philosophy, ancient Indian wisdom, Shakespeare, and Milton made no contribution to our understanding of human life?

Against the backdrop of self-important claims such as this, I'm tempted to point out that the social sciences and humanities may well be one of the last strong-holds against the overly pragmatic, results-oriented tenor of our society. I'm by no means anti-science. But neither would I ever concede that science alone can adequately deal with every facet of human life, including our psychological, emotional, ethical, and existential conundrums. Asking science to explain the meaning of our lives, help us on our deathbeds, resolve our moral dilemmas, capture the subtleties of our feelings through metaphor, or offer us a piercing image of irony, tragedy, or sublimity won't get us very far. It can't do these things, which in turn means that elevating it to the pinnacle of human creative capacity is to impoverish us in a fairly drastic way.

Perhaps even more astonishing is the sexual fantasy that animates Miller's assessment of the superior prowess of science (and scientists). It all starts innocently enough, with the following statement: "Science is a set of social institutions for channeling our

sexually selected instincts for ideological display in certain directions according to strict rules. These rules award social status to
individuals for proposing good theories and gathering good data,
not for physical attractiveness." But then things heat up nicely:
"Science separates the arenas of intellectual display (conferences,
classrooms, journals) from other styles of courtship display ...
Scientists are required to provide intellectual displays to young
single people (through undergraduate teaching, graduate advising,
and colloquium-giving), but are discouraged from enjoying any
sexual benefits from these displays, so are kept in a state of
perpetual quasi-courtship until retirement" (424–5). So scientists settle for brilliant intellectual displays because they can't
have sex with their students? And the rest of us within the
academy? Are we merely spinning webs of ideology, blinded by
our "romantic obscurantism" (427), and incapable of any rigorous
intellectual exertion? And what exactly does this picture of virile
(presumably male) scientists strutting their stuff, writing ground-
breaking journal articles, and stunning their students with their
dazzling classroom sublimations reveal about the unconscious
lives of evolutionary psychologists? Miller writes: "The scientific
traditions are ingenious ways of harnessing human courtship effort
to produce cumulative progress towards world-models that are
abstract, communicable, and true ... . [Science] is one of the most
sophisticated arenas for human courtship" (425). If this is true, I
think we're all in trouble. One can only hope that Sarah Hrdy is
right when she states, "Sooner or later in science, wrong assumptions get revised."[13]

4

The Downfall of the Coy Female

Before the war on drugs, the war on terror, or the war on cancer, there was the war on female sexual desire. It's a war that has been raging far longer than any other, and its victims number well into the billions by now. Like the others, it's a war that can never be won, as the declared enemy is a force of nature. We may as well declare war on the cycles of the moon.

CHRISTOPHER RYAN AND CACILDA JETHÁ

1

Given evolutionary psychology's Victorian sensibilities, it's hardly surprising that it is the image of the coy female that has, in recent years, become one of its weak links. If the standard narrative is showing signs of fraying, it's in part because its depiction of reticent female sexuality has become harder and harder to justify not only in terms of modern social realities but also in purely evolutionary terms. One of the greatest services rendered by Ryan and Jethá's *Sex at Dawn* is to reveal just how flimsy—and how ideologically saturated—is the "science" that has been used to advance the standard narrative's take on female sexuality. To begin with, primates that are most similar to humans both in terms of genetic makeup and social organization, such as the bonobos, display a robust female sexuality that is a far cry from the Victorian imagery promoted by Wright and his colleagues. Ryan and Jethá assert that it is only by ignoring the sexual culture of our closest relatives that evolutionary psychologists have been able to broadcast the backward ideals of female chastity and sexual reluctance. Bonobo females copulate numerous times a day, often with many different males, and they also routinely engage in sexual activities that are not in any way directly related to reproduction; they have sex, including lesbian sex, for pleasure, and they like to have a lot of it. What's more, bonobo societies are relatively egalitarian, displaying little of the male aggression that many evolutionary psychologists take for granted. Furthermore, both males and females have multiple sexual partners, which makes it hard to argue for the "naturalness" of the double standard of promiscuous males and strictly monogamous females.

Ryan and Jethá observe that if evolutionary psychology has routinely sidelined the bonobos in favor of other primates that are further from humans in evolutionary terms, it is because its standard narrative has been motivated to defend a particular story about human sexuality—a story that, as I have shown, has more in common with Victorian morality than with the principles of science; the evolutionary record, in other words, has been obscured by the demands of cultural mythology. Ryan and Jethá call this process "flintstonization": the tendency to project current (or historical) human social arrangements back onto the evolutionary past, as well as onto the animal societies that are used to back up a specific version of this past, so as to arrive at a representation of human evolutionary development that is socially palatable. Note the insidious circularity of this process: first one "finds" current inequalitarian social arrangements everywhere in the evolutionary past, and then one refers to this past to "prove" the naturalness— and therefore the validity—of the social arrangements in question. As Ryan and Jethá remark, "Despite high-minded claims to the contrary—often couched in language chosen to intimidate would-be dissenters—science all too often grovels at the feet of the dominant cultural paradigm."[1] Flintstonization, they specify, "has two parents: a lack of solid data and the psychological need to explain, justify, and celebrate one's own life and times" (32).

Using evidence from primate societies closely resembling human societies, hunter-gatherer cultures, the archeological record, and human anatomy, Ryan and Jethá hypothesize that it is actually extremely unlikely that patriarchy, monogamy, and coy female sexuality characterized the social organization of our ancestors. Rather, the evidence points to the likelihood that our ancestors lived in small informal bands where men and women were relatively equal and where both genders had several sexual partners. This in turn spells trouble for the standard narrative. As Ryan and Jethá state, "If human sexuality developed primarily as a bonding mechanism in interdependent bands where paternity certainty was a nonissue, then the standard narrative of human sexual evolution is toast. The anachronistic presumption that women have *always* bartered their sexual favors to individual men in return for help with child care, food, protection, and the rest of it collapses ... where women feel no need to negotiate such deals" (149). That is, if the standard narrative relies on a deeply patriarchal vision of human prehistory, the collapse of this vision immediately leads to the collapse of the narrative, which is precisely why so many evolutionary psychologists adhere to this vision even in the face of overwhelming evidence to the contrary. They know that the minute they surrender this vision, they lose the cornerstone of their whole enterprise: the iconography of randy males and coy females. This is why they keep trying to prove that a patriarchal version of female sexuality—one that runs from the chastity belts of feudal times to the double standard of Victorian England, to the practice of female circumcision in some contemporary societies, all the way to the persistent rhetoric of female purity (and the value placed on female virginity) in modern America—represents the natural state of women.

2

Noting that egalitarianism and an ethos of sharing is found in many still existing hunter-gatherer societies, Ryan and Jethá argue that patriarchal social arrangements are a relatively recent invention, coinciding with the invention of agriculture around ten thousand years ago (which, in evolutionary terms, is very late). It is the hunter-gatherer societies specifically that are still facing conditions that are somewhat similar to those of evolutionary history, which is why it makes more sense to use them as a point of comparison than it does to refer to social structures that obviously have a more recent origin. After all, human societies altered radically with plant cultivation and the domestication of animals: suddenly private property became an issue, and with it emerged the desire to pass it onto one's offspring. This, in turn, meant that certainty about paternity—the knowledge that one was actually passing one's property to one's own children—became important in ways that it might not have been before ("property" in hunter-gatherer societies is largely portable, which immediately limits its size). This explains the rise of patriarchal social arrangements where men sought to control female sexuality in order to ensure that their children, in fact, were theirs. In this new system, women became pawns in the transmission of property through marriage, and their value depended primarily on their chastity, which is why their sexuality became so strictly monitored. This monitoring wasn't merely a matter of sexual prohibitions but included a vast machinery of psychological conditioning designed to make the very idea of sleeping with someone besides their husband unpalatable to most women. The traces of this mentality are still discernible in even the most gender-egalitarian societies. But this doesn't mean that it reflects human "nature." Rather, it reflects a very particular social organization that came into being quite late in human history.

Ryan and Jethá write: "The biggest loser (aside from slaves, perhaps) in the agricultural revolution was the human female, who went from occupying a central, respected role in foraging societies to becoming another possession for a man to earn and defend, along with his house, slaves, and livestock" (14). Helen Fisher likewise traces the emergence of the sexual double standard to the emergence of agriculture. Emphasizing that women are just as likely as men to philander in societies that don't punish them for doing so, Fisher draws the same link as Ryan and Jethá do between the development of agriculture and private property on the one hand and the ideal of the pure female on the other.[2] The problem—one that we still have not been able to transcend—is that over time this ideal became so naturalized that people lost track of its agricultural origins and started to think of it as an indicator of women's innate predilections. More specifically, by the time evolutionary biology started to devise theories of human sexuality, everyone took it for granted that women were largely asexual. As Fisher exclaims in relation to the arguments of Donald Symons: "Man the natural playboy, woman the doting spouse—Americans already believed it. Because of our agrarian background and sexual double standard it became acceptable to view men as would-be Don Juans and women as the more virtuous of the genders. So when Symons presented an evolutionary explanation for men's philandering nature, many scholars bought it like a better chocolate bar. The idea that men crave sexual novelty more than women do now saturates academic books and academic minds" (89).

Fisher reminds us that "it is an old axiom in science that what you are looking for, you tend to find," adding that "there is no evidence whatsoever that women are sexually shy or that they shun clandestine sexual adventures" (95).[3] Yet Westerners, curiously enough, "cling to the concept that men are the seducers and women the coy, submissive recipients of male overtures" (32). Like Ryan and Jethá, Fisher turns to the bonobos for proof of how indefensible this view really is, noting that bonobo females are not known for their reticence. The same can be said of chimps: "Chimp females are sexually aggressive," and "adolescent females are sometimes insatiable, even tweaking the flaccid penises of uninterested companions" (132). And since neither the bonobos nor the chimps are monogamous, Fisher concludes that monogamy, in human societies, is most likely a recent invention. This in turn implies that the high rate of divorce we are witnessing in today's society might be a fallback onto our evolutionary history rather than a deviation from it. If the development of agriculture is to blame for the constraints on female sexuality, then it makes sense that in post-agricultural societies such as the United States we might be reverting back to the greater sexual freedom of earlier eras. Moreover, it's hardly a secret that women's economic independence is directly related to their sexual freedom, including divorce. In the United States, divorce rates have risen with the greater independence of women for the simple reason that, to borrow from Fisher, "a woman with a salary is often less tolerant of marital despair than one dependent on her spouse to provide the evening meal" (107).[4] Perhaps this is why Wright is so keen to endorse polygamy—rather than women's greater economic independence—as a solution to American poverty. Since divorce is the thing he most wants to prevent, keeping women economically enslaved to their husbands might seem like the most expedient solution for him.

Fisher also maintains that, contrary to the arguments of the standard narrative, monogamous pair-bonding might not be any more evolutionarily adaptive to females than it is to males, for "a male can be more trouble than he is worth"; indeed, Fisher continues, "if a female needs a male for protection, why not travel in a mixed group and copulate with several males—the common tactic of female chimps" (150). Besides better protection, Fisher lists three other evolutionary reasons for why female promiscuity might have been adaptive in the past: access to the resources of multiple men, more varied DNA, and the acquisition of better genes. Along related lines, Ryan and Jethá argue that it is likely that sexual competition between men didn't take place on the level of individuals—that the image of several men fighting for one woman is probably completely inaccurate. Rather, sexual competition between men might have taken place on the level of sperm: in species where females routinely copulate with multiple males, it is the strongest sperm, not the strongest male, who wins the evolutionary race. Why else, Ryan and Jethá ask, would women have developed the capacity for prolonged sexual arousal, including multiple orgasms, which makes it possible for them to have sex with a number of men in quick succession? And why would they have developed their notorious noisiness during sex—what in the field is known as "copulatory vocalization"—if not to alert the males of the neighborhood to the fact that they were having sex, thereby inviting males roaming nearby to participate in the fun? In sum: if women really are as uninterested in sex as the standard narrative tells us, why would human females have evolved such an abundant sexual capacity: among other things, the desire for sex even when they are not ovulating (unusual in the animal world, though shared by our closest cousins, the bonobos); loud sexual vocalization (which advertises to the rest of the world, including straight men other than their current partner, the extent of their sexual pleasure); and an orgasmic capacity that arguably trumps that of most human males (as Tiresias, the ancient seer, already admitted)?

3

Historically, our society has striven to conceal women's sexual voraciousness. Many Westerners gasp in horror when they hear about female circumcision—which in many cases entails the excision of the clitoris, thereby making female orgasm difficult to attain—in some far-flung contemporary cultures. Yet our own culture engaged in comparable practices well into the twentieth century while simultaneously disseminating a widespread rhetoric on female sexual purity. Ryan and Jethá report that as late as 1936, a respected medical school text "recommended surgical removal or cauterization of the clitoris as a cure for masturbation in girls" (251). This idea had its roots in the once popular theories of a British gynecologist named Isaac Baker Brown, who argued that many women's diseases derived from an overexcitement of the nervous system, and particularly of the pudic nerve, which runs to the clitoris. He maintained that the removal of the clitoris was the best way to prevent the evils triggered by female masturbation, such as hysteria, epilepsy, idiocy, mania, and death (250). While Baker Brown was eventually discredited, his theories became popular in the United States, where clitoredectomies were performed as a cure for hysteria, nymphomania, and female masturbation well into the twentieth century (251). While it was common for nineteenth-century medical experts to vilify masturbation for men and women alike, and to align it with various ailments, such as syphilis, smallpox, infertility, insanity, and blindness, it was women in particular who bore the physical burden of this repressive sexual culture.

Strangely, all of this was going on at the same time as medical experts and cultural authorities alike proclaimed that women had no sexual feelings to begin with. The famous German neurologist, Richard von Krafft-Ebing, for instance, insisted that when a woman is "normally developed mentally and well-bred, her sexual desire is small. If this were not so, the world would become a brothel and marriage and a family impossible."[5] This was 1886. But how far is this really from the rhetoric of the contemporary religious Right, or even from the evolutionary psychological rhetoric of someone like Wright? Clearly, time has not been able to entirely erase the uniquely satisfying image of women as innocent guardians of the hearth, caretakers of children, and purifiers of men's dirty minds. But to make matters even more contradictory, this image had its heyday at a point in history when doctors were routinely masturbating female patients to an orgasm as a treatment for a variety of ailments, such as hysteria, anxiety, irritability, nervousness, and insomnia.[6] In other words, there was an implicit acknowledgement that women, like men, needed orgasms to maintain health of both body and mind at the same time as some doctors were removing women's clitorises in order to render orgasm impossible. We are talking about a literal neutering, and one can only wonder about the feat of logic that made it possible *both* to insist that women had no sexual feelings whatsoever *and* to engage in the most brutal conceivable repression of these feelings. Why was it necessary to resort to such drastic measures to repress the very sexuality that was not supposed to exist in the first place?[7]

All of this suggests that it is patriarchy rather than female "nature" that has created the ongoing situation where many women don't (seem to) want sex and where many men are chronically frustrated by its scarcity. First *some* men—by no means all, but the power-hungry and shortsighted ones—devise a patriarchal system that seeks to snuff out all signs of female sexuality. Once this system is in place, they announce that women aren't sexual creatures. And then they use their science to "prove" this. I can't imagine a more self-undermining strategy if sex is what you want. To be sure, the control of female sexuality may have given some men access to more sex, but over time it created an environment where many women became so paranoid about their sexuality that they actually ended up suppressing it. Straight men might have gained a sense of power (and certainty about paternity) from all of this, but they certainly didn't improve their own sex lives. As Ryan and Jethá playfully write, "Rather than feel threatened, we'd recommend that our male readers ponder this: Societies in which women have lots of autonomy and authority tend to be decidedly male-friendly, relaxed, tolerant, and plenty sexy. Got that, fellas? If you're unhappy at the amount of sexual opportunity in your life, don't blame the women. Instead, make sure they have equal access to power, wealth, and status. Then watch what happens" (133–4).

Amen. Independent and lively women—women who aren't ashamed of their bodies or their sexuality—make exciting sexual partners. And nonpatriarchal, emotionally evolved men make good lovers. In short, greater gender equality equals better sex for everyone. From this perspective, patriarchy—and particularly patriarchal religion—not only controls women's sexuality but also places restrictions on male sexuality. In extreme cases, it keeps women secluded so that men can't even see them. In less extreme ones, it tends to make women so conflicted about their sexuality that it becomes a source of anxiety for them. And it doesn't help that many men, like many women, have been indoctrinated into retrograde erotic paradigms. Many American men, for instance, seem to *like* "their" women demure even as they simultaneously whine about the lack of sex in their lives. They don't seem to understand that they can't have it both ways: as long as women stay demure in the traditional sense, they won't be very likely to satisfy men's need for hot sex. Simply put, a sexually repressed woman is not going to be offering gobs of sex, let alone soul-piercing sex. That is, a woman who has heard all her life that women are—and should be—modest creatures might find it psychologically impossible to envision any other way of expressing her sexuality. In this sense, men have themselves to blame for their sexual aggravation, and doubly so because many of them seem to still hugely enjoy the idea of having to work for it. They have been taught to think that sex is somehow better (and more proper) if it doesn't come too easily. But if they aren't willing to revise this belief, then they have no choice but to reconcile themselves to their fate: they must stop complaining about their lack of satisfaction, for they can't expect women to be generous with their sexuality as long as men keep sending them the signal that there is something wrong with them if they are.

Some female readers might be saying to themselves: "But it's true, I don't have a strong sex drive." But think about it. Is your lack of sex drive inherent, biological? Or is it a result of years of socialization telling you that good girls don't put out. It seems glaringly obvious that patriarchal norms regarding female sexuality do not mirror an essential female nature but rather seek—sometimes quite violently—to *shape* that nature into the desired configuration. In other words, the double standard and the valorization of female sexual purity that still to some extent characterize our society do not reflect a chaste female sexuality but rather work overtime to bring it into being. A related way of thinking about the issue is the following: is your foundering libido due to some basic flaw in your biological design or might it have something to do with the fact that you're trying to get excited about a guy you've spent the last ten years with? These are two very different things. Were you uninterested in sex when you first met your husband (or long-term partner)? I doubt it. I bet you were at it like bunny rabbits, unless your religion or social upbringing prohibited it. If you're not feeling the spark now, it's not because you don't have a sex drive but because you can't get that thrilled about the guy who snores in your bed night after night. If I put a 32-year-old Italian god in front of you, would you not feel the spark? You might still refuse the guy because of loyalty to your partner. But this is not the same thing as you not feeling the spark.

Modern, postindustrial societies may no longer engage in a literal neutering of female sexuality through surgery. But the metaphorical neutering continues, not only in evolutionary psychological tomes but also in popular self-help guides that inform us that women are less sexual than men. John Gray, for instance, insists in his 2005 *Mars and Venus Starting Over* that women don't need a sexual release as much as men do.[8] Men's hormones pressure them to have sex, he informs us, which is why sex "is to men what marriage is to women," namely "the highest reward of love" (191). Women, in turn, "generally don't feel the pull of sexual attraction unless their hearts open" (208–9). In other words, women need a long process of emotional closeness—it helps if the guy shows up with a stack of bridal magazines—to feel any sexual passion:

> Maybe women in the movies get turned on right away but, in the real world, it takes time and loving communication. In real life, the women who find lasting love are not immediately aroused. The passion they eventually feel takes time to develop. This is not the same for a man. A man may feel the sexual passion right from the beginning. Men are wired differently. They first feel their sexual attraction, and gradually it develops into affection and then interest. Women are wired to experience interest first, and then sexual attraction. (195)

Apparently I'm not living in the real world. Alternatively, I'm not a real woman. But let's not allow these details to derail us. Let's complete Gray's thought: "When a woman experiences sexual attraction right away, it is clearly a warning signal. When a woman is attracted to finding passion, she lives in a world of disappointment. The only men that make her feel that passion are in some way dangerous. Like the mountain climber who needs danger to feel, the race car driver who needs speed, the alcoholic who needs a drink, this woman needs a man who is dangerous. She is automatically attracted to men who can hurt her in some way" (195–6). So not only are women less prone to passion than men but their quest for it—when they're stupid enough to embark on it—is bound to end badly, in despair and disappointment. Gray is essentially telling us that any woman capable of feeling sexual arousal without feeling a deep emotional connection has a dangerous addiction.

Gray's book on male and female sexuality—*Mars and Venus in the Bedroom*—may well be the most nauseating reading experience I've ever had. Imagine a whole book based on the by-now familiar themes of male sexual gluttony and female reluctance, but with a peculiar twist: women need to *always* be available for sex when men want it while staying deeply respectful of the rare times when men might not want it. That is, if a guy doesn't want sex when a woman does, she needs to back off; but she can't expect a man to back off when she's not in the mood. Rather, she needs to do everything in her power to accommodate him, and this is the case even when she's feeling ill. After all, "a woman can easily hide her lack of arousal and pretend that everything is fine."[9] In lieu of going further into the excruciating details of Gray's argument, let me quote a few poignant reader responses from amazon.com:

1   In which year was John Gray born, some time in 1870???
    I can't believe this book is for real. The intro is promising,
    but then it goes off on the premise that women are
    generally frigid and men are sex animals. The repetitive
    theme is how important sex is to men, and how women
    should always agree to have it … . The overriding theme
    is stroking the male ego, as men need to have sex to feel
    loved. The importance of sex and orgasms to women is
    all but dismissed totally. In fact, Gray even presumes that
    orgasms are not important to women.

2   What did I get from reading this book? A feeling that Gray
    fanatically believes men are the hunters and sex is a male
    domain, and women are the prey and merely the sexless

toys of men ... . His pointers to women have nothing to do with her as an individual, but how to overcome her innate sexual shyness and slow arousal time ... . he thinks women are lacking in sexuality, or that it is some vague defused sexuality, only stimulated by words of love. In short, women don't have eyes or sex drive, and it has to be guided by the man into some kind of romantic fog in order for women to function. On the other hand, Gray believes men are the only visual creatures who have to hold back these animal sex drives which are only tamed by honorable gentlemanly controls ... . Basically men want sex and women want love, this is the "fact" Gray is trying to pound into the reader.

3 My husband was really insulted that Gray made men out to be sex machines who require an orgasm in order to love and feel. I was upset that women were characterized as essentially sexless, needing our male counterparts to coax us into having intercourse. Even more annoying though, Gray devalues female orgasms almost completely, and at no time is it appropriate for a woman to decline sex ... . On the other hand, according to Gray, it's hard for a man to say no to sex, so if he does, a woman should take care of things herself.

4 This book insists that a woman is sexless and needs to be cattle prodded to bed. Every stereotype about female sexuality is in this ridiculous story about the monster sex drive male and the helpless female.

5 He also states that at certain times of the month many women don't feel the need to have an orgasm. I know LOTS of women and none of them will tell you orgasms are not important!

6 At first I was astonished, thinking, certainly John Gray is joking ... . [The book] is so biased toward a woman doing everything for the man to make sure his poor little ego isn't bruised and his libido is satisfied. He occasionally mentioned that once in a while it is okay for the woman to have an orgasm, although she many times doesn't want one. Excuse me????

7 I would not recommend this book to any couple that has a relationship based on mutual love, respect, trust, and

partnership, for it clearly "encourages" a woman to "give, give, give" and a man to "take, take, take" when it comes to intimacy.

These excerpts are obviously taken from the one-star pile. As a matter of fact, what is most noteworthy about them—because it tells us something quite chilling about our culture's general attitude toward female sexuality—is that they are the exception: the vast majority of readers believe that Gray is giving them useful, scientifically sound advice on the divergent sexual natures of men and women.[10] My survey of self-help literature from the last decade revealed that similar attitudes are common among relationship experts (though admittedly, most of them do not tell women to fake orgasms to keep their men happy). If our movies and television shows—as I argued in the previous chapter—tend to display relatively progressive models of female sexuality, our self-help gurus seem for the most part to agree with our evolutionary psychologists that sex is less important to women than it is to men. And like Gray, whose vocabulary of the different "wiring" of men and women indicates that he's thinking in terms of inborn predilections, many self-help gurus take it for granted that women's (presumed) lesser interest in sex is due to biological rather than social factors. Such convictions are one reason that the idea that men are constantly looking for a quick physical fix whereas women need intimacy persists in our culture despite the fact that it doesn't necessarily reflect the sexual realities of many men and women, particularly younger ones.

In this context, it's instructive to note that a 2006 study on porn—outlined by Ryan and Jethá—shows that, contrary to cultural expectations, not only do women respond strongly to porn but they do so more indiscriminately than men. If straight men tend to get aroused by pictures of naked women, and gay men tend to get aroused by pictures of naked men, straight women seem to get excited by just about anyone (men, women, straights, gays, bonobos, etc.) engaged in sexual activity of any kind. Yet many of them won't report their excitement. What the researchers found was that even though the physical measurements used in the study clearly indicated high levels of excitement, many women continued to deny being turned on by the images in front of them.[11] Undoubtedly, this is in part because women know that, culturally speaking, they aren't expected to respond to porn, so that admitting to a response becomes equivalent to admitting that they might not be "normal" women. That is, the neutering of female sexuality in our culture has been so effective that women themselves either don't recognize their sexual feelings or feel compelled to hide these feelings out of shame or fear of being judged slutty, sinful, or otherwise deranged. Equally importantly for our purposes, that many women in this study consistently denied sexual arousal that was evident in their bodily reactions showcases just how easy it is to end up with misleading results in so-called "scientific" studies. If the researchers of this study had taken the women at their word— as did, for example, Buss and his associates when they surveyed the mating preferences of men and women—they would have wound up with skewed results that would have confirmed the pre-existing hypothesis about women not responding to visual erotic stimuli. Fortunately for us, they introduced the control mechanism of measuring physical indicators of sexual arousal.

4

At this juncture, it may be worth revisiting the evolutionary psychological mantra that men get jealous about sexual infidelity whereas women get jealous about emotional infidelity (and upset about being deserted). Even Fisher, who otherwise sidesteps many of the clichés of the standard narrative, endorses this notion without question, arguing that women "are more likely than men to overlook a mate's 'one-night stand' or temporary sexual fling." According to Fisher, this makes "Darwinian sense," for—and we already know how this argument goes—"if men fear being cuckolded, women fear being abandoned—emotionally and finan-cially … . if a woman thinks her mate is building a serious emotional attachment to another woman, or knows he is spending valuable time and money on this competitor, she can become exceedingly jealous."[12] But researchers who decided to measure women's physical responses to the matter found that, on the level of their bodily reactions, women disliked the idea of sexual infidelity just as much as they disliked the idea of emotional infidelity. Yet they still *claimed* to be more bothered by emotional infidelity, perhaps because they know that this is what they are supposed to say. Furthermore, the very distinction between sexual and emotional infidelity is artificial to begin with in the sense that one usually bleeds into the other: a woman who suspects her partner of sexual infidelity is going to suspect him of emotional infidelity as well (and vice versa), so that the very idea that her responses to these could be measured separately is somewhat naïve. That earlier studies on the topic were set up around the binary of sexual versus emotional infidelity reveals that those conducting such studies knew ahead of time what they were hoping to find. Indeed, when researchers added a third option that allowed women to report that they found sexual and emotional infidelity equally disturbing, this is exactly what women did report.[13]

This is why it is useful to maintain a degree of skepticism when evolutionary psychologists report, say, that their surveys reveal that men are more promiscuous than women, for it is well known that straight men tend to exaggerate the number of their sexual partners whereas women tend to underreport this number. Ryan and Jethá explain that when researchers decided to take a closer look at the matter, they found the following: "Women who thought their answers might be seen reported an average of 2.6 partners (all the subjects were college students younger than twenty-five). Those who thought their answers were anonymous reported 3.4 partners, while those who thought their lies would be detected reported an average 4.4 partners. So, while women admitted to 70 percent more sexual partners when they thought they couldn't fib, the men's answers showed almost no variation" (277).[14]

Ryan and Jethá further note that when researchers surveyed women between the ages of twenty-two and fifty-seven, they found that 61 percent of those under thirty-five maintained that their primary motivation for sex was emotional rather than physical, but that among those over thirty-five, only 38 percent claimed that their relational motivations were stronger than their physical urges (289).[15] This suggests that women's motivations may change with age, but it also suggests—as Ryan and Jethá correctly argue—that women might quite simply become less apologetic about their sexuality as they mature. A younger woman may well feel the social pressure for "emotional," "relational" sexuality—the kind of sexuality that the John Grays of the world tell her is the only *properly* feminine sexuality—more than older women, who may have learned to read their sexuality independently of culturally coercive ideologies. That is, a woman who has had sex hundreds of times might be less inclined to let cultural ideals dictate the meaning of sex for her than a woman who is less experienced. Moreover, the study Ryan and Jethá refer to was published in 1989, at the threshold of the Mars-Venus era. My bet is that the percentage of women willing to admit that physical release is one of their reasons for seeking sex would be much higher now. With the rise of sex toy stores, workshops on masturbation, the college hookup culture, and television shows with strong female characters with strong sex drives, it seems probable that more women would be likely to divulge that sex, for them, is not always a matter of emotional connection, even if it clearly sometimes is, as it is for many men as well.

Ryan and Jethá humorously propose that young American women filling out questionnaires for their psychology professors might be especially embarrassed about their sexuality, and that this embarrassment might have caused a great deal of "scientific" confusion with regard to female sexuality (289). This may seem like a minor point, but it's actually quite important. A lot of evolutionary psychological data collection has been done on college students, and it would be imprudent to underestimate the extent to which the specificity of this sample (very young women who haven't yet reached their sexual maturity), as well as the specificity of this sample's relationship to the person collecting the data (often a professor or a graduate student assistant in relation to whom the students are in a subordinate position), might have distorted the results. Even "anonymous" surveys always have an implied audience. It is, for instance, unlikely that a nineteen-year-old female student taking Evolutionary Psychology 101 with a fifty-five-year-old male professor will admit in a survey collected from that class that she actually gets pretty horny at times. *Of course* she's going say that she is looking for an emotional connection. She knows that this is what she is expected to say. And let's not forget that she knows this particularly well if she has just sat through a whole semester of the said professor lecturing to her about the inherent weakness of the female libido. She doesn't want to come across as an oversexed nympho, particularly to folks who will be grading her, so she'll say whatever she thinks they want to hear.

Guys, in contrast, won't have the same qualms because they know that it will only increase their status to brag about being a little sex-crazed. And they will particularly know that it's okay to take pride in their vigorous sexuality if they have had the privilege of hearing an authority figure—this same fifty-five-year-old male professor—repeatedly tell them that, when it comes to sex, men just can't help themselves, that evolutionary psychology "proves" that men are born randy. Indeed, having just listened to a whole semester's worth of "scientific" dogma that brainwashes them to think that it's their masculine mission to overcome the inborn resistances of female sexuality, they are likely to be feeling pretty good about being men. The idea that you can spend a semester approvingly outlining the kinds of theories of human sexuality that I have (not so approvingly) foregrounded in this book, and that you can then produce a set of survey results that isn't tainted by these theories, is laughable. And even if you end up conducting your survey in unrelated courses, you can't evade the problem of study subjects reporting what they know is expected of them, for the theories in question are so prevalent in our culture that it's hard for any twenty-year-old to not be impacted by them.

Even when such psychological factors don't play a part, practical considerations might. From my own experience as a university professor, I know that the mere mention of concepts such as orgasm, masturbation, or sexual arousal instantly results in an ocean of downcast eyes and flushed cheeks, and this is sometimes even the case in graduate seminars. I can imagine that a comparable flustering might happen in the process of filling out surveys about sexual behavior, particularly when there is any possibility that the professor (or graduate student assistant) might be able to match specific responses to specific students. There is a reason professors don't see the course evaluations that students fill out at the end of each course until final grades have been submitted: many of us have virtually photographic memories when it comes to handwriting samples and the kinds of pens students have used during the semester. Even if a student doesn't write anything on the evaluation form but merely marks the boxes indicating satisfaction or dissatisfaction with different aspects of the course with an X, I can sometimes tell who filled out the evaluation just by the color of the ink used. Computerized survey methods have now eradicated this problem, but this was not the case in decades past when much of evolutionary psychological data was collected. Imagine, then, the hesitation of female students checking boxes on a survey that aims to capture the intimate details of their sex lives.

5

Ryan and Jethá's critique of the coy female is related to their critique of the idea that human beings are naturally monogamous. If monogamous marriage is the "natural" configuration of human relationality, they ask, then why do our societies and religions find it so necessary to prop it up with tax breaks and other supports? On the flipside, why do they resort to various forms of moral censorship and punishment to hold us within its confines? Why, in short, does it take so much effort to guarantee the success of something that is supposed to come "naturally" to us?[16] And why are our societies—not to mention individual people—so willing to undertake this effort given that marriage is a source of misery for so many people? As Ryan and Jethá declare, "We've been misled and misinformed by an unfounded yet constantly repeated mantra about the *naturalness* of wedded bliss, female sexual reticence, and happily-ever-after sexual monogamy—a narrative pitting man against woman in a tragic tango of unrealistic expectations, snowballing frustration, and crushing disappointment" (40-1). "Conventional marriage is a full-blown disaster for millions of men, women, and children right now," they conclude: "Emotionally, economically, psychologically, and sexually, it just doesn't work over the long term for too many couples" (308-309).

Ryan and Jethá assert that if evolutionary researchers were less committed to socially convenient interpretations of human prehistory, they would have to admit that there is nothing inherently monogamous about humans. They would have to admit that "the amoral agencies of evolution have created in us a species with a secret it just can't keep," namely that "*Homo sapiens* evolved to be shamelessly, undeniably, inescapably sexual" (46). They would have to admit that of all the Earth's beings, "none is as urgently, creatively, and constantly sexual as *Homo sapiens*" (47). "No animal," Ryan and Jethá stress, "spends more of its allotted time on Earth fussing over sex than *Homo sapiens*," so that "the percentage of our lives we human beings spend thinking about, planning, having, and remembering sex is incomparably greater than that of any other creature on the planet" (85-86). And if most species in the animal world have sex only when the female is ovulating, humans "can do it week in and week out for nonreproductive reasons" (85). From this viewpoint, human sexuality doesn't make us "animalistic" but rather showcases how different we are from most other animals. And as much as our societies try to curtail this overflowing sexuality, as much as they throw guilt, fear, shame, bodily mutilation, and even death at us as punishments for it, they can't repress the fact that we are "a species with a sweet tooth for sex" (3).

Ryan and Jethá remind us of just how uncommon monogamy really is in the animal world: "For starters, recall that the total number of monogamous primate species that live in large social groups is precisely *zero* ... The few monogamous primates that do exist (out of hundreds of species) all live in the treetops. Primates aside, only 3 percent of mammals and one in ten thousand invertebrate species can be considered sexually monogamous" (97). Furthermore, even though most major religions of the world punish women (and often also men) for extramarital sex, adultery persists around the world, including in societies "in which fornicators are stoned to death": "It's hard to see how monogamy comes 'naturally' to our species. Why would so many risk their reputations, families, careers—even presidential legacies—for something that runs *against* human nature? Were monogamy an ancient, evolved trait characteristic of our species, as the standard narrative insists, these ubiquitous transgressions would be infrequent and such horrible enforcement unnecessary. No creature needs to be threatened with death to act in accord with its own nature" (98). Against this backdrop, Ryan and Jethá note the oddity of the fact that evolutionary theorists tend to turn to the monogamous gibbons whenever they are trying to trace the evolutionary origins of human sexuality; isn't it quite bizarre, Ryan and Jethá wryly ask, that when it comes to pretty much any other question about the roots of human behavior, we look to chimps for clues, but when it comes to sex, "we prudishly turn away from these models to the distantly related, antisocial, low-I.Q., *but monogamous* gibbon? Really?" (246)

Ryan and Jethá view the tendency to use the gibbons as a model for human sexuality as a glaring example of flintstonization: it is an instance of seeking far and wide for the one example that seems to confirm our cultural ideals regarding sexuality, and of doing so even when it's obvious that the antisocial gibbons are otherwise quite different from humans (who, like other apes, are deeply social). The reasoning runs something like this: the gibbons confirm our sexual ideals; thus it must be the case that they represent an accurate evolutionary model for human sexuality. Fisher still subscribes to this view, albeit with some difficulty and with some serious qualifications. Among the latter is the admission that our early ancestors "probably lived in communities much like modern chimps," where everyone "copulated with just about everybody else" (154). Fisher in fact gives a fairly convincing account of the evolutionary origins of the dual system of serial monogamy and philandering (for both men and women) that we still live with in those societies that don't place severe punishments on female philandering. Like us, she claims, "our ancestors fell in love, paired, philandered, abandoned each other, and paired again, then settled down as they got older or had more young" (292). Fisher thus speculates that serial monogamy, rather than lifelong monogamy, is our evolutionary heritage: "Most Americans idealize lifelong marriage; they equate divorce with failure, as many peoples do. From a Darwinian perspective, however, there were advantages to serial monogamy millennia ago" (159). Likewise, "divorce, single parents, remarriage, stepparents, and blended families are as old as the human animal" (304).

Ultimately, though, Fisher, a bit like Wright, ends up arguing that we should strive to transcend this heritage of serial monogamy and philandering. Indeed, she ends up back-pedaling on some of her own observations, such as the fact that the pointedly promiscuous sexuality of bonobos is the closest to human sexuality that we can find in nature. In order to protect the contemporary cultural ideals of long-term pair-bonding and nuclear family, Fisher declares that bonobos "do not qualify as a useful model for life as it was some twenty million years ago" (121) because they do not "raise their young as husband and wife" (131). "Can we rise above our natural heritage?" Fisher then asks: "Of course we can. Our contemporary marriage patterns are a testament to the triumph of culture and personality over naturally human tendencies. Almost half of all American marriages last for life; about half of all marital partners are faithful to their spouses. The world is full of people who marry once and forgo adultery" (161). Somewhat justifiably, Ryan and Jethá make tremendous fun of the "double backflip" (74) that Fisher performs here in order to rescue monogamy. They point out that it is strange that Fisher spends so much time outlining the obvious similarities between human and bonobo sexual behavior only to turn around in the last minute and deny that these similarities are important, explaining that the bonobos are, after all, an extreme case, that their sex lives are very different from those of other apes, and therefore not an appropriate comparison point for humans.

6

Ryan and Jethá's criticism of Fisher's inconsistency with regard to bonobos and humans is entirely valid but—and I say this as someone who disagrees with Fisher's gender profiling tendencies—I think that it misses the larger point she is making. Fisher is not arguing that lifelong monogamy is natural. She is merely saying that cultural values—such as our contemporary valorization of monogamy—have the power to trump our evolutionary legacies. Fisher of course does disagree with Ryan and Jethá on a fundamental level in the sense that she advances the abovementioned theory of serial monogamy and clandestine adultery as our evolutionary heritage whereas Ryan and Jethá are convinced that humans are essentially promiscuous. For my purposes, it doesn't much matter which theory is more accurate, for I merely wish to note that the argument that Fisher makes about cultural factors wielding an enormous degree of sway in human societies is similar to what I have been saying all along, namely that the importance of culture makes it overly reductive to interpret human behavior solely on the basis of its biological underpinnings. Personally, I don't care whether a given individual chooses to be monogamous or promiscuous—and I also don't have any stake in our culture's ideal of lifelong monogamy—but I agree with Fisher that it would be unwise to deny the power of this ideal, including the ways in which it molds our emotional reactions, psychological processes, and relationship objectives. Ryan and Jethá sometimes speak as if the fact that humans are naturally promiscuous—which I don't doubt—meant that it should be easy for all of us to chuck our desire for sexual faithfulness. But things are not this simple, precisely because of the hold that socialization and cultural ideals have on us. .

In Chapter 1 I expressed some frustration at Wright's efforts to resurrect Victorian sexual norms. This wasn't because I was skeptical of the capacity of these norms to do the work he wants them to do, but because I was aggravated by his refusal to admit that our modern norms—ones that value gender equality—are just as powerful. My position was to argue that if we are to look for productive paradigms of gendered behavior, surely our own more progressive values are a better place to start than the oppressive and female-denigrating norms of Victorian England. As I demonstrated, Wright's fetishization of Victorian ideals arises from his (dubious) conviction that these ideals reflect the realities of our evolutionary history. In contrast, my point—and this may be Fisher's point as well—is that cultural ideals, *regardless of whether or not they reflect our evolutionary heritage*, can shape human behavior, and that they do so just as effectively, if not more effectively, as this heritage. While I would like to see us revise our more retrograde ideals, I would never want to downplay the power that cultural ideals, generally speaking, have. This is why I believe that Ryan and Jethá engage in their own version of biological reductionism when they suggest that a more accurate understanding of our evolutionary heritage should automatically lead to new configurations of sexuality. I don't think that the recognition that humans are biologically designed for promiscuity—however true this may be—can instantly erase our allegiance to ideals of romantic love and sexual faithfulness, at least not for everyone.

In the previous chapter, we saw that Miller hypothesizes that even though sexual loyalty isn't natural to humans, evolutionary history may have taught our ancestors to value it to such an extent that it over time became a desired fitness indicator in a potential mate. This may or may not be true. I don't know whether our appreciation of fidelity is a result of evolutionary development or purely cultural or both. Indeed, one of my arguments in this book has been that it may be impossible to distinguish between the two. What matters in the present context is that we don't need a scientific study to know that sexual loyalty is highly meaningful to many of us. The idea that we should toss it out the window now that we know that our sexuality is like that of the bonobos is a little like saying that we should give up our flushing toilets because we understand that, underneath our social personas, we are no different from other animals. As Laura Kipnis—a cultural critic I will be drawing on in the next chapter—states: "Harkening back to some remote evolutionary past for social explanations does seem to be a smoke screen for other agendas ... When sociobiologists start shitting in their backyards with dinner guests in their vicinity, maybe their arguments about innateness over culture will start seeming more persuasive."[17]

I use this rather crude example to illustrate that the right question to ask may not be, How can we live more in accordance to our biological makeup, but rather, Which of our cultural norms do we wish to continue to uphold and which do we wish to discard? Personally, I'm happy to give up the ideal of lifelong monogamy, though I admit liking serial monogamy. And I think—and this is a political, ideological preference—that it would do us a lot of good to loosen the cultural mores that demonize nonreproductive sexuality. But this doesn't mean that I wish to overlook the very real emotional investment that many people have in sexual loyalty, or the very real suffering that ensues when this investment is violated. Because so many of us are socialized to expect faithfulness from our partners—as well as to experience pain when this expectation is not met—we will be very hurt when our partners betray us. Our cognitive understanding that humans are, biologically speaking, close to the bonobos won't change this. I suppose that, in the final analysis, I would say that I favor the lifting of sexual restrictions on the collective level without at the same time wishing to impose my particular preferences on anyone who wishes to live differently. I'm furious at Wright for his tendency to use his "science" to convince us that we should all behave like repressed Victorian gentlemen and ladies. But I'm also a little mad at Ryan and Jethá for implying that we should all act like the bonobos. I agree with them that moralizing about human sexual behavior is socially coercive. But this hardly means that we can simply just disregard the centrality of culture in human life.

Along closely related lines, though I'm just as annoyed at the worldwide cultural and religious restrictions placed on human sexuality—particularly on female sexuality—as Ryan and Jethá are, I think that we need to recognize that it is impossible to understand human life without acknowledging that a degree of sexual restraint is foundational to human societies. That is, the fact that humans have learned to control their sexuality more than the bonobos is not unrelated to the fact that humans have also managed to construct a more complicated cultural edifice than the bonobos. In this sense, there is no human culture without a degree of sexual prohibition. As Sigmund Freud already recognized, it is in part because human sexuality is constrained that we are capable of cultural production: what he called "sublimation." This is because human sexual energy is so malleable that it can be directed at a countless number of substitute satisfactions when direct satisfaction is not available. We are used to thinking about sublimation as a matter of intellectual or artistic exertions. But more broadly speaking, pretty much anything we do in our lives (outside of having sex) could be considered a form of sublimation: a way of channeling our erotic reserves into non-erotic pathways.

Like Ryan and Jethá, Freud criticized our society for its excessive prudishness, emphasizing that too forceful a repression of sexuality leads to various pathologies. And interestingly, he was ahead of his time in underscoring that the repression of female sexuality in particular was causing a lot of unnecessary suffering. But this doesn't change his basic insight that *some* degree of repression is necessary for human life—that we would not have reached our current level of sociocultural sophistication without learning to curtail our sexual urges. This is why Freud famously posited that a degree of "discontent" was the inevitable price of "civilization."[18] Ryan and Jethá maintain that "any attempt to understand who we are, how we got to be this way, and what to do about it must begin by facing up to our evolved human sexual predispositions," adding that there is something artificial about the fact that "so many forces resist our sustained fulfillment" (47). I agree—to a point. But I wouldn't want to lose track of the fact that who we are and how we got to be this way has a lot to do with how our sexuality has been regulated. After all, the various prohibitions on our sexuality have not merely constricted the realm of what is sexually possible for us but also, and equally, generated a whole host of sexual practices that do not exist elsewhere in nature. This includes everything from the common habit of pining for one's soulmate to S&M. Neither is it something that other animals seem interested in, and if humans do, it's precisely because their sexuality has been touched by culture. In this sense, every cultural attempt to restrict sexuality brings new forms of sexuality into existence. This is why it makes absolutely no sense to talk about human sexuality outside of its social environment; human sexual expression is so thoroughly steeped in cultural meaning that it seems pointless to look for a biological baseline that would somehow entirely escape this meaning.

Humans spend a lot of time doing things—such as getting educated, working long hours, building things, creating things, and talking about things—that bonobos don't do. And it's the fact that we don't (usually) have sex dozens of times a day that allows us to do these things. So, let's not pretend that the differences between humans and bonobos don't matter: unless we are willing to give up our shoes, books, showers, microwaves, and airline tickets, it's probably best not to insist that our sex lives should be *just like* those of the bonobos. I hope I have left no doubt about my wish to liberate women from the shackles of a repressive sexual culture. And I also hope that I have been clear about my belief that old-school evolutionary psychologists would benefit from taking seriously the parallels between human and bonobo sexual cultures. But let's not go overboard. Indeed, the lifestyle of having sex dozens of times a day would probably bore most of us—randy guys included—quite quickly. It might be fun for a weekend or even a few weeks. But eventually even sex can become tedious if it's not interspersed by other activities. And we all know that absence makes the heart grow fonder—that our level of desire increases when we are deprived for a while. In a sense, one of the distinguishing qualities of humans is that we have learned to turn deprivation not only into something productive but even into something delicious. There are even those who desire to desire (yearn to yearn) more than they actually desire to be satisfied. Their sense of fulfillment, in other words, requires obstacles. What Freud called "the repetition compulsion"—our tendency to repeat painful relational scenarios—is one way in which we accumulate such obstacles, one way in which we ensure that our satisfaction gets delayed. This is not a matter of horny men running after reluctant women, but of the uniquely human capacity to take pleasure in the postponement of pleasure.

7

Given how vehemently Ryan and Jethá condemn the cultural ideal of monogamy, and given how strongly (and convincingly) they attack the notion that lifelong marriage is our natural state, it's more than a little surprising that they end their book by defending marriage, and even go as far as to imply that women should learn to forgive their philandering husbands in order to save their marriages. It seems that the acceptance of the double standard is so deep-seated within evolutionary psychology that even its most innovative practitioners cannot in the final analysis entirely resist its siren song. After having spent much of their book proving to us that women are highly sexual, and that women, as well as men, are naturally promiscuous, Ryan and Jethá end on a strangely gender dichotomized note when they claim that it is men specifically who need sexual novelty. This claim comes in the context of their attempt to explain why so many middle-aged men feel compelled to leave their wives for younger women. Having quoted the heart-rending testimonial of Phil, a man who cheated on his wife—and who reported that his yearning for sex with a woman other than his wife felt like "a life-or-death situation" (291)—Ryan and Jethá sympathetically state, "Variety and change are the necessary spice of the sex life of the human male" (292). Fair enough. But what about the human female? Why is it the male specifically who is suddenly the one who can't live without variety? After their wonderful arguments about how social norms often make it hard for women to express the truth about their sexuality, it's bizarre that Ryan and Jethá fail to consider the possibility that if women don't report their need for variety as readily as men do, it may not be because they don't feel this need, but because they don't feel like they can admit to it without being ostracized.

Ryan and Jethá make their argument about the male need for sexual variety against the backdrop of calling for greater overall sexual openness. I certainly don't have a problem with this. But what is troubling is that they suddenly fall back on the by now familiar tropes of masculine randiness and feminine indifference. And they also suddenly resort to the kind of gender profiling that (thankfully) didn't characterize the rest of the book. Reporting that Phil's professional success, good looks, and wonderful personality generated a constant stream of sexual opportunity for him, so that the fact that he cheated on his wife comes as no surprise, Ryan and Jethá create a gender-divided world of imaginary respondents: "Many male readers are probably thinking, '*Of course* he was sleeping with another woman—or two! Come on!' But if you're a woman, you may be thinking, '*Of course* his wife and daughters locked the pig out'" (291). But I'm not at all sure that gender alone would dictate readers' responses. I think that a great deal might depend on a particular reader's social, political, and religious views, as well as on his or her personal experience. And I also think that there might be quite a few of us with enough intellectual capaciousness to empathize with *both* Phil and his wife and daughters. Speaking for myself only, I can certainly understand why a guy who is bored with his marriage might be tempted to stray. But I can also understand why his wife and daughters would feel terribly betrayed by this. In other words, it seems to me that we here have yet another example of how gendered thinking immediately oversimplifies the picture, creating the kinds of stark dichotomies that might not in any way reflect people's complicated feelings and assessments.

Ryan and Jethá begin their analysis of the so-called male midlife crisis by asking what could possibly motivate men who are otherwise smart, caring, loving, and cautious to risk so much for a fleeting sexual thrill. Their answer has all the banality of the utterly predictable: men aren't biologically designed to live without sexual variety. Even though they themselves have presented a number of compelling evolutionary arguments for why women specifically might benefit from having multiple partners—such as the aforementioned theory of sperm competition—by the end of the book, we have returned to the idea that men are, by nature, more promiscuous than women. From here there is a very small step to the very standard narrative that Ryan and Jethá have sought to discredit. They cite writer and film director Nora Ephron on the oversexed male libido: "The problem with men is not whether they're nice or not. It's that it's hard for them at a certain point in their lives to stay true. It just is. It's almost not their fault" (292). I love Ephron's work, but in this instance even she can't rise above a cultural cliché. And let's also note how easily the biological argument gets turned into a justification: "It's almost not their fault." I may have more sympathy for men who cheat—and for women who cheat—than many other readers, but let's not go crazy with forgiveness: if a guy cheats on his wife, it *is* his fault.

Ryan and Jethá's "evolutionary" justification for the double standard—for why wives might want to look the other way—is that men's need for sexual variety arises from their need to avoid incest. They argue that men who have been married to the same woman for a long time come to regard her as "family," almost like a sister, so that sexual distaste for this woman is almost inevitable. We learn that "to avoid the genetic stagnation that would have dragged our ancestors into extinction long ago, males evolved a strong appetite for sexual novelty and a robust aversion to the overly familiar" (293). One can only wonder why women didn't develop the same aversion. Along related lines, Ryan and Jethá approvingly report on the findings of the anthropologist William Davenport, who lived among a group of Melanesian islanders in the 1960s. These islanders didn't have many sexual hangups and all the women claimed to be highly orgasmic, "with most reporting several orgasms to each of her partner's one" (294). Davenport explains that, despite this, the islanders took it for granted that, after a few years of married life, the husband's interest in his wife would pale and he would take a younger lover. Apparently, wives on the island regarded such mistresses as status symbols and showed no jealousy over their husbands' extramarital sexual escapades. This is all fine and good. But one still wonders what these wives were supposed to do with their highly orgasmic bodies once their husbands started having sex with other women.

Ryan and Jethá further note that back in America, William Masters and Virginia Johnson reported that "loss of coital interest engendered by monotony in a sexual relationship is probably the most constant factor in the loss of an aging male's interest in sexual performance with his partner" (294). I'm sure this is true. But are we to believe that the same is not true for women—that there is no connection between women's lagging libidos and marital monotony? One of the most persistent tidbits of sexual lore in our culture is that married women rarely want sex. To the extent that this is in fact the case, what is keeping us from concluding that their lack of interest has the same cause as men's lack of interest? Those who circulate this lore almost invariably attribute it to women's innate sexual reluctance. But it seems to me that marital monotony is a much more plausible argument. I'm happy to accept the possibility that a man who has been married to the same woman for a decade might be looking for some sexual variety. But let's extend the same reasoning to the woman who has been married to this same man for all those years. The fact that she might be less likely to act on the urge doesn't mean that the urge isn't there; it just means that the social prohibitions against it are more powerful.

8

One such prohibition is the iconography of motherhood that dominates our society: the fact that there seems to be something inherently antithetical about the roles of mother and lover. As Sarah Hrdy notes in *Mother Nature*, "It was no accident that first moralists and then Victorian evolutionists looked to nature to justify assigning to female animals the same qualities that patri-archal cultures have almost always ascribed to 'good' mothers (nurturing and passive). Women were assumed to be 'naturally' what patriarchal culture would socialize them to be: modest, compliant, noncompetitive, and sexually reserved. This, I suspect, is the main reason why *sexuality* has always been studied separately from *maternity*, as if sex had nothing to do with maternity" (xvii). Hrdy proceeds to deconstruct this binary, showing that sexuality and maternity are far from being adverse to each other. But this dichotomy has an incredible grip on our psyches even in contemporary culture (a grip that can be traced at least as far back as the idea that Mary was able to give birth to Jesus while remaining a virgin). We saw a stark example of this in Wright's Madonna-whore model, but its influence reaches beyond the retrograde musings of a conservative evolutionary psychologist: the ideal of the coy female is the cornerstone of the sacredness of the nuclear family in the sense that the possibility of a randy mother would immediately shatter the cozy image of family life that our culture likes to advocate. The idea that motherhood and sexuality don't mesh—should not mesh—permeates our society, with the result that women who are mothers might find it quite difficult to stay in touch with their sexuality. Moreover, if they are less likely than their husbands to seek outside lovers when the marital spark dies, this surely has something to do with the fact that they don't want to be bad mothers. While it's not exactly a badge of good fatherhood to stray either, the philandering father is still to some degree conceivable in our cultural imagination. The philandering mother, in contrast, is the kind of cultural taboo that few women are willing to violate.

Ryan and Jethá write: "Many female readers aren't going to be happy reading this, and some will be enraged by it, but for most men, sexual monogamy leads inexorably to monotony" (295). I'm one of those female readers who is enraged by this, but not for the reason Ryan and Jethá assume. I have no problem with the idea that long-term monogamy leads to boredom. By all accounts, this is obvious. What enrages me is the idea that this only happens to men. And what follows enrages me even more: "If it's true that most men are constituted, by millions of years of evolution, to need occasional novel partners to maintain an active and vital sexuality throughout their lives, then what are we saying to men when we demand lifetime sexual monogamy? Must they choose between familial love and long-term sexual fulfillment? Most men don't fully appreciate the conflict between the demands of society and those of their own biology until they've been married for years—plenty of time for life to have grown very complicated, with children, joint property, mutual friends, and the sort of love and friendship only shared history can bring. When they arrive at the crisis point, where domesticity and declining testosterone levels have drained the color from life, what to do?" (298). The implied answer to this rhetorical question is: let men stray; and if you're the wife, forgive. Indeed, Ryan and Jethá report appreciatively that the sociologist Jessie Bernard argued in the 1970s "that increasing men's opportunities for sexually novel partners was one of the most important social changes required in Western societies to promote marital happiness" (295). Likewise, they comment sympathetically on the decision of Roy Romer, the governor of Colorado back in the 1980s, to tell the reporters who were haunting him about his extramarital affair that his wife had known about the affair all along and accepted it (310–11). Good for Romer and his wife. But is this really the best we can do to resolve the problem of philandering husbands?

When it comes to Ryan and Jethá's attempts to revise married life, they arrive at the same solution as Wright did: let men stray while asking their tormented wives to meekly accept their lot of being chronically cheated on. This again leaves us with the question I raised above in the context of the Melanesian islanders, namely what we are to do with all the wives who are now getting even less sex (and who may be just as bored with their marriages as their husbands, and who may have lives that are just as complicated, just as riddled with responsibilities, as their husbands do). How can it be that these two evolutionary thinkers who have spent half their book talking about women's intense sexuality are now completely oblivious to the fact that their proposed solution doesn't exactly work for women, either sexually or emotionally? Sexually, they are asking women to increase their level of frustration so that *men* can have more sex; emotionally, they are asking women to do what other cultural authorities have told them to do for centuries: stop complaining about aspects of male nature that can't be changed. Ryan and Jethá seem to assume that if women just simply accepted some basic facts about men's evolutionary heritage, they might find it easier to tolerate men's sexual indiscretions. But this once more reveals the narrowness of the evolutionary approach—the ways in which it fails to account for human psychological complexity. A mere rational understanding of sexuality doesn't erase the emotional responses—such as jealousy—that we have to it, so that telling women not to be hurt by their husbands' philandering is like telling a five-year-old that he shouldn't cry when his sister gets the model train he asked for for Christmas. You can try to tell women that they shouldn't take it personally. But they probably will. Likewise for a guy who discovers that his wife has cheated on him. Can we expect him to just merrily go on with his marriage? No? If we see the *no* so clearly for the man—as even conservative evolutionary psychologists do—then shouldn't we be able see the same for women?

Ryan and Jethá claim that one of their hopes for their book is to allow couples to arrive at "a deeper, less judgmental under-standing of the ancient roots of ... inconvenient feelings and a more informed, mature approach to dealing with them" (305). Placed in the context of their argument about philandering husbands, this amounts to advising women that they should take a more "mature" ("less judgmental") attitude to the matter by learning to better deal with their "inconvenient feelings." Indeed, speaking of the aftermath of an affair, Ryan and Jethá write, "Once the transitory thrill passes, these men are left once again with the realities of what makes a relationship work over the long run: respect, admiration, convergent interests, good conversation, sense of humor, and so on. A marriage built upon sexual passion alone has as much chance of enduring as a house built on winter ice. Only by arriving at a more nuanced understanding of the nature of human sexuality will we learn to make smarter decisions about our long-term commitments. But this understanding requires us to face some uncomfortable facts" (297). The idea here seems to be that if women were able to "face" the "uncomfortable fact" that their husbands are bound to philander, they would be able to make smarter relationship decisions. Perhaps they might patiently wait for their husbands to return to them once the thrill passes rather than ending their marriage? Perhaps they might be more forgiving? What gets completely brushed under the rug here is that women are being asked to carry the emotional burden of their husbands' wounding behavior. This is a fairly blatant example of blaming the victim, of telling women that if they had a "more nuanced understanding of the nature of human sexuality," then they wouldn't be so hurt. In this way, women become responsible for their own suffering: it is no longer their husbands' philandering that hurts them but rather their own unreasonable reactions to this philandering.

9

Why are Ryan and Jethá so keen for women to forgive their philandering husbands? The rather astonishing answer is that, in the end, and despite their own withering criticisms of the institution, they seem just as keen to preserve the sanctity of marriages as Wright is, and even agree with his assessment that serial monogamy is one of the biggest problems in our society. Here their reasoning is in fact identical to his: "Though often presented as the *honorable* response to the conundrum [of adultery], the serial monogamy cop-out has led directly to the current epidemic of broken homes and single-parent families" (299–300). Ryan and Jethá's antidote to this epidemic is to take sex less seriously: "When it's just sex, that's all it is. In such cases, it's not love … . Or a good reason to destroy an otherwise happy family" (301–2). But isn't it stretching things a bit to argue that adultery could take place within an "otherwise happy family"? And how, exactly, is it progress to suggest that women should hold their families together without the expectation that their husbands will remain monogamous? Ryan and Jethá's fear of broken families—the tenacious fear that so many American thinkers cling to even though there is plenty of evidence from other parts of the world that it's not broken families but rather the poverty that often accompanies them that causes problems—prompts them to advocate the double standard over serial monogamy although the latter is arguably a fairly good solution to the predicament of monogamy leading to monotony. Why, one might ask, is it a better solution to stay with your cheating husband, no matter how unhappy this makes you, than to look for new love with another man? And what's so wrong with what people in our society are already doing in droves: divorcing, remarrying, forming blended families, reconfiguring kinship systems, and (hopefully) leading more rewarding sex lives?

The answer is, once again, predictable: serial monogamy hurts children! Mocking the idea that abandoning one's family is the "adult" option for dealing with the conflict between romantic ideals and sexual desire, Ryan and Jethá ask, "How is it 'adult' to inflict emotional trauma on our children because we're unable to face the truth about sex?" (300). This implies that while children will be terribly traumatized if their father leaves the family, they will be entirely fine if their father sleeps around and their resentful mother sits at home mourning her non-existent sex life (not to mention her shattered self-esteem). It implies that a young girl will be better off with a philandering father than a mother who might over time find a loving boyfriend who is not her father. The fact that the former arrangement sends the girl the message that her mother is unlovable (and that women can be mistreated) whereas the latter signals that her mother is lovable doesn't seem to be a part of the equation. I know many people who sincerely wish that their parents had gotten divorced when they were young because they grew up in dysfunctional families that made them wretched. But for Ryan and Jethá the quality of children's family life apparently has no bearing on their well-being as long as the family stays intact. It's as if, having written the first twenty chapters of their book, they had hired Wright to write Chapter 21, so that we are suddenly faced with the following question: "Apart from death itself, what causes as much human misery as the ongoing demise of marriage?" (302). Apparently nothing.

It's hardly a coincidence that it is in the context of male philandering that conservative social ideology, along with gender profiling, raises its ugly head within an otherwise refreshingly progressive evolutionary tome, for there seems no escaping from the icon of the randy male in evolutionary theory. After having told us that if couples wish to reignite their passion for each other, they need to have intimate conversations about their feelings, Ryan and Jethá state: "We don't mean to suggest these will be easy conversations. They won't be. There are zones where it's always going to be difficult for men and women to understand one another, and sexual desire is one of them. Many women will find it difficult to accept that men can so easily dissociate sexual pleasure from emotional intimacy, just as many men will struggle to understand why these two obviously separate (to them) issues are often so intertwined for many women" (304). Infuriatingly, we have once again been ushered into Mars-Venus land, caught up in the stalest gender banalities conceivable, and the discrepancy between this rhetoric and Ryan and Jethá's earlier rhetoric of robust female sexuality is startling. As a matter of fact, early in the book they themselves make fun of experts who "opine that women need commitment to feel sexual intimacy because 'that's just the way they are'" (23). So what happened? There is absolutely nothing about their own analysis of the evolutionary record that lends credibility to the kind of gender stereotyping that they resort to in the final pages of their book. Presumably bonobo females do not need long walks on the beach or heart-felt conversations by the fire as a prelude to sex. Yet somehow we end up with the same old story: men want sex; women want intimacy; woman can't separate sex from intimacy; the two are easily separable for men.

To make matters even worse, Ryan and Jethá conclude their book by comparing men and women to the sun and the moon, attributing to men the sun's constancy and power and to women the moon's changeability, beauty, and monthly cycles. So we end on a note of constant and powerful males and irrational, PMS-ing females (who at least get to be pretty). Given the foregoing analysis of inevitable male philandering, the attribution of "constancy" to them seems a little far-fetched. At this stage, heteronormativity also makes a belated entrance, as it tends to do whenever gender profiling reaches a high pitch. We are told that in a total solar eclipse, "the disc of the moon fits so precisely over that of the sun that the naked eye can see solar flares leaping into space from behind" (311). That is, the sun and the moon complement each other like men and women, the implication being that two suns or two moons can't quite make the same seamlessly blended couple. And of course, this complementarity has a natural basis: "While they *appear* precisely the same size to terrestrial observers, scientists long ago determined that the true diameter of the sun is about *four hundred times* that of the moon. Yet incredibly, the sun's distance from Earth is roughly four hundred times that of the moon's, thus bringing them into unlikely balance when viewed from the only planet with anyone to notice ... . Like our distant ancestors, we watch the eternal dance of our sun and our moon, looking for clues to the nature of man and woman, masculine and feminine here at home" (311–12). Heteronormativity, the natural complementarity of men and women, and gender profiling—these seem inevitably to go hand in hand. And let's also not forget that, despite appearances, the (masculine) sun really is four hundred times bigger than the (feminine) moon.

5

The Cruelty of Optimism

A relation of cruel optimism exists when something you desire is actually an obstacle to your flourishing.

LAUREN BERLANT

1

The standard narrative may be increasingly under attack, but its repercussions continue to be tremendous in our society: since 2000, scientific journals have published more than 30,000 articles on the differences between men and women[1]; neuroscientists are tracking variations in male and female brain functioning; education experts are busy devising differentiated learning strategies for boys and girls based on the idea that they have contrasting strengths (e.g. boys excelling in mathematical tasks and girls excelling in verbal tasks); self-help authors continue to advise women to play hard to get, withhold sex, accentuate their "feminine" vulnerability, and downplay their ambitions and achievements in order to manipulate men; and pickup artists are educating men in the "hunter's art" of seducing women. I am not saying that evolutionary psychology alone is responsible for all of this—far from it. Gender profiling is so endemic in our society that it is impossible to point to a single explanation for its persistence. My argument in this book has merely been that evolutionary psychology has played an influential part in lending "scientific" credibility to our culture's obsession with the idea that Mars-Venus can tell us something meaningful about men and women. Precisely because many Americans already hold a gender-bifurcated worldview, it doesn't take a great deal to convince them that this view reflects the realities of nature. Even worse, to the extent that they believe that what is "natural" should not be tampered with, they tend to translate the idea that the social dominance of men may have natural causes to the idea that it is irreversible (and perhaps even acceptable).

We're dealing with a classic chicken-and-egg scenario: on the one hand, preexisting cultural mythologies about gender and sexuality infiltrate our science, and on the other, our science is used to justify these very same mythologies. The minute these mythologies show any signs of waning—the minute people start to question the rhetoric of men *this* women *that*—science steps in to tell us that it has "proven" that men "really" are this way whereas women "really" are that way. This obviously makes it harder for the rest of us to loosen the norms of gender and sexuality that have for so long handicapped us as a society and as individuals. To be sure, for increasing numbers of people there is no going back to traditional arrangements of gender and sexuality for the simple reason that the new arrangements are not just more fair but more interesting. But there is no doubt that our modern gender profilers can still cause a lot of havoc. It's not a coincidence that the scientific insistence on the archaic models of gender and sexuality that I've outlined in this book coincides with the considerable victories of feminism and gay, lesbian, and queer struggles. As I've shown, evolutionary psychology is, in part at least, a backlash phenomenon, and the fact that it can so easily don the cloak of scientific objectivity makes it all the more dangerous.

Because I first encountered the problem of gender profiling in the context of self-help literature aimed at straight women, I'm keenly aware of the ways in which it is being used to persuade them that they have no choice but to reconcile themselves to men's hurtful behavior. Take the idea that men are hardwired to cheat on women. The minute scientists start telling us that this is a scientifically proven fact, it becomes the perfect excuse for men to step out on their partners. It's in men's genes, so the poor sops can't help themselves. This in turn means that they can't be held responsible for it. We have seen that Wright readily admits that this is the logical result of evolutionary attempts to prove the genetic foundations of the sexual double standard. As soon as women believe that men's propensity to stray is intrinsic to their biological makeup, there really isn't much they can do about it besides resigning themselves to their sorry lot, maybe crying a little and eating a pint of Chunky Monkey. I'm not saying that men are inherently faithful. As I hope to have made clear, I believe that all of us—men and women alike—are prone to promiscuity. And I'm not in the least bit interested in moralistic efforts to curtail it. My point is rather that the *gendering* of promiscuity—the idea that it is a specifically masculine predilection—puts extreme pressure on women to be forgiving about male sexual behavior that they may experience as acutely wounding. Likewise, if a man doesn't want to listen to a woman's emotional troubles, it's not because he's lazy, selfish, or just plain incompetent; it's because he's a *guy* so she better cut him some slack. Commitment phobia? Well, that's also in his genes. This type of thinking serves the interests of patriarchal men who are likely to mistreat women for the simple reason that they think that they have the right to do so. What's so problematic about evolutionary psychology is that it's asking women to celebrate this version of masculinity as men's innate "nature."

On the flipside, both evolutionary psychology and self-help literature try to console women by reassuring them that they are good at all the things that our society has traditionally *devalued*: talking, emotions, empathy, compassion, altruism, intuition, and nurturing. I'm not saying that it's bad to be good at these things— not at all. But these traits have throughout the ages been used to justify the idea that women's place is in the home, taking care of the young, smoothing over ruffled feathers, propping up male egos, and generally speaking, making sure that relationships survive. Telling women that they are better than men at, say, emotional intelligence may seem like a compliment. But on another level it's merely an invitation to work harder than the guy does. John Gray writes, "On Venus, everyone studies psychology and has at least a master's degree in counseling. They are very involved in personal growth, spirituality, and everything that can nurture life, healing, and growth," adding that "Venusians are very intuitive. They have developed this ability through centuries of anticipating the needs of others."[2] How handy for men. They don't need to lift a finger to make their relationships work because women are innately so good at it.

Why, then, are so many women so charmed by the gender

profilers of our society? Why do they keep devouring self-help literature, magazine articles, talk shows, and others sites of popular culture that engage in the practice? As I mentioned in the introduction to this book, a big part of the appeal arises from the notion that learning to profile men will deliver women to the gates of happiness and romantic fulfillment; the simplicity of the Mars-Venus mentality offers a quick fix for relationship problems. The idea that gender differences are the primary cause of relationship troubles makes it possible to ignore a whole host of other possible causes having to do with the almost inevitable tensions of relating; it may be easier to assume that gender is the problem than to admit that the very task of relating is extremely complicated—that there is never any guarantee that two singular individuals will be able to build a union that will work in the long run. Gray promises in the opening pages of *Men Are from Mars, Women Are from Venus* that his book "reveals how men and women *differ in all areas of their lives.* Not only do men and women communicate differently but they think, feel, perceive, react, respond, love, need, and appreciate differently. They almost seem to be from different planets, speaking different languages and needing different nourishment" (xxx; emphasis added). "When you remember that your partner is as different from you as someone from another planet," Gray continues, "you can relax and cooperate with the differences instead of resisting or trying to change them" (xxx). This is because "men and women are *supposed to be different*" (2; emphasis added). "Expecting or demanding that men and women think, feel, react, and respond in the same way," he notes, "will only set you up for failure and disappointment in your relationships" (xix). And finally, "When you remember that men are from Mars and women are from Venus, everything can be explained" (3). *Everything?* This is a bold claim, but many women have found it a compelling one. Who, after all, wouldn't want a definitive solution to the tangles of relating?

Perhaps even more insidiously, one of the main reasons our gender profilers have been so successful among women is that they are extremely good at implying that deviating from the traditional "feminine" profile will result in the lack of love. Gray bluntly states that when women become "overly self-sufficient," they often "unknowingly push love away."[3] Other authors tend to be more diplomatic about the matter, but the implicit message of many self-help guides is that any woman who refuses to abide by normative definitions of femininity risks losing her man; the punishment for not performing one's gender correctly is misery, loneliness, desolation, and lack of romantic fulfillment. Our gender profilers have thus figured out that the best way to flood women with antifeminist ideas is to make them feel insecure about their basic desirability. Even educated women who have carved out impressive careers, and who expect quite a bit from their friends and colleagues, seem willing to put up with denigrating relationship advice when they fear that their "unfeminine" success might have rendered them unlovable. This is why I think that dominant codes of romantic behavior are—along with economic disparity—one of the last strongholds of patriarchy in our society, that they are a means of feeding otherwise confident women a hefty dose of submissiveness when their defenses are down. This is how many women come to buy into one version of what Lauren Berlant calls "cruel optimism"; it is how they come to place their faith in the kinds of gender-bifurcated relational models that are very unlikely to satisfy them.

2

Berlant defines cruel optimism as the stubborn, irrational belief that social arrangements, ideologies, and ways of life that hurt us will eventually pay off and make us happy. Among other things, cruel optimism entails the fantasy that the belief systems we have inherited from our society and families will bring us the love, intimacy, success, security, financial reward, or the so-called "good life" that we crave even when they are extremely unlikely to do so. Berlant explains, for instance, that the economically disadvantaged may at times form optimistic attachments to the very power structures that oppress them, so that a poor person might support a conservative political agenda even when it is clear that this agenda will never help him or her overcome poverty. Or the daughter of working-class parents who has watched her parents toil without reward for two decades might still place a great deal of faith in the ideals of hard work and social mobility, hoping against hope that the American dream will one day rescue her even if it didn't rescue her parents. Such an optimistic attachment to potentially damaging ways of life tends to arise from our desire to feel normal: we want to feel like we are a part of something familiar, like we "belong" to the world in which we live, with the result that we go along with the norms that make our social environment intelligible to us. As Berlant specifies, our investment in the notion of a "dependable life" can be so strong that we remain wedded to certain fantasies of satisfaction even after they have disappointed us.[4] We, in short, endorse forms of life that are not in the least bit good for us, coming, as it were, to "misrecognize the bad life as a good one" (174).

One reason gender profiling has been so effective in our society is that it has managed to infiltrate our collective fantasies of satisfaction: it relies on the ruse of misrecognition Berlant highlights, repeatedly causing people to believe that what is bad for them (limiting, coercive gender models) is the cornerstone of the good life. Because our cultural authorities align gender profiling with the promise of happiness, they cause many women to enter into a vicious cycle of hope and disappointment where they are willing to work extremely hard at securing their romantic fulfillment even when there is absolutely no evidence that their exertions are bringing them any closer to their goal. The dynamic is somewhat like the one that Barbara Ehrenreich outlines in the context of the all-American penchant for positive thinking: many Americans are so conditioned to be optimistic that they have an almost unbounded faith in their ability to succeed, harness a fortune, bring about miraculous reversals of fortune, attract good things to their lives merely by imagining them, or beat the odds of cancer even when their chances of doing so are extremely slim.[5] Likewise, many women run after the promise of fulfilling love, and are willing to give up a great deal to keep this promise alive, even when they have been repeatedly disappointed.

Many of us—men and women alike—have been trained since early childhood to dwell within such a vicious cycle of hope and disappointment. As Berlant explains, children often form an optimistic allegiance to "attachments they never consented to making," and they do so even when these attachments are inherently unsatisfactory: "They may even come to be in love with the promise of the promise that there will be a moment of reciprocal *something* between themselves and the world, if they're good, that is, *if they become a good subject of the promise*, and they may mistake love for subjection to the will of others who have promised to care for/love them" (184). That is, children frequently form attachments to deeply wounding intimate bonds for the simple reason that they don't have a choice: their very survival depends on the people who surround them so that, regardless of how badly such people treat them, they develop an emotional loyalty to them. Children are looking for recognition, reciprocity, and affection, and if these come packaged in problematic bundles of intimacy, they are obliged to accept the bad along with the good. This is exactly why so many of us spend much of our lives trying to overcome hurtful patterns of behavior we internalized at an early age—why the legacies of our formative years can be so difficult to transcend. And it's also one reason the cycle of romantic hope and disappointment remains, for many of us, the status quo of our lives, why many of us remain caught up in self-undermining attachments to devastating intimate scenarios.

When it comes to gender profiling specifically, deeply ingrained patterns of intimacy intermingle with collective cultural norms that dictate the proper parameters of masculinity and femininity. The fact that many of these norms are inherently unjust doesn't make them any easier to discard as long as they sustain the fantasy of satisfaction. The hope that effort will eventually pay off, that things will eventually get better, keeps many women loyal to relational paradigms that undermine them; they are so seduced by the mirage of happiness (of the good life, self-completion, and intimate gratification) that seems to await around the corner that they stay patient even when they shouldn't. They consent to a narrative—the standard narrative of evolutionary psychology or the Mars-Venus model of self-help literature—even when the price of doing so is a big chunk of their dignity. In part because, as Berlant remarks, "the desire for a less-bad life" (180) often entails a fantasmatic attempt to imagine the kind of happiness that one has never experienced but that one insists on thinking is nevertheless possible, many women keep placing their faith in dominant practices of gender profiling even though these practices are unlikely to reward them with the kind of intimacy they are looking for; in this way, they are induced to participate in a system that guarantees their misery at the same time as it relegates them to a secondary status.

3

Obviously, some women see through the ruse. Some refuse to participate, which is one reason increasing numbers of women these days choose to stay single or opt for egalitarian relationships over gender-bifurcated ones. But it would be hard to overestimate the damage done to women's lives by our gender profilers. Moreover, it barely needs stating that there is a direct link between gender profiling and reproductive heteronormativity. It would be hard to find a clearer example of "the fascism of the baby's face" that Lee Edelman criticizes in *No Future* than the standard narrative of evolutionary psychology.[6] As we have seen, this narrative reduces the complex edifice of sexuality and intimate relationality to the mandate to secure the survival of the species—and in particular the survival of one's own gene pool—by producing children. The alluring iconography of the child as the guarantor of the (heteronormative) future—the iconography that Edelman adroitly dissects—is nowhere as transparently manifest as it is in evolutionary theories of human mating. The child in these theories becomes the justification for the existence of its parents, for without the child, or at least the promise of the child, the parents, quite literally, do not have a reason for existing. I've emphasized this specifically in the context of the evolutionary reduction of women to the lifespan of their ovaries, but it is foundational to evolutionary theory generally speaking: both men and women exist in order to bring children into the world; whatever else they might wish to do with their lives is incidental and largely beside the point. The child, the promise of the child, represents the end-game of human life, and one is justified in doing "whatever it takes" (to return to Wright's unfortunate wording) to be successful at this game.

What leaps out from my survey of evolutionary psychology is the field's fear of dissociating sexuality—particularly female sexuality—from reproduction. To be sure, there are proponents of the field, such as Ryan and Jethá, who recognize that sexual expression may have nothing to do with reproductive aims. But for many evolutionary psychologists, the equation of sexuality with reproduction seems more or less automatic. And given that there is, in our society as in most others, a straight line from reproduction to marriage, we are looking at the scientific side of what, following Michel

Foucault, we might characterize as the biopolitical management of human relationality. Foucault defined biopolitics as the kind of largely invisible but pervasive edifice of power that guarantees the smooth running of postindustrial capitalist society.[7] It includes the more or less systematic supervision of "human resources" through the governmental monitoring of births, deaths, and health policy. But it also includes more subtle forms that penetrate the most intimate corners of our lives. The social pressure on people to get married and reproduce is among the most influential of the latter. Most people in our society believe that their decision to marry is a "choice." But from a biopolitical perspective, it is the result of a complex machinery of cultural conditioning that presents marriage as the most reasonable and rewarding way to organize our romantic lives. And, as I have already emphasized, persuading people to marry is a tremendously effective means of producing a population that acts in relatively predictable, relatively responsible ways. Simply put, married people are more likely to show up at work every morning than people who choose to approach their sex lives in less conventional ways.

I do not want to suggest that biopolitical control is the only reason people marry. In addition—and I want to be very clear about this—I have absolutely no wish to vilify people who are happily married. But I think that it is useful to recognize that marriage has historically served, and continues to serve, as a means of disciplining the unruliness of desire. It of course routinely fails at this task, as is obvious from the prevalence of infidelity. But all things considered, marriage is a remarkably efficient way of making sure that desire gets channeled toward reproductive ends. And it is also an efficient way of producing citizens whose emotional lives mirror the collective needs of our society. Every society has a stake in producing the kinds of personalities, the kinds of character types, that suit its socioeconomic purposes. Marriage has always been a means of molding such characters, of creating psychological structures that reflect the normative codes of our culture, including its economic imperatives. By offering us a very specific blueprint for happiness—for what the good life is supposed to look like—it makes it hard for us to even begin to envision different ways of living and loving.

The early-twentieth-century Italian philosopher Antonio Gramsci notes that Henry Ford was among the first to recognize the socioeconomic benefits of marriage. When Ford updated the technology of his car factories in the 1920s—shifting to an assembly line process that hugely increased his workers' productivity (while arguably eroding the quality of the hours they spent at work)—he capitalized on the link between marriage and (presumed) productivity by demanding proof of marital status as a precondition of higher wages. He even had a cadre of investigators who conducted spot-checks at workers' homes to verify that their domestic arrangements were what they had reported. This is because he understood that stable domestic arrangements tended to produce more stable, and therefore more efficient, workers. As Gramsci states, "The new industrialism wants monogamy: it wants the man as worker not to squander his nervous energies in the disorderly and stimulating pursuit of occasional sexual satisfaction. The employee who goes to work after a night of 'excess' is no good for his work. The exaltation of passion cannot be reconciled with the timed movements of productive motions connected with the most perfected automatism."[8] In this sense, the precision of industrial labor benefits from an ideology of family values.

Along related lines, Herbert Marcuse noted in the mid-1950s that our society—like perhaps all societies—seeks to channel sexual desire into specific pathways in order to generate the necessary discipline for a well-oiled economic order. Marcuse argued that Western societies are governed by what he called "the performance principle": an ideal of productivity and efficiency, for the sake of which we are asked to sacrifice a big portion of our pleasure, particularly of our sexual pleasure.[9] This principle asks us to perform on higher and higher levels of productivity and efficiency even though our societies are already generating an excess of goods, services, and commodities. In addition, to compensate for the pressures of keeping up with the system—the fact that we are working much harder than our survival would, strictly speaking, require—the system produces substitute pleasures in the form of consumables and luxury items as well as in the form of an extensive entertainment system that keeps us glued to our television sets (and, increasingly, our computers) at night. Such substitute pleasures do not detract from the performance principle but instead feed it by making sure that our bodies and minds get to recharge at night so that we are ready to tackle the task of productivity and efficiency the next morning. But the system is much less tolerant of pleasures that don't bolster its needs, which is precisely why it seeks to control sexuality by restricting it to the confines of marriage.

In the context of the performance principle, sexuality is a "useless" pleasure: outside of reproduction it doesn't "lead" to anything. It's therefore not surprising that our society strives, much like Henry Ford did, to promote the connection between sexuality and reproduction. And marriage is obviously an excellent way of doing this. What's more, by rendering marriage the thing that everyone is supposed to want, our culture ensures that we no longer see it as a tool of social discipline. As Marcuse writes, "The restrictions imposed upon the libido appear as the more rational, the more universal they become, the more they permeate the whole of society. They operate on the individual as external objective aims and as an internalized force ... In the 'normal' development, the individual lives his repression 'freely' as his own life: he desires what he is supposed to desire; his gratifications are profitable to him and to others; he is reasonably and often even exuberantly happy" (46). When marriage becomes a nearly universally desired institution, we no longer recognize it as a means of restricting our libido but freely (and happily) walk into its cage. To be sure, we joke about "the ball and chain" that marriage represents, thereby revealing that, underneath the social ideology of the happily-ever-after, we do have an awareness of the repressive aspects of marriage. But for the most part, we stifle such doubts, seeing in marriage the very fulfillment of our existence. This is one way in which, as Marcuse states, man's "erotic performance is brought in line with his societal performance" (46).

4

Once again, I am not saying that the disciplinary aspects of marriage sum up the entire institution. Obviously, for marriage to have survived throughout the centuries, it must offer its proponents some very compelling rewards and pleasures.[10] But I want to focus on the coercive side here because this is harder for us to recognize for the simple reason that biopolitical control is, as I noted above, invisible: it is not the kind of power that is held by specific individuals but rather a nebulous network of sociocultural influences that permeate our collective world; because it has no clearly discernible center, no one can be held directly responsible for it. Precisely because of this, its tentacles can reach the furthest reaches of our psyches without our conscious awareness. I'm not saying that we are powerless against it, for this would amount to the kind of social determinism that would replicate some of the worst aspects of the biological determinism that I have criticized in this book. But I think it would be a mistake to ignore the various ways it can subtly manipulate us into conventional, collectively condoned patterns of behavior.

Among the most remarkable of such patterns is our willingness to work at our marriages even when they make us miserable. In her scathing critique of marriage, Laura Kipnis deftly captures the paradox that characterizes the lives of so many married people: the very alliance that was supposed to usher them to the heart of the good life is making them despondent. In our society, we are taught to expect from marriage an almost miraculous power to right all the wrongs of our lives, heal the wounds of our past, make us blissfully happy, and grant us enduring satisfaction. Yet the realities of married life are often quite removed from this fantasy. It seems safe to say that the institution is failing to live up to its promises more often than it succeeds: not only do half of all marriages end in divorce but many of the ones that survive are far from the haven of harmony we have been taught to imagine. Many married people experience their marriages as deadening, suffocating, frustrating, and sometimes even frightening. Sniping, sarcasm, resentment, the silent treatment, and other forms of psychological warfare seem to be among the standard devices of modern marriage. Speaking of the high levels of everyday irritation that often accompany married lives, Kipnis notes that relatively trivial things—such as who forgot to run an errand, take out the recycling, return the scissors to their designated spot, or leave the toilet seat the way it's supposed to be—serve as emotional trigger points that govern the tone of a couple's daily interactions. "Considering the amount of psychological space such issues come to occupy," Kipnis states, "irritation would seem to be domestic coupledom's default setting."[11] And to confuse things even further, you can irritate your partner not just when you seem to care too much—also known as nagging—but also when you don't seem to care enough.

Faithful to Foucault's analysis of marriage as a tool of biopolitical manipulation, Kipnis stresses that the ideology of romantic love that underpins our vision of married life is one way in which social norms penetrate the deepest recesses of our interiority: "Has any despot's rule ever so successfully infiltrated every crevice of a population's being, into its movements and gestures, penetrated its very soul? In fact it creates the modern notion of a soul—one which experiences itself as empty without love. Saying 'no' to love isn't just heresy, it's tragedy: for our sort the failure to achieve what is most essentially human. And not just tragic, but abnormal" (26). In this way, Kipnis proposes that the very ideal of romantic love that our culture holds in such high regard is an instrument of social normalization: "Whether or not we fancy that we love as we please, free as the birds and butterflies, an endless quantity of social instructions exists to tell us what it is, and what to do with it, and how, and when. And tell us, and tell us: the quantity of advice on the subject of how to love properly is almost as infinite as the sanctioned forms it takes are limited" (40–1). Kipnis further observes that domesticity—the form of love promoted by our society—is the mechanism by which our ideal of love is enforced: "Imagine the most efficient kind of social control possible. It wouldn't be a soldier on every corner—too expensive, too crass. Wouldn't the most elegant means of producing acquiescence be to somehow transplant those social controls so seamlessly into the guise of individual needs that the difference between them dissolved?" (39). Foucault already argued that societies invent institutions such as factories, schools, prisons, and asylums to guarantee that people can be disciplined into predictable routines, which is why they tend to regulate both mobility and timetables (forcing people's lives to conform to enclosed spaces and the ticking of the clock). Against this backdrop, Kipnis asks: "What current social institution is more enclosed than modern domesticity? What offers greater regulation of movement and time, or more precise surveillance of body and thought to a greater number of individuals?" (93). The answer to this rhetorical question is, of course, that there is no modern institution that tames people more effectively than marriage.

Let me state this again: I have nothing against happy marriages. I believe that all social institutions—even marriage—can be revitalized, so that it's conceivable to be married without buying into the repressive ideologies that have traditionally accompanied marriage. At the same time, it's impossible to deny that the social glorification of marriage as the pinnacle of happiness serves to hide the fact that, as Kipnis puts it, "toxic levels of everyday dissatisfaction, boredom, unhappiness, and not-enoughness are the functional norms in millions of lives and marriages" (190). Far from the "mature" form of relating that our society portrays, marriage is often an ongoing attempt to keep the keg of irritation from exploding. Kipnis is onto something when she claims that "*Would you please stop doing that?*" constitutes the "deep structure" of modern coupledom (82). From bedroom to bathroom, kitchen to garage, married couples bicker, quarrel, squabble, and sometimes even scream at each other. Alternatively, they spend countless hours negotiating, adjusting, and resolving their "issues," frequently even paying therapists to play umpire to their domestic dramas. Sometimes the mere tone of a mate's voice demands numerous therapy sessions to work through, for even a hint of disapproval can open the floodgates of a long history of bruised egos, callous rejections, hurtful letdowns, and stinging disappointments. And strangely enough, we have come to take this as the status quo of married life, so that if we dare to complain about it, we are told to grow up, become more realistic, and learn to ask less from our marriages. As Kipnis points out, marriage researchers, relationship experts, religious authorities, and couples' counselors are all telling us that the secret to a good marriage is to lower our expectations (173–5). That this "Ask Less from Life plan" (175) directly contradicts the cultural hype about marriage being the cure for all of our problems—social and personal alike—seems to go unnoticed, as does the fact that lowering our expectations hardly represents the solution it professes to be.

Those who dare to complain about the state of their marriages are often met with a wall of rhetoric along the lines of "everyone has problems," "no one said it would be easy," "it could be worse—count your blessings," or "marriage takes hard work." This last notion—that marriage takes hard work—has become so widely accepted that it's these days almost impossible to talk about marriage without immediately conjuring up the language of mines, factories, sweatshops, and chain-gangs. "Yes, we all know that Good Marriages Take Work," Kipnis quips: "we've been well tutored in the catechism of labor-intensive intimacy. Work, work, work: given all the heavy lifting required, what's the difference between work and 'after work' again? Work/home, office/bedroom: are you ever *not* on the clock? Good relationships may take work, but unfortunately, when it comes to love, trying is always trying too hard: work doesn't work" (18). Yet many of us are prepared to work at our marriage to an almost irrational degree. We "work at" intimacy, at getting along, at not getting on each other's nerves, at doing what we are supposed to do, at not doing what we are not supposed to do, and so on. Indeed, as Kipnis observes, one of the incredible feats of our social order is to make "working for love" (20) sound admirable—as the thing we should all want to do. And even though we may have moments of yearning for something different, we often don't act on these yearnings because we have already invested so much of ourselves in our marriage that we can't bear the thought of losing it all. So we work even harder. We even work at sex. As Kipnis poignantly asks, "When did sex get to be so boring? When did it turn into this thing you're supposed to 'work at'?" (5–6).

A good question—and one that many married couples seem afraid to ask because they know that doing so might rock the foundations of their well-organized life. From a certain perspective, when you have to work at sex, let alone love, something has already gone wrong. Yet many of us take it for granted that "grown-up" love is going to be a labor-intensive enterprise. And perhaps most strangely of all, we even elevate this type of love, a "love" that feels like an endless bootcamp, over less permanent but more uplifting affairs. We are trained to equate love with longevity to such an extent that we tend to think that a relationship that lasts is a success regardless of how wretched it makes us. Conversely, we tend to think that a relationship that doesn't last is a failure regardless of how joyful—how alive, vitalized, and transformed—it might have made us feel. The association of love with long-term stability is so ingrained in our minds that few of us dare to seriously entertain alternatives. Even those of us who get a divorce are usually on the lookout for a new partner we might be able to marry. To be sure, we may fantasize about other possibilities (the cute guy or gal at work), and sometimes even act on our fantasies (having an affair with the said guy or gal), but such interludes are usually thought to be deviations from the script we are supposed to follow: lapses, missteps, digressions, or even tragic mistakes. In other words, even our indiscretions don't usually cause us to question the ideal of an enduring marriage that lends comfort to the lives of both partners for as long as they live.

Perhaps we *should* question this ideal, given how rarely it actually bears any resemblance to reality. Perhaps we should start taking seriously the possibility that there might be better ways to arrange our love lives. Who is to say, for instance, that a lifelong marriage that offers security but no passion is better than a dozen ardent affairs that don't endure? Kipnis writes: "As we know, 'mature love,' that magical elixir, is supposed to kick in when desire flags, but could that be the problem right there? Mature love: it's kind of like denture adhesive. Yes, it's supposed to hold things in place; yes, it's awkward for everyone when it doesn't; but unfortunately there are some things that glue just won't glue, no matter how much you apply" (34). Is it really the case that the endless repetition of arguments, the gnawing sense of being disrespected, the monotony of overfamiliarity, the tedium of routines, and the aggravation of daily torments is invariably worth the trouble? Are the rewards and pleasures of marriage really worth the emotional deep freeze that seems to hover over so many marriages? And can they compensate for the sacrifice of libido that seems almost always to accompany married life, for sex lives that have shriveled to a hushed, insipid, slightly embarrassing, and largely unappetizing task—one that we are relieved to check off our to-do list for the month? True enough, some couples "muster the requisite fizz to achieve sexual congress on a regular basis," Kipnis jokes: "And true enough, some couples do manage to perform enough psychical retooling to reshape the anarchy of desire to the confines of the marriage bed, plugging away at the task year after year like diligent assembly line workers (once a week, same time, same position), aided by the occasional fantasy or two to get the old motor to turn over, or keep running, or complete the trip" (66). This pathetic picture has nothing to do with the aliveness of desire or the longings of the soul. Yet many people put up with it for economic reasons, because they need emotional reassurance, out of habit, or for the sake of their children, creating a nation of erotic workaholics: people who believe that if sex is not fulfilling, it's because they aren't working hard enough at it.

Kipnis argues that it's difficult to imagine "a modern middle-class marriage not syncopated by rage" (35). While this—as so much else about Kipnis's polemic—may be an overstatement, it's not entirely false. This is one reason it's genuinely sad that the dominant cultural narrative regarding marriage implies that there is something laudatory, even "noble" about the incessant effort to hold a marriage together against all odds (and regardless of how much repressed rage it generates). Kipnis is right to suggest that if so many married people have affairs, it's not just because they are looking for sexual novelty but because they are desperate for a little taste of the vitality that marriage has beaten out of their lives. Our society may try to tell us that the durability of our marriage is its own reward—and even a sign of our moral fiber—but this narrative can't always stifle the realization that there is something deeply antithetical about marriage as a long-term arrangement and the realities of human desire, about the social institution and the cravings of the body and soul. Social critics have long argued that desire—eros in its unshackled form—is one of the most antisocial forces under the sun. To put the matter bluntly, desire is not in the least bit interested in the viability of the cultural order. It couldn't care less about tax breaks, joint bank accounts, or our children's education. When it overflows the restrictions that are designed to contain it, it wreaks havoc with everything that is organized and well-established about our lives. And its force is often so overwhelming that we're willing to risk just about everything for just a moment's satisfaction, as is proven by politicians, celebrities, and other persons of social prominence who routinely tarnish their reputations by having affairs.

5

Our social order has a strong investment in making sure that we don't spend too much time thinking about the contradiction between marriage and desire—that we don't dwell on the possibility that our married lives might not be giving us everything we want from life. Particularly now that marriage is ailing, that more and more people are getting divorced or bowing out of marriage altogether, our society resorts to various tactics to distract us from the realization that marriage might not be the zenith of our lives after all. One of the most effective of these tactics is what Kipnis calls "the well-publicized desperation of single life." "Much as the grimness of the USSR once was used against anyone misguided enough to argue for systematic social reforms," Kipnis specifies, the threat of singleness is now being used against anyone questioning the delights of married life, so that *"Hey, if you don't like it here, just see how you like it over there"*—among those miserable singles—has become the motto leveled against anyone hesitating to step into the promised land of marriage (23). Michael Cobb, another interpreter of the costs of modern coupledom, agrees, explaining that one reason so many people think that marriage is a good choice is that they have been conditioned to think that "it is terrible to be single." "I could immediately rattle off 'proof' of its horrors," Cobb humorously continues: "the scent of rotting vegetables and unused product portions drifting out of my fridge; the numerous wedding invitations with 'and guest' violently scrawled next to my name; the pitying glances of people saddened that I often have nothing of substance to report about a 'love life' (and the relieved glee when sometimes I do have things to report); the sad knowledge that not even the commodity form often fits the single; and the perplexed utterances of wait staff asking me, 'Just you?'"[12]

Our society is so unsympathetic to the idea of singleness—and so determined to turn single people into coupled ones—that it's not terribly surprising that so many people seek shelter under the umbrella of marriage. Among other things, being single carries the double mark of failure: undesirability and unhappiness. At worst, it is a reviled state of being; at best, it is, as Cobb puts it, "a conundrum to be solved by coupling off, and as soon as possible" (4). Our society, in short, makes it very difficult to fathom what it might be like to lead a rewarding single life, and ultimately, as Cobb notes, "no one is *really* supposed to be single": "there are no *real* single people out there—they're all just waiting for the chance to find that special someone, sometime soon" (5). That is, our culture is so strongly oriented toward enduring intimate relationships that being single is always seen as a transitory state, something to be overcome rather than something to be enjoyed for its own unique rewards and pleasures. A single person is in some ways always read as someone who has somehow—perhaps by some fault of his or her own or due to some past personal trauma—missed the opportunity to become coupled. As Bella DePaulo, who has written extensively about the ways in which singles are shunned in our society, bemoans: "Tell new acquaintances that you are single and often they think they already know quite a lot about you. They understand your emotions: You are miserable and lonely and envious of couples. They know what motivates you: More than anything else in the world, you want to become coupled … . They also believe they know something about your psychological development and your psyche: You are just not as mature as the other people your age who are coupled. And at heart, you are basically selfish." You of course don't have any important people in your life, or even a life to speak of, so that "you can be asked to stay late at work or do all the traveling over the holidays."[13] And if all else fails, the promoters of coupledom deliver the final threat: "You will grow old alone. Then you will die alone" (3).

To be single in our society is to bear the stigma of loneliness, emptiness, sexlessness, and lovelessness. This implies that you have failed on a number of levels, but above all else, it signifies a fundamental existential failing because, as Cobb, echoing Kipnis, observes, in our society "you're not allowed to be without love"; love is "not merely an activity one adds to a list of things that have to get done in this life … but life itself" (18). As a result, to be single is—to borrow from DePaulo—to lose by definition: "No matter what you can point to on your own behalf—spectacular accomplishments, a lifelong and caring convoy of relatives and friends, extraordinary altruism—none of it redeems you if you have no soulmate. Others will forever be scratching their heads and wondering what's wrong with you and comparing notes (he's always a bit strange; she's so neurotic; I think he's gay)" (4). You'll be shown some leniency if you exhibit signs of a serious effort to secure a partner. But otherwise you get little sympathy. For instance, singles who have satisfying sex lives are often branded as loose and promiscuous. At the same time, those who are not having sex are pitied for not "getting any." Singles who are successful at their jobs are seen as overcompensating for not having a love life. And if they think they are happy, they are just deluding themselves: everyone knows that one can't be genuinely happy without a partner. Single women are warned that if they postpone having children for too long, their dried-up eggs will be good for nothing. And those who might want to opt out of motherhood are told that they will regret this later, that they will miss out on their life's calling, that their lives will forever be incomplete, and that to their dying breath (and particularly as they draw that breath) they will wish that they had understood earlier what being a woman was really all about.

Men, in turn, are cautioned that, in DePaulo's words, "without the civilizing hand of a woman, they will run amok with slovenliness, horniness, and criminality" (16). As we saw in Chapter 1, this was one of Wright's tactics for cajoling men to marry.

6

This bleak picture of single life of course frequently has nothing to do with the realities of single people, who often (not always, but often) lead rich and rewarding lives with thriving careers, friendships, and social support networks, not to mention plenty of amorous adventures and passionate sex. In this sense, to make singles bear the burden of being labeled lonely outcasts is to project a lot of the misery of coupledom—including the fact that many married people are desperately lonely—onto singles. DePaulo highlights the extent to which marriage in our society is considered the benchmark of personhood by noting that there is something strange about the very fact that single people are called "unmarried." Given that "it is singlehood that comes first and then is undone—if it is undone—by marriage," "why aren't married people called 'unsingle'" (3)? The answer of course is that our society doesn't consider you a full person unless you're married or at least coupled up: marriage is the gold standard of personhood, and it doesn't seem to matter whether you are happy or unhappy as long as you have a marriage certificate. And as we know, this certificate comes with a whole host of social perks, rewards, and privileges: access to your spouse's social security benefits, health-care plan, hospital room, and the life-and-death decisions that sometimes come with that hospital room. Even hotel rooms, vacation packages, and club memberships cost less if you're coupled up. As Cobb remarks, there are huge social, political, and economic stakes in dividing people into those who are legally married and those who are not (17), which is one reason gay marriage has become such a charged issue in contemporary politics.[14]

One reason singles threaten the social status quo is that their lifestyle choices—from single gays who favor promiscuous sex over monogamy (which is not to say that all single gays do) to single women who opt out of motherhood (which is not to say that all single women, gay or straight, do) all the way to single straight guys who prefer rock music to fatherhood (which is not to say that all single straight guys do)—undermine the conservative ideal of social stability. And the more this ideal flounders, the more it frays around the edges, the more nervous the dominant cultural establishment gets. DePaulo stresses that now that increasing numbers of people no longer see marriage as an essential component of their lives, our culture is engaged in a frantic effort to "instill in an entire populace the unshakeable belief that marriage is exactly what it is not: utterly and uniquely transformational" (13). According to this mythology, DePaulo continues, marriage "transforms the immature single person into a mature spouse. It creates a sense of commitment, sacrifice, and selflessness where there was none before. It is the one true place where intimacy and loyalty can be nurtured and sustained. It transforms a serious sexual partnership from a tryout to the real thing. Before, you hoped you were each other's everything; now you really are. Marriage delivers as its ultimate reward the most sought-after American prize: happiness. Not just garden-variety happiness, but deep and meaningful well-being. A sense of fulfillment that a single person cannot even fathom. Marry, the mythology promises, and you will never be lonely again" (13). Along similar lines, Cobb argues that in our cultural imagination, marriage is supposed to end "our tragic twists and turns, nullifying all the bad feelings of misunderstanding and misconnection that preceded it. Could you even imagine a president who could be elected if she or he were single?" (13).

Though the household consisting of a married couple and their children was in the minority by the beginning of the twenty-first century, overtaken by households with single people living alone (and DePaulo specifies that most single people don't actually live alone), the reification of marriage as the only really desirable way to live continues more strongly than ever. Indeed, now that Americans have so many other options—now that it has become possible to attain outside of marriage many of the things that were once only available within its confines (such as sex, intimacy, and economic viability)—the propaganda machine that fetishizes married bliss has only intensified its efforts to paint a rosy picture of the institution. DePaulo calls this propaganda machine "matrimania" (10). And because it is women specifically who have gained from the collapse of traditional marriage—who can now have sex, intimacy, and careers outside of marriage—they are the ultimate target of matrimania: "If marriage is to be restored to an undisputed place of honor and privilege, then women especially need to be convinced that it is marriage, above all else, that they should wish for, work for, yearn for" (16). That this is what our society is doing is beyond doubt. As we have seen, both evolutionary psychologists and self-help gurus are keen to convince women that they would be happiest in the folds of married life, where their economic interests would be protected at the same time as their flagging libidos would not be overtaxed. The entertainment industry, in turn, though for obvious reasons much less interested in flagging libidos, stages a relentless effort—from *The Bachelor* and *Marry a Millionaire* to the plot lines of many hit dramas—to remind women that all roads should lead to the altar. Add to this the equally tireless efforts of relationship guides, internet sites, and advice columns to convince them of the same, and it becomes clear why resisting marriage can be so very difficult. Isn't the celebrity wedding album today's equivalent of the *Playboy* centerfold?

That we no longer have to get married to lead satisfying lives has been liberating to many. But it has been deeply alarming to those who would prefer a more traditional relationship culture. The latter seem to look back at the 1950s as the golden era of American life, when marriage seemed to render everyday lives both predictable and meaningful. We tend to imagine this time as one of safety, warmth, comfort, and moral rectitude so that, as DePaulo asserts, "The more complicated, unsettled, and contentious our current American lives and American values seem to be, and the more these complexities seem threatening rather than freeing, the more we yearn for the way we believe things used to be" (12). Yet by all accounts, the 1950s were a historical anomaly, a bizarre social climate generated in part by the fact that countless women were forced out of the workforce when veterans of World War II returned home to claim their jobs. Women who had been economically independent became once again dependent on their husbands, which is one reason traditional marriages thrived. Moreover, mortgage breaks and tax advantages for married couples ensured that marriage became an economically desirable arrangement. Mainstream culture pitched in by turning house-keeping into an art form, by warning women about the dangers of mixing careers with motherhood, and by elevating motherhood to a woman's sacred (and natural) calling. The result? The baby boom, which locked many women into the role of mother and wife, at least until the emergence of feminist consciousness during the 1960s. While contemporary culture is more tolerant of the idea of working women than the ethos of the 1950s was, there are still considerable pressures on women to fulfill their calling of motherhood first and foremost. If a woman doesn't have children, the assumption is that she is infertile, couldn't find a man, or is otherwise unfit to be a mother. The idea that she might have chosen not to have children seems very hard for many Americans to wrap their heads around.

Though things have changed for the better, and though many married people these days consciously strive for egalitarian partnerships (and frequently succeed in creating such partnerships), it would be useless to deny that, generally speaking, old gendered connotations still hang to the corners of marriage. Take the ideal of the coy female I've criticized throughout this book: this ideal bolsters the seamless operation of society by turning women into wives and mothers who support the stability of the nuclear family. If women thought of themselves as highly sexual creatures—with strong sexual needs—they might be more likely to seek sex outside of marriage, with the result that they would have less energy to devote to their husbands and children. And obviously, from the perspective of conventional gender roles, nothing is as important as women devoting themselves to their husbands and children; there is nothing as important as the idea that women will spend the bulk of their energies serving their family. A sexually adventurous woman might not do so, which is why it's in the interest of traditional marriage (and of the social order that this marriage supports) to convince women that, really, they don't need sex very much. Referring to the needs of consumer society, Kipnis states: "A citizenry who fucked in lieu of shopping would soon bring the entire economy grinding to a standstill" (36). Similarly, one could say that wives who fucked frequently—or fucked outside the marital bedroom—would quickly bring the institution of marriage to its knees. Nothing is more essential to the ideal of traditional marriage as the sexually repressed female, which is exactly why our gender profilers are so keen to tell us that women are incapable of desire independently of emotional commitment. More generally speaking, what I've tried to illustrate in this book is that the more the realities of American men and women have started to diverge from our society's time-honored gender norms, the more desperate our gender profilers have gotten about convincing us that these norms captured something about the essential natures of men and women.

7

As I've already implied, what is so insidious about this process of domestication is that it's all done in the name of happiness. The feminist philosopher Sara Ahmed proposes that because virtually no one in our society contests the idea that happiness should be the goal of human existence, how we are taught to conceptualize its parameters has an immense impact on how we end up living our lives. In other words, because there exists a nearly unanimous consensus in our society that happiness is what everyone wants, the cultural portraiture of happiness that surrounds us is one of the most powerful (biopolitical) influences in our lives, dictating which life directions we choose to pursue and which to avoid. And, as I've been stressing, one of the primary social indicators of happiness is marriage. As Ahmed writes, "Marriage [is] defined as 'the best of all possible worlds' as it maximizes happiness. The argument is simple: if you are married, then we can predict that you are more likely to be happier than if you are not married. The finding is also a recommendation: get married and you will be happier!"[15] Marriage as an ideal gives us a very specific image of what our future should look like, in many ways teaching us how we are supposed to experience pleasure. Ahmed notes that in every society, the promise of happiness clings to particular goals—goals that are deemed necessary for the attainment of the good life—so that those who are perceived as falling short of such goals are also perceived as falling short of happiness. In our society, heterosexual marriage, with its expectation of lifelong monogamy, gender-differentiated tasks, and reproductive aims, is foremost among such privileged goals, which is precisely why it can be so hard to choose a different kind of life; it can be hard to avoid the sense that if one opts out of marriage, one opts out of happiness.

Ahmed points out that the "happiness scripts" (90) that govern our society are almost invariably gendered scripts that orient us toward marriage as a culmination of heterosexual desire (which, needless to say, is the only kind of desire that is considered to lead to happiness). As I've attempted to show in this book, the dominant happiness script for a straight woman—propagated by evolutionary psychologists and self-help authors alike—is to settle down with a good man who will complete her being, provide her with security, and act as a reliable father to her children; to deviate from this script is to be threatened with unhappiness. Ahmed specifies that, historically, the danger of unhappiness for women was often associated with having too much curiosity about other possibilities, too much imagination about scripts other than the marriage script. This is one reason feminists are often characterized as killjoys, as women who suck the joy out of life by daring to pursue scripts other than the dominant happiness script.[16] Likewise, in today's society, queers are portrayed as troublemakers who threaten the dominant happiness script, sometimes because they, by pursuing promiscuous lifestyles, shun the kind of intimacy that underpins the ideal of married monogamy, other times because they are demanding admission to the folds of this very ideal. In this sense, queers are doomed whether they reject or uphold the ideal, in the former instance because they express sexuality in ways that don't fit the script, in the latter because they are asking the script to be revised so that they can also participate. Either way, the establishment resists because it is wedded (pun intended) to a very particular version of the happiness script—one premised on the ideals of gender profiling and the (presumed) "natural" complementarily of men and women.

Our dominant happiness script aims at gender-bifurcated domesticity. It admits more and more overlap between men and women as long as it's still clear to everyone that when it comes to basic psychological, emotional, and sexual responses, men and women are completely different. Moreover, the cultural efforts to draw women back into the circuit of domesticity are considerable. Ahmed gives a poignant example of this by quoting Darla Shine, the author of *Happy Housewives*: "Being home in a warm, comfy house floating around in your pajamas and furry slippers while sipping coffee as your babies play on the floor and your hubby works hard to pay for it all is not desperation. Grow up! Shut up! Count your blessings!" (52). As Ahmed correctly notes, Shine presents a very specific image of what makes a housewife happy:

one sated with white middle-class leisure, comfort, affluence, and ease. The implication is that this is the kind of life women gave up when they embraced feminism, choosing careers over homemaking. Yet this life was never available to most women in the past. Nor is it available for many women in the present—even those who might want it. And, as might be expected, Shine leaves out of the picture all the ways in which the life of the "happy housewife" might not always be that happy after all. The idea that there might be a gap between the ideal of the happy housewife and the realities of being a housewife cannot be admitted to Shine's universe for the simple reason that the intelligibility of this universe demands that house-wives be by definition happy.

A related example Ahmed offers is the expectation that the bride should invariably be happy. In fact, the wedding day should by definition be the happiest day of a woman's life, so that a bride who doesn't experience it as such is more or less incomprehensible in our social context. "If the bride is not happy on the wedding day and even feels 'depressed and upset,'" Ahmed remarks, "then she is experiencing an 'inappropriate affect'" (41). To correct her mistake—to "save the day"—the bride must be able to make herself feel happy or at least "pass" as being happy, so that everyone can say with conviction that "the bride looked happy." More generally speaking, any woman who has ever been harassed on the street by a strange man telling her to "smile" has had a small taste of the violence entailed in the notion that it's women's cultural role to project happiness even when they don't feel happy. It never seems to occur to the guy asking you to smile that you might be having a miserable day, that you might be besieged by a swarm of worries, or that your grandmother might have died earlier in the week: as far as he's concerned, it's your duty to reassure him that everything is well in the (patriarchal) world by beaming at him while trying to catch the next train uptown. This is why the feminist Shulamith Firestone called for a "smile boycott," telling women to abandon their "pleasing" smiles, "henceforth only smiling when something pleased *them*." Firestone writes: "In my own case, I had to train myself out of the phony smile, which is like a nervous tic on every teenage girl. And this meant that I smiled rarely, for in truth, when it came down to real smiling, I had less to smile about."[17] The feminist who refuses to smile when she is not happy, Ahmed adds, "wants a more exciting life" (69). She is not necessarily resisting the idea of being happy; but she is resisting the cultural pressure to appear happy even when she is not. She wants to find alternative ways of procuring satisfaction, of living the kind of life that feels worth living to her specifically.

What is so devastating about the dominant scripts of femininity—scripts that often presuppose a degree of alienation from the truth of one's inner states—is precisely that they blind us to alternative ways of attaining happiness. I agree with Ahmed's assessment that feminism, at its best, is an attempt to widen our horizons, to open up "the places where we can look." "The fact that any such opening is read as a sign of hostility, or of killing other people's joy, tells us something," Ahmed continues: "The public investment in happiness is an investment in a very particular and narrow model of the good" (70). In this context, it may be useful to recall the extremes to which some social conservatives, such as Wright, are willing to go to portray feminism as killing the joy of women (so that feminism, by some wild twist of logic, becomes what oppresses women). While it is true that there have historically been some forms of feminism that have been prudish and restrictive—the antisex rhetoric of some of the second wave feminists jumps to mind—for the most part feminism has always been an attempt to expand the array of life options for both men and women. That so many people find this attempt so menacing says a great deal about our cultural reluctance to step outside the lines of the happiness scripts we have inherited. Our commitment to such scripts can in fact be so strong that when a given script doesn't deliver what it promises, when it makes us unhappy rather than happy, we don't think of questioning the script itself (say, the marriage script) but instead assume that somehow we have failed to live out the script correctly. In other words, when we have been invested in the notion that a certain kind of life is the happy life, it can be very difficult for us to admit that this life hasn't actually made us happy; it can be hard to admit that our faith in a specific happiness script has led us astray. Indeed, we are often kept from acknowledging our unhappiness by our very hope that if we just keep at it, if we just try hard enough, this script will eventually deliver us to the threshold of happiness.[18]

As we saw above, this is Berlant's definition of cruel optimism: we keep hoping that one day our life choices will give us the desired result even when it is highly unlikely that they ever will. And it is our very failure to be conscious of alternative ways of organizing our lives that, in Ahmed's words, "blocks other possible worlds, as a blockage that makes possibles impossible, such that possibles are lost before they can be lived, experienced, or imagined" (165). That is, a huge array of alternative existential paths are lost to us before they even become possibilities, before we even get a chance to imagine what it would be like to pursue them. And sadly, we are often not in the least bit aware of what it is that we are giving up. Ahmed in fact specifies that it is not only social prohibitions— "don't do that"—that lead to such personal sacrifices but, equally importantly, the affirmations we receive—"yes, that's good"—that direct us to certain existential orientations. As a matter of fact, the latter are more difficult to resist because it's harder to see them as tools of social conditioning. With prohibitions, we are usually to some degree aware that our desire is being disciplined, that we are told to desire in specific ways. With affirmations, in contrast, it's harder to see the machinery of disciplining at work; it's harder to understand that we are getting an education in how to desire. As Ahmed states, "We can hear the 'no' in part as it asks us to stop doing something. It might be harder to hear the 'yes words' … because the words seem to 'go along' with or affirm what we are already doing" (48).

8

Is there, then, no force capable of thwarting the disciplinary processes that seek to convince us that traditional marriage with its gender-specific roles represents the cradle of happiness? There is: desire. Thus far I've highlighted the ways in which our desires can be molded to fit the needs of the collective order. In the same way that consumer culture teaches us to desire specific items (cars, shoes, clothes, watches, computers, body shapes, hair styles, breast sizes, and a countless number of other items and ideals), our society teaches us to desire specific intimate formations. The fetishization of marriage I've analyzed, for example, is meant to persuade us that what we gain from investing our desire in one person for the rest of our lives is far more valuable, far more precious, than what we lose. And perhaps it is for many people. Yet despite all these efforts at curtailing desire, a portion of it always escapes; even if our desire can be socially conditioned, it can rarely be completely colonized. Indeed, as I've observed, the countless social restrictions that have historically been placed on desire—particularly on female desire—only prove how difficult it is to fully contain. There is always a limit to the degree of renunciation our desire is capable of tolerating; there is only so much dissatisfaction it is willing to endure. And dissatisfaction, as Kipnis astutely states, "gives people 'ideas'," sometimes even critical ones: "First a glimmering, then an urge, then a transient desire, soon a nascent thought: '*Maybe there's something else*'" (45). In this sense, there is a direct line from the dissatisfaction of desire to the realization that there should be "something more" to life than what we are experiencing. And once such a notion of "something more" has been introduced, we are on our way to rebelling against the habitual parameters of our lives.

Kipnis likens this to what happened early in the twentieth century, when workers started demanding shorter workdays. "A few troublemakers got fed up with being treated like machines, word spread, and pretty soon there was a whole movement" (45), she explains, adding that "there were wildcat strikes long before there was a labor movement" (139). This is because "'wanting more' is a step on the way to a political idea" (45). It is, in fact, the basis of all utopian thinking, of the kind of thinking that hankers for a state of affairs that is different from the current one. Desire, in turn, is just another word for "wanting more," which is precisely why it can be so difficult to keep within the bounds of marriage. Desire is always driven to ask, "Could things be different?" This question might not always be fully thought out or conscious, but it is what lurks behind our fantasies, which are, at bottom, nothing but an attempt to imagine what "something more" might consist of. Our fantasies are a form of utopian thinking that rejects—that rebels against—the drudgery of our lives. As Kipnis states, "Here we come to the weak link in the security-state model of long-term coupledom: *desire*. It's ineradicable. It's roving and inchoate, we're inherently desiring creatures, and sometimes desire just won't take no for an answer, particularly when some beguiling and potentially available love-object moves into your sight lines, making you feel what you'd forgotten to feel, which is *alive*, even though you're supposed to be channeling all such affective capacities into the 'appropriate' venues, and everything (Social Stability! The National Fabric! Being a Good Person!) hinges on making sure that you do" (44).

Marcuse proposes that in "a repressive order, which enforces the equation between normal, socially useful, and good, the manifestations of pleasure for its own sake must appear as *fleurs du mal*" (50). Pleasure for its own sake, sexuality as its own end—which nonreproductive sexuality is—is disruptive of the social order, not in small doses perhaps but when it becomes frequent and widespread, which is exactly why this order seeks to marginalize it in the ways I've outlined. But this effort is destined to fail: there are always going to be singles, queers, and straight married folks who have sex just because they happen to like it. Moreover, of particular interest in this context is the fact that the family values rhetoric of our society can't keep married people—even super-conservative ones—from cheating on their spouses, with the result that adultery is, paradoxically enough, one of the forms that rebellion takes in our society. As I revealed in Chapter 4, I'm personally not a huge fan of adultery. But as a cultural critic, I must admit that Kipnis is right when she asserts that adultery tends to throw a monkey wrench into the performance principle that our society tries to uphold. Speaking of the effects of adultery on our work morale, Kipnis writes, "*Fuck work*': if adulterers ever adopt a slogan, this could be it. A close contender: *'stolen moments'*" (109). Or consider this more detailed portraiture: "Instead of Bartleby hunched dutifully over the project or report that was due days or weeks ago, there you are on the computer composing witty novella-length e-mails to your beloved. Every time you hit 'send' you're redirecting resources: your productivity, your attention, the boss's dollar. Rebellion? It's virtually industrial sabotage. From upstanding citizen to petty thief: pilfering from the company stockroom, poaching in the boss's pond, as useless to the forces of production as a lovestruck hormonal teenager or a Romantic poet—no, you're hardly going to make Employee of the Year" (108).

In a society that uses marriage to prop up the productivity of its workers, this type of deviation from the dominant happiness script is disastrous. Suddenly your desire is no longer serving the larger social good but rather turning you into a dissenter—and this is the case even when dissension is not your conscious aim. "If stumbling into the wrong bed with the wrong partner and getting lost in reverie and losing track of time refashions ordinary citizens into default social critics and heirs to Romantic protest," Kipnis muses, then "perhaps social conservatives and marital moralizers are onto something when they fret about sexual transgression. Maybe there really is some sort of a domino effect, and the social fabric *is* being irrevocably sullied and torn asunder" (112–13). Kipnis therefore accepts the possibility that social conservatives are correct in drawing a link between non-marital, nonreproductive sexuality and the erosion of the traditional cultural order. The difference, of course, is that she doesn't mind this erosion whereas social conservatives do. This is exactly why they meet all deviations from the marriage script with the chastising rhetoric of brimstone and punishment. As Kipnis states, "When possibilities for altering life conditions do very occasionally force themselves into daylight like tiny, delicate sprouts struggling up through the hard dirt, what an array of sharp-bladed mechanisms stand ready to mow them into mulch before they manage to take root!" (137). But even this is to a large extent a losing battle, for once our desire has had a taste of freedom, "it becomes hard to refute the idea that *something's* missing" (196). It keeps nagging us with the question of what, and how much, we are "allowed to want from life" (136). How much more waiting are we supposed to endure?

I've underscored that at the core of cruel optimism resides the fact that we are often willing to wait indefinitely for whatever it is that we think will give us satisfaction. And, as Ahmed notes, the longer we wait, the harder it becomes for us to deviate from our path for the simple reason that the longer we stay on the path, the more we invest in that path (236). Against this backdrop, what makes desire such a rebellious force is that it refuses to wait: it wants satisfaction *now*. It causes us to lose our patience, thereby inciting us to question the path we are on; it jolts us to a new life because it is no longer willing to stay sheepishly devoted to the old one. "It is no accident that revolutionary consciousness means feeling at odds with the world, or feeling that the world is odd," Ahmed explains: "You become estranged from the world as it has been given" (168). In this sense, the flipside of a new desire is an alienation from previous forms of life. In Ahmed's words, "you feel against the world and the world feels against you"; you are "no longer well adjusted: you cannot adjust to the world" (168–9). Such alienation is often the precondition of one's ability to reject the dominant happiness scripts of one's society, for it forces one to recognize just how limiting such scripts can be, to "become conscious of how much one's being has been stolen" (167). From this viewpoint, rebelliousness is in part a matter of becoming aware of one's suffering. This can apply to various types of suffering, such as political oppression or socioeconomic deprivation. But it can also apply to the suffering of desire.

Illegitimate desires can be a way of questioning happiness scripts that we have been accustomed to accept. And once we become aware of how such scripts curtail our lives—what we have sacrificed in order to stay faithful to them—modalities of life that might have formerly seemed unintelligible become intelligible: we start to see other possibilities, other modes of satisfaction. More concretely speaking, when our desire is suddenly revived—when we meet a new person who is able to awaken the dormant yearning within us—we experience a rebirth. Suddenly we feel fully alive, buoyant, reinvented, in touch with ourselves; everything seems richer, brighter, more intense. It's hard to deprive ourselves of such feelings once they have been roused. As Kipnis posits, once we open the can of worms that contains our repressed desires, "those worms clearly aren't going to just crawl willingly back into their can" (9). In this sense, it's in the nature of desire to be transformative. It connects us to disclaimed dimensions of ourselves—dimensions that we have had to suppress to sustain the life that we have been living. Such disclaimed dimensions may have for the most part stayed hidden, but they are never fully suppressed. And when the right occasion arises, they start to clamor for recognition. They remind us of the alternative life that we could have lived—and that we might still be able to live. We may not always act on our new information, our new inclinations. But neither can we pretend that this information, these inclinations, aren't now a clandestine element of our lives. Most likely, they will lie in wait for the next opening, the next time our desire is unexpectedly stirred. And the more we strive to suppress them, the more momentum they are likely to gather.

9

The gender profiling practices I've analyzed in this book are one way to curb the rebelliousness of our desire, to keep us on the straight and narrow. And one reason they are so powerful is that they can be traced back to our families of origin—the fact that, for many of us, our families are where we first internalized the ideology of gendered lives. A big part of the dominant happiness script—the marriage script—is the belief that our happiness depends on our ability to reproduce the forms of family life we ourselves experienced. Of course, if we had an unhappy childhood, we are not expecting to imitate everything about our family. But the basic parameters of the nuclear family—mother, father, children—are a largely unquestioned ideal in our society; they are an object of desire for many people. Indeed, for many, a happy family seems indisputably necessary for the good life. This is the message not only of our government, our schools, our churches, and our parents but also of the countless movies and television shows that reproduce the image of the happy nuclear family. To take just one randomly chosen example, in Season 2 of the teen hit *Pretty Little Liars*, Hanna—one of the main characters—is shown wishfully looking at a couple with two small children at a neighborhood café. She turns to her friend, Caleb, and says, with reference to her own broken family, "We'll never be that." The implication is that if there were a way to keep her family intact—in this case by preventing her father from remarrying—everything would automatically be okay: there would be no more pain, suffering, or disappointment. That this is a wholly unrealistic portrayal of what actually takes place in the daily lives of many families is irrelevant. What we are being sold is the myth of the happy family that would instantly erase all of our problems.[19]

The family values rhetoric of social conservatives depends on the same mystification. Yet this vision of happy families is also losing credibility. As Kipnis asserts, "To those who want to maintain that non-divorced families turn out less neurotic or happier adults, the evidence supporting such views is a little scanty: please look around. Are traditional families really such happy, neurosis-free places?" (140–1). Hardly. More generally speaking, the answer to the question of whether or not divorce hurts children depends on how you set up the comparison. If divorce is what gets a child out of an environment of fighting, yelling, bickering, and constant fear and anxiety (not to mention physical abuse), then clearly that child is going to be better off. But if divorce ushers mother and child below the poverty line—as it often does in the United States—then perhaps it's true that the child would have been better off with an intact family. Yet it's also the case that if this child received the necessary social supports to keep him or her above the poverty line, he or she might benefit from escaping a bad marriage that the spouses hold together just for the sake of their children. Make no mistake: families are frequently ways of transmitting trauma, of passing the wounds of parents, particularly their shame and guilt, onto children in an endless chain of emotional misery. As Kipnis points out, "Unfortunately what 'for the sake of the children' really means is multi-generational training grounds for lowered expectations as an affective norm" (141). That is, families are often a means of reconciling children to the idea that they shouldn't have high expectations, that life is hard, and that having any unusual ("unrealistic") aspirations is a recipe for disappointment. And they are often also a crucible for the notion that life is always going to be the way it is at present, that any hankering after "something more" is a waste of energy.

Kipnis is also correct in unveiling the hypocrisies of the governmental rhetoric of trying to save marriages "for the sake of the children." She remarks that this notion—that we are doing things for the sake of our children—"is rather a selective enterprise, holding sway far more frequently when it comes to guilty matters like divorce than when it comes to pocketbook issues like education spending" (139). The United States, after all, ranks behind most other industrialized countries in money spent on education. The country is similarly dismal when it comes to other indicators of childhood health and well-being: it ranks behind most Western nations in infant mortality, and more American children than children of any other industrialized country live in poverty. This prompts Kipnis to note that "sentimentality about children's welfare comes and goes apparently: highest when there's the chance to moralize about adult behavior, lowest when it comes to resource allocation" (140). She finally draws the same conclusion I've drawn throughout this book, namely that it is not divorce but rather the fact that women's income tends to drop as a consequence of divorce that is the main problem. Kipnis specifies that Sweden's system of guaranteed child allocations proves this "with its childhood poverty rate of under 3 percent compared with 22 percent with our preferred method—which is to ignore reality, let everyone fend for themselves, and blame the consequences on lax morals or not working hard enough—whether at marriage or the minimum wage jobs that produce the poverty in the first place" (140).

DePaulo in turn challenges the idea that marriage is the communal glue that holds our society together, pointing out that singles often have much more extensive social networks than married people. While many married couples spend the bulk of their time within the walls of their home, reluctant to venture beyond their privacy, singles are busy creating alternative communities, kinship structures, and modes of relating. As DePaulo puts it, for many married couples, the home is their castle, "with a moat around it" (258). This is not to say that married people are somehow intrinsically less active or generous than singles but, as DePaulo notes, singles do seem to have a greater interest in forms of human connectedness that reach beyond the intimate sphere of the home. This makes it all the more frustrating that marriage keeps being touted as the cornerstone of our social order. As DePaulo writes, "There sure has been a lot of bedrock talk of late, as when marriage is described as the bedrock of society or the foundation of civilization. Such proclamations seem to imply that if society were to implement the dismantling of marital privileges … all of civilization would collapse" (255).

Like DePaulo, I obviously don't believe that the erosion of marital privileges would cause civilization to collapse. But one of the things I've attempted to argue in this chapter is that it might cause civilization to swerve into a new direction, and that this new direction might actually be quite desirable. Again, my argument is not meant to discredit happy marriages. If you are happily married, good for you. My objective, rather, has been to question the value of unhappy marriages. And it has also been to illustrate that there is a great deal that is problematic about our cultural valorization of marriage, particularly as this valorization tends to be accompanied by rampant gender profiling and massively outmoded gender roles. It is certainly possible to be married without buying into the latter. But our social rhetoric—the rhetoric we are hearing not only from social conservatives but also from our "scientists" and relationship "experts"—hasn't caught up to this new reality, with the result that when these scientists and experts talk about marriage, they tend to talk about modes of relationality that, to me, seem like the very antithesis of the good life. This is one reason I'm interested in the kinds of relational possibilities that are made available to us when we discard the idea that gender stereotypes sum up the truth about men and women and that heterosexual reproduction is the end-game of all romantic relationships.

Fortunately, more and more people in our society are finding traditional ideals of gender and sexuality both tyrannical and mind-numbingly boring. And they are realizing that there are massive advantages to recognizing the versatility of human relational capacity. This doesn't necessarily mean that things have gotten easier, that there is less confusion about relationships, for it can be demanding to negotiate the parameters of our intimate lives without the safety-net of tradition. Yet the more we are able to do so—the more open-minded we remain about other people—the more considerate, and perhaps even more ethical, our relation-ships become: when we no longer assume that we "already know" what being a man or a woman consists of, we might actually make a genuine effort to understand the people we invite into our lives. Many of us are relieved by this new reality. But others feel menaced by it, as if the increase in relational suppleness automati-cally led to an increase in social instability (and as if instability were invariably a bad thing). This is why gender profiling is such an important component of the conservative backlash, for it seems to offer an antidote to instability: it reintroduces clear divisions, clear categories, clear blueprints for behavior in a world that some experience as too chaotic. But the price we pay for this is too high in the sense that the more we cling to inequalitarian traditions, the less we are able to imagine viable alternatives; we lock ourselves into outdated modalities of romantic behavior that can ultimately only shrink the relational possibilities available to us.

CONCLUSION

Love at the beginning of the twenty-first century has been defused and discredited... . We inhabit a world in which every aspect of romance from meeting to mating has been streamlined, safety-checked, and emptied of spiritual consequence. The result is that we imagine we live in an erotic culture of unprecedented opportunity when, in fact, we live in an erotic culture that is almost unendurably bland.

CHRISTINA NEHRING

To the extent that we are unable to imagine viable alternatives to outmoded relational paradigms—and to the gender profiling tendencies that accompany these paradigms—we, as Christina Nehring observes, live in an impoverished erotic culture. One reason for this is that, as I have underscored throughout my discussion, gender profiling is ultimately quite tiresome: there is something utterly deadening about the incessant repetition of stereotypes. Moreover—and this has been another important theme in this book—the practice of gender profiling gives us the illusion that we can control our romantic destinies. This is the aspect of our romantic culture that Nehring calls attention to, albeit without the emphasis on gender that I have adopted. Both Nehring and I are disturbed by the fact that our society tries to persuade us that romantic relationships are (or should be) a rational enterprise that can be manipulated into the desired outcome. When it comes to evolutionary psychology specifically, the main idea seems to be that the better our "scientific" understanding of how men and women "function," the more efficiently we can manage our relationships (and the happier our lives will be); gender profiling, as it were, serves as a kind of "user's manual" to men and women. From my point of view, this is just about the most tedious—not to mention the most reductive—approach we could ever take to the adventure of intimacy.

That such a levelheaded (or faux-scientific) approach has gained prominence in our day is due in some part to the fact that the tenor of our society is thoroughly pragmatic: in all areas of life, we are supposed to get results; we are expected to fix all problems that arise so that we can move on with the rest of our lives (whatever that means). To some degree, this explains why, as we saw in the last chapter, we are conditioned to think that "true" love is a matter of being able to keep going even when ardor has been lost. "Real" love, we are told, is utilitarian, best realized in cozy, secure, and enduring marriages that transcend the volatility of passion. To be sure, the breathtaking fantasies of head-over-heels romance disseminated by our entertainment industry guide us toward the more irrational aspects of love. But the dominant message of our romantic culture, particularly of our "scientific" and self-help culture, is that love is an activity that we should be able to manage like any other.

If gender profiling is so popular in our romantic culture—if evolutionary arguments about men and women have been so influential in this culture—it's in part because it promises to insulate us against love's power to devastate, disorient, disappoint, and disillusion us. By giving us the impression that gender differences offer us valuable information about our partner, it causes us to assume that we can minimize the risks of relating, rendering it as safe and predictable as choosing the right lamp for our living room. This is of course not true: no amount of gender profiling is going to protect us against love's capacity to ravage us. But if, as Nehring maintains, "romance in our day is a poor and shrunken thing,"[1] it's in part because many people in our society do seem to believe that gender profiling can tame love's more unruly frequencies. In other words, those who place their faith in gender profiling seem primarily interested in making sure that love fits their preconceived notions—that there won't be any surprises. The worst, for them, seems to be the idea that they might not be able to tell ahead of time how things are going to unfold.

I understand the wish to avoid pain; I understand why people might not want to subject themselves to love's obsessions and illogical passions. But isn't there something rather sad about the idea that love is a matter of finding a mate who brings into the union a slew of stereotypical characteristics? It seems to me that the more we resort to this type of thinking—thinking based on caricatures—the more likely we are to stifle what is most inspiring and life-altering about romance. When romance becomes reduced to a gendered strategy—let alone some sort of a battle of the sexes—it becomes just about as unsexy as the process of shopping for our lamp. I can't in fact think of anything that is more antithetical to the ethos of eros than the belief that we can trick it into submission. If anything, the more we try to stage-manage it, the less likely it is to reward us, for it's not in the least bit interested in our gendered games. It aims at the very core of our being—at what makes each of us a unique and inimitable creature—so that when we insult it with our gendered thinking, it turns away in boredom.

But gender profiling is not just devitalizing; it's unethical. If there is one thing I would like you to take away from this book, it's the recognition that gender profiling is a violent way of going about relationality. For starters, the more we fixate on what makes men and women different from each other, the less we are able to see the singularity of others, including those we profess to love. Gender profiling covers over the idiosyncratic doubts, desires, struggles, anxieties, insecurities, confusions, and aspirations of others, thereby making it all the more difficult for us to build meaningful relationships with them. Because it turns men and women into cardboard cut-outs, it tempts us to read people through a narrow lens that causes us to neglect all the ways in which a given person is a thousand other things besides being male or female. To be sure, there are some individuals in our society who have internalized collective gender stereotypes so seamlessly that they do act in ways that conform to these stereotypes. But even with such individuals, we won't get very far if the stereotypical picture is where we stop at, if we assume that it somehow captures the full humanity of the person we are dealing with. If anything, for every tidbit of insight that stereotypes seem to give us, they deliver a mass of misinformation, in part because they leave out of the picture everything that doesn't fit neatly within its parameters. In this sense, the more we rely on stereotypes, the more shallow our relationships remain.

I doubt that our culture's gender platitudes can aid us with what is, after all, a fairly complex endeavor, namely the attempt to lead rewarding lives and forge respectful, mutually satisfactory relationships. Those who swear by gender profiling seem to presume that they can classify a person before they even make his or her acquaintance—that gender *alone* can tell them what sort of a person they are dealing with. Yet even a moment's reflection reveals that this is a fairly moronic way of approaching people. Making assumptions about others based on stereotypes doesn't make us smarter; it makes us intellectually sloppy. It deludes us into thinking that we understand others even when we don't; by offering us a convenient formula for reading others, it lulls us to the idea that people are easy to categorize—which they are not. And as a guide to complicated emotional realities, it's more or less useless because it causes us to focus on the most superficial aspects of relating imaginable—such as who is supposed to do what in a given interaction—when what is called for is a degree of sensitivity to the particularity of the situation at hand.

Take, for instance, the private background of suffering that has formed each of us. Some of us have suffered a lot more than others, but it's safe to say that none of us has been able to fully escape heartache, disappointment, disenchantment, and other forms of emotional pain. The distinctiveness of our suffering has contributed to the distinctiveness of our character, so that it would be impossible to dissociate what is singular about us from the singularity of our history of suffering. The effort to reduce a given man or woman to the coordinates of gender blinds us to this intricate reality, making it impossible for us to respond appropriately when the ghosts of past suffering populate the relational space of the present, as they are prone to do, as they often insist on doing. That is, because stereotypes make us emotionally robotic rather than innovative, they thwart our ability to adequately deal with the more pain-saturated dimensions of another person's experience; they cause us to fall into overly simplistic patterns of relating that will in no way help us with the interpersonal challenges we face.

We are fooling ourselves if we believe that gender profiling doesn't hurt us. When we operate in a world of stale assumptions about the proper natures (and roles) of men and women, we forget to do the work of relating, thereby thwarting the very possibility of a genuine human connection. Furthermore, it's useless to pretend that gender profiling doesn't feed sexism, for it's in the nature of binary thinking to imply that one side of the divide is superior to the other. Take young versus old. All you have to do is to browse the skin-care selections of your local drugstore to see that this is not an innocent binary—that we live in a society that is vehemently "anti-age." Or take white versus black. Whiteness tends to be associated with good things from the purity of Snow White to the luminescence of God. Blackness, in turn, tends to connote things that are evil, dirty, sinister, shameful, or touched by the Devil. The problematic racial implications of this are obvious, which is one of many reasons to start admitting shades of gray into our thinking. Binary thinking is violent precisely because it excludes all gradations in order to forge an easy-to-digest representation of the world. It insists on stuffing people into tidy little boxes so as to stomp out everything that is eccentric and incomparable about them. And it callously leaves out those who can't conform, or who can't be made to conform, signing them off as irrelevant "anomalies." How exactly is this supposed to help us? As tempting as it may be to assume that binaries offer clear-cut answers to life's messy problems, there is no way to avoid their oppressive undercurrents; with respect to the gender binary specifically, there is no way around the fact that the more "different" men and women are thought to be, the more unequal they also become.

What's more, in the same way that Team A versus Team B on a football field signifies a battle, men versus women signifies a fight. In this context, it may be useful to recall that politicians tend to resort to binary logic whenever they need to foster a dog-eat-dog mentality. For example, the first step in an effective military strategy is to divide the world into Good and Evil and to convince one's own camp that the enemy embodies the latter. Those belonging to the enemy are painted as inhuman monsters who have absolutely nothing in common with decent, civilized folks such as ourselves. And of course the enemy is doing exactly the same, working overtime to depict us as soulless, murderous fiends. Within the framework of war, the purpose of binary thinking is to produce an enemy that can be attacked without remorse because we no longer see the similarities between "them" and ourselves; its purpose is to help us silence our ethical qualms so that we can wage violence without feeling too badly about it. To pretend that gender profiling is doing something more dignified is to be woefully naïve, for it merely makes it easier for men to mock women and for women to turn every man into a potential villain. This can be seductive because the more disparaged the "opposite" side becomes, the more the self seems to gain in strength and prestige. But is this how we want to conduct our relationships, particularly intimate ones? Personally, I can't imagine anything more damaging to romance than the idea that your partner is an opponent to be defeated. If it's cruel optimism to think that the caveman will make you happy, it may also be cruel optimism to think that treating love as a battle of the sexes is going to give you the loving relationship you're looking for. Isn't there in fact something quite twisted about the idea that a courtship based on gendered schemes of manipulation will eventually result in an honest, cordial, and reciprocal relationship?

The more we focus on gender differences, the more we fortify them. In contrast, if we chose to highlight what unifies men and women—say, our vulnerability to suffering—we would quickly demolish the status quo of gendered thinking because we would invite both genders to step outside the borders of what they have been culturally conditioned to believe is their proper domain; we would expand the range of human potentialities available to all of us. Those who resist this type of opening up of the gender terrain often do so because they are unable (or unwilling) to embrace the uncertainties of relating, including the fact that there is no way for any of us to fully know the person we love. They find the rhetoric of our gender profilers reassuring because it makes it sound like we can. But, as I've illustrated in this book, this is a delusion, a culturally (and scientifically) generated fantasy. It would serve us much better to admit that whenever two people—men or women, straight or gay, or anything in between—relate on an intimate level, they must be prepared to deal with a degree of murkiness. It's not just that another person is never fully transparent to us; it's also that this person might not be fully transparent even to him- or herself. After all, many human motivations remain unconscious, so that we can hardly expect any more clarity from others than we can expect from ourselves. In this sense, our ability to relate to others ethically may, in some measure at least, be a matter of patience in relation to what remains opaque about them.

By this I don't mean to imply that we should remain patient in every situation. There are circumstances where others take advantage of our patience, where they expect us to tolerate their ambivalence, hesitation, or lack of clarity to the point that our patience starts to hurt us. People who can't make up their minds, who can't express their feelings sincerely, who string us along because they aren't sure of what they want, who keep us on the backburner indefinitely "just in case" they might one day need us, or who refuse to reject us cleanly often act as if any sign of impatience on our part was an ethical failure. I'm therefore not arguing that there is invariably something noble about being able to resist the temptation to demand a clear accounting of motivations; the emotional wishy-washiness of others can sometimes be virtually unbearable. At the same time, it seems to me that a big part of being able to relate to others ethically, with kindness and generosity, is being able to defy the urge to jump to conclusions about them before we have attempted to understand what is going on in their private universe. The ethics of relationality, in other words, means accepting that some things will always remain tangled, muddled, and unsettled. This is what contemporary theorists refer to as the willingness to dwell within aporias and existential conundrums.[2] From this perspective, there is something deeply ethical about lingering within relational impasses instead of insisting on their hasty resolution. And when it comes to the main theme of this book, the lesson, obviously, is that we can't even begin to behave ethically if we are not able to reject the conceptual shortcuts that our gender profilers are so keen to market to us, for there is absolutely nothing ethically defensible about the idea that the intricate reality of a given person can be reduced to his or her gender.

The psychoanalyst Adam Phillips proposes that we may even be fundamentally misguided when we think that knowing people is the best way to go about relating. The problem, according to Phillips, is not merely that we might violate other people by "our assumed knowledge about them—as in racist and sexist fantasy—but that it is misleading to assume that it is knowledge that we want or that we have of people, any more than it is knowledge we get from listening to music. (Perhaps bodies simply affect each other, or evoke each other.)"[3] The intimate space between two people is always filled with mystery. When two individuals come together, they bring their unconscious lives and personal histories, including the aforementioned histories of suffering, into the mix. That this can generate wave after wave of confusion is hardly surprising.

What *is* surprising is that we seem so surprised by this confusion—that we expect anything different. For instance, the movements of our desire are never wholly predictable; they are never just a matter of bodily impulses but include bits of social conditioning, cultural imagery, personal background, and unconscious fantasy. To attempt to impose clarity on this inherently obscure reality by, for example, squeezing it into a theory of gendered reproductive strategies, is to be downright dim-witted. Similarly, the effort to account for the densities of emotional life through something as simplistic as Gray's Mars-Venus model is to be borderline abusive to the people we are supposed to love.

I'm not saying that we shouldn't try to understand others. Indeed, the claim that we can't is sometimes a sign of ethical complacency, as when we declare that we can't comprehend someone from another culture when in fact we are simply too lazy to make an effort. Along related lines, one of the maddening things about the rhetoric of gender profiling is that, on the one hand, it implies that stereotyping helps us understand the "opposite" sex but, on the other, it offers a convenient excuse for those times when we can't be bothered to attempt to bridge the gap between self and other. In such instances, men get to hide behind the notion that women are too different, perplexing, mystifying, or irrational whereas women get to hide behind the notion that men are too infuriating or unreliable (note that the two sides in the end amount to something quite similar even though the vocabulary used is designed to create a divide). This is merely yet another way of fanning the hostility between men and women, of pretending that it is gender that is causing us to stumble when in fact it is our unwillingness to exert ourselves that is tripping us up. But equally often, it is the pretense that we understand others when we actually don't—which is what gender profiling almost automatically implies—that is ethically questionable. And the idea that gender profiling might have something to do with love seems more or less unjustifiable.

Because we cannot ever fully know the person we love, it is, in the final analysis, impossible to love without exposing ourselves to the possibility of pain. Because the other always remains to some degree beyond our reach—and certainly beyond our control—there is no way to guarantee the safety of our emotional investments. But this is not a calamity; it's not a tragic flaw in the grand design of love. It's what makes love a genuine exploration, a genuine site of discovery. From this viewpoint, "mature" love is not the kind of hardnosed love that strives to rid romance of its illusions. Rather, it's a matter of being able to cope with the fact that we can never entirely grasp the other's reality; it's a matter of courageously stepping into the ambivalences of relating. Among other things, when we admit that the other is always to some extent unknown and unknowable, we create space for transformation. If rigid assumptions about the other—including rigid gender stereotypes—impede change, the act of discarding our preconceived notions gives the other the permission to evolve in directions that have nothing to do with our expectations. This type of flexibility, this type of interpersonal generosity, is what our gender profilers, inexplicably, cannot handle and often even ridicule. Because they are convinced that gender profiling can help us avoid relationship failures, that it can fend off any and all unpleasant surprises, they are willing to trade away the one thing that seems essential to love, namely the willingness to honor the other's integrity as a multifaceted individual. They treat people as pawns in a gendered game, obstinately clinging to the old order of gender relations while the rest of us step forward. They don't seem to understand that the future belongs to those who are able to overcome what was misguided about the past.

NOTES

Introduction

1 See Mari Ruti, *The Case for Falling in Love: Why We Can't Master the Madness of Love – and Why That's the Best Part* (Chicago: Sourcebooks Casablanca, 2011).

2 Coyne makes this statement in "Of Vice and Men: A Case Study in Evolutionary Psychology," *Evolution, Gender, and Rape*, ed. Cheryl Travis (Cambridge, MA: MIT Press, 2003).

3 Robert Wright, *The Moral Animal: Evolutionary Psychology and Everyday Life* (New York: Pantheon Books, 1994), 52 (emphasis added). Further references to Wright are from this source.

4 David Buss, *The Evolution of Desire: Strategies of Human Mating* (New York: Basic Books, 2003), 270–5. Further references to Buss are from this source.

5 Buss maintains that it is "startling that a recent study discovered that pregnancy rates resulting *from penile-vaginal rape among reproductive-age women* are extraordinarily high—6.42 percent—compared to a consensual per-incident rate of only 3.1 percent. This finding can be partially explained by selection bias in the victims whom rapists target—young fertile women. Nonetheless, even controlling for age, the authors find a rape-pregnancy rate that is roughly 2 percent higher than the consensual-sex pregnancy rate" (273–4).

6 Jonathan Gottschall and Tiffani Gottschall, "Are Per-Incident Rape-Pregnancy Rates Higher than Per-Incident Consensual Pregnancy Rates?," *Human Nature*, vol. 14 (1) (2003), 2.

7 Buss is here referencing a study by Martin Lalumiere.

8 Joan Roughgarden, *Evolution's Rainbow: Diversity, Gender, and Sexuality in Nature and People* (Berkeley: University of California Press, 2004), 173. Further references to Roughgarden are from this source.

9 In relation to Coyne's outburst, Roughgarden writes, "What provoked such an unusual declaration? The recent publication of yet another theory of the naturalness of rape supposedly based on evolutionary biology. The idea is that men unable to find mates in the 'usual way' can reproduce thróugh rape. Genes for rape then increase, leading to the brain's acquisition of a 'rape chip.' All men are therefore potential rapists, although they do not necessarily act on this potential, depending on external circumstances. Coyne points out that this I-can't-fight-evolution theory is falsified by the facts that one-third of all rapes are of women too young or too old to reproduce; 20 percent do not involve vaginal penetration; 50 percent do not include ejaculation in the vagina; 22 percent involve violence in excess of that needed to force copulation; 10 percent of peacetime rapes are in gangs, thus diluting each man's chance of reproducing; wartime rapes usually culminate in the murder and sexual mutilation of the victim; some rapists are wealthy, giving them access to women without coercion; and many rapes are homosexual. So many rapes are nonreproductive that rape can't plausibly be viewed as a means of sperm transfer for disadvantaged men to achieve reproduction. Like other mating acts, rape is about relationships – in this case, domination" (173–4).

10 Quoted in Roughgarden, 173–4.

11 Wright notes that while bonobos and humans diverged about eight million years ago, orangutans and humans diverged sixteen million years ago (49).

12 Geoffrey Miller, *The Mating Mind: How Sexual Choice Shaped the Evolution of Human Nature* (New York: Doubleday, 2000), 427–8. Further references to Miller are from this source.

13 As Miller writes, "A woman might have written a book about mental evolution through sexual selection with different emphases and insights. Indeed, I hope that women will write such books, so we can triangulate on the truth about human evolution from our distinctive viewpoints. Evolutionary psychology has made rapid progress in part because it includes a nearly equal sex ratio of researchers, with both men and women drawing upon their experiences to develop new ideas and experiments. Personal experience is not very useful in testing scientific theories, but it can be invaluable in formulating and refining them. I hope that each sex will continue to correct the other's biases and oversights within the scientific arena" (428).

14 Sarah Hrdy is perhaps the most well known of the female researchers who have challenged the notion of female coyness.

15 Donald Symons, *The Evolution of Human Sexuality* (Oxford: Oxford University Press, 1979), v.

16 See, for instance, Buss, 251.

17 For details of this quarrel, see Ullica Segerstrale, *Defenders of the Truth: The Battle for Science in the Sociobiology Debate and Beyond* (Oxford: Oxford University Press, 2000). Further references to Segerstrale are from this source.

18 O. E. Wilson, "Human Decency Is Animal," *The New York Times Magazine*, October 12, 1975, 38-50.

19 Helen Fisher, *Anatomy of Love: A Natural History of Mating, Marriage, and Why We Stray* (New York: Ballantine Books, 1992). Fisher writes, "Men vary; women vary. In fact, there is more variation within each gender than there is between them" (191).

20 Christopher Ryan and Cacilda Jethá, *Sex at Dawn: The Prehistoric Origins of Modern Sexuality* (New York: Harper, 2011).

21 Alan Miller and Satoshi Kanazawa, *Why Beautiful People Have More Daughters: From Dating, Shopping, and Praying to Going to War and Becoming a Billionaire – Two Evolutionary Psychologists Explain Why We Do What We Do* (New York: Perigee, 2008); Jena Pincott, *Do Gentlemen Really Prefer Blondes? Bodies, Behavior, and Brains – The Science Behind Sex, Love, and Attraction* (New York: Delta, 2009); Roy Baumeister, *Is There Anything Good About Men? How Cultures Flourish by Exploiting Men* (Oxford: Oxford University Press, 2010); Larry Young and Brian Alexander, *The Chemistry Between Us: Love, Sex, and the Science of Attraction* (New York: Current Hardcover, 2012).

22 I also wrote a number of follow-up posts, all of which received the same aggressive response. These posts, along with the responses, can be viewed at http://www.psychologytoday.com/blog/the-juicy-bits

23 A commentary on this post can be found at http://feministing. com/2011/05/16/racist-psychology-today-article-claims-black-women-are-objectively-less-attractive-than-other-women/

24 See David Buss, *Dangerous Passion: Why Jealousy Is as Necessary as Love and Sex* (New York: Free Press, 2011).

25 See Anne Fausto-Sterling's *Sexing the Body: Gender Politics and the Construction of Sexuality* (Basic Books, 2000) and *Sex/Gender: Biology in the Social World* (New York: Routledge, 2012).

Chapter 1

1 David Buss, for instance, draws on O. E. Wilson to argue that homosexuals can "increase their reproductive fitness by investing heavily in their genetic relatives, such as their sister's or brother's children" (David Buss, *The Evolution of Desire: Strategies of Human Mating* [New York: Basic Books, 2003], 251; further references to Buss are from this source).

2 Geoffrey Miller, *The Mating Mind: How Sexual Choice Shaped the Evolution of Human Nature* (New York: Doubleday, 2000), 140. Further references to Miller are from this source.

3 William Acton, *The Functions and Disorders of the Reproductive Organs in Childhood, Youth, Adult Age, and Advanced Life Considered in the Physiological, Social, and Moral Relations* (Charleston, SC: BiblioLife, 2008; originally published in 1857), 162.

4 Donald Symons, *The Evolution of Human Sexuality* (Oxford: Oxford University Press, 1979), vi.

5 Robert Wright, *The Moral Animal: Evolutionary Psychology and Everyday Life* (New York: Pantheon Books, 1994), 30. Further references to Wright are from this source.

6 See Sarah Hrdy, *The Woman that Never Evolved* (Cambridge, MA: Harvard University Press, 1981).

7 *The Correspondence of Charles Darwin*, ed. Frederick Burkhardt and Sydney Smith (Cambridge: Cambridge University Press, 1985–91), vol. 1, 460.

8 Christopher Ryan and Cacilda Jethá, *Sex at Dawn: The Prehistoric Origins of Modern Sexuality* (New York: Harper, 2011), 35. Regarding Darwin, Ryan and Jethá note: "Though he certainly didn't originate this narrative of the interminable tango between randy male and choosy female, Darwin beat the drum for its supposed 'naturalness' and inevitability. He wrote passages like, 'The female ... with the rarest exception, is less eager than the male ... [She] requires to be courted; she is coy, and may often be seen endeavoring for a long time to escape the male.' While this female resistance is a key feature in the mating systems of many mammals, it isn't particularly applicable to human beings or, for that matter, the primates most closely related to us" (27). "In questions of human sexual behavior, Darwin had little to go on other than conjecture" (31), Ryan and Jethá conclude: "Darwin was a genius and a gentleman for whom we have endless respect. But as is often the case with gentleman geniuses,

he was a bit clueless when it came to women" (30). Further references to Ryan and Jethá are from this source.

9 Joan Roughgarden, *Evolution's Rainbow: Diversity, Gender, and Sexuality in Nature and People* (Berkeley: University of California Press, 2004), 168. Further references to Roughgarden are from this source.

10 Roughgarden explains, "*Mating is not primarily for sperm transfer.* The purpose of mating, both heterosexual and homosexual, is more often to create and to maintain relationships than to transfer sperm. Sexual selection theory requires that mating be primarily about sperm transfer, whereas the amount of mating that actually takes place is a hundred to a thousand times more frequent than that needed for conception alone" (171).

11 This, by the way, is statistically impossible, unless one assumes that prostitutes and a handful of aberrantly "loose" women supply the main outlet for straying men.

12 Buss reports that a cross-cultural study of conjugal dissolution "found polygyny to be a cause for divorce in twenty-five societies, largely because of conflict among the man's co-wives" (179). Helen Fisher in turn asserts that "as more women have regained economic power in recent decades, fewer are willing to weather the favoritism, jealousy, and bickering that sharing a husband brings" (*Why We Love: The Nature and Chemistry of Romantic Love* [New York: Henry Holt and Co., 2004], 213). Are we to believe that American women are an exception to this?

13 In this context, Wright notes, "We needn't worry about creeping determinism muting a victim's rage. But the rage of spectators may wane as they come to believe that, for example, male philandering is 'natural,' a biochemical compulsion – and that, anyway, the wife's retributive furor is an arbitrary product of evolution. Life – the life, at least, of those other than ourselves, our kin, and our close friends – becomes a movie that we watch with the bemused detachment of an absurdist" (357).

14 Wright does admit that criticism by one's peers is an important part of science.

15 Miller, for instance, argues that nineteenth-century biologists rejected Darwin's idea that females exercise sexual choice, explaining that this rejection "was cloaked as scientific argumentation, but the motivations for rejection were not scientific. Many male scientists at the time wrote as if female humans were barely capable of cognition and choice in any domain of life" (51).

16 See Philip Kitcher, *Vaulting Ambition: Sociobiology and the Quest for Human Nature* (Cambridge, MA: MIT Press, 1985).

Chapter 2

1 David Buss, *The Evolution of Desire: Strategies of Human Mating* (New York: Basic Books, 2003). Buss's book also draws on countless smaller studies conducted by him or his associates or by other researchers in the field. Unless otherwise indicated, further references to Buss are from this source.

2 As Ryan and Jethá warn us, "The holy grail of evolutionary psychology is the 'human universal' ... Because evolutionary psychology is all about uncovering and elucidating the so-called *psychic unity of humankind*—and because of the considerable political and professional pressure to discover traits that conform to specific political agendas—readers need to be cautious about claims concerning such universals. Too often, the claims don't hold up to scrutiny" (*Sex at Dawn: The Prehistoric Origins of Modern Sexuality* [New York: Harper, 2011], 115).

3 Consider, for example, the following statement: "The averages mask a wide variability in individual circumstances. Ultimately, a person's value as a mate is an individual matter and is determined by the particular needs of the individual making the selection" (186).

4 The articles in question are: David Buss, "Sex Differences in Human Mate Preferences: Evolutionary Hypotheses Tested in 37 Cultures," *Behavioral and Brain Sciences* (1989), vol. 12; and David Buss et al., "International Preferences in Selecting Mates: A Study of 37 Cultures," *Journal of Cross-Cultural Psychology* (1990), vol. 21 (5). Further references to these articles will be specified by year of publication. Where no year is indicated, the reference is to Buss's book, *The Evolution of Desire*.

5 Robert Trivers, "Parental Investment and Sexual Selection," *Sexual Selection and the Descent of Man*, ed. Bernard Campbell (Chicago: Aldine de Gruyter, 1972), 153.

6 Robert Wright, *The Moral Animal: Evolutionary Psychology and Everyday Life* (New York: Pantheon Books, 1994), 103. Further references to Wright are from this source.

7 This statement is made by Mildred Dickemann.

8 Helen Fisher, *Why We Love: The Nature and Chemistry of Romantic Love* (New York: Henry Holt and Co., 2004), 107–8.

9 Far from admitting that we experience some people as irreplaceable, Buss argues that evolutionary reasoning dictates that it might be advantageous for us to desert "a bad mate" who doesn't help us successfully pass on our genes. He points out that "losing an infertile mate serves the goal of reproduction for ring doves better than remaining in a barren union" (11). The next sentence informs us that the same logic holds for humans. Yet this jump from ring doves to humans cannot possibly be justified, for humans – at least those living in modern societies – do not usually abandon their mate just because he or she proves infertile. Not surprisingly, similar unwarranted jumps from various animal species to humans abound in evolutionary psychological literature. Buss himself has no qualms about drawing analogies between weaverbirds, lovebugs, and scorpionflies on the one hand and humans on the other (see Chapter 1 of *The Evolution of Desire*).

10 This quotation is from *Sex, Power, Conflict: Evolutionary and Feminist Perspectives*, ed. David Buss and Neil Malamuth (Oxford: Oxford University Press, 1996), 306.

Chapter 3

1 Judith Halberstam, *The Queer Art of Failure* (Durham, NC: Duke University Press, 2011), 40. Further references to Halberstam are from this source.

2 Ryan and Jethá note that penguins have at least two dozen families in a lifetime, each pair lasting only a year. They further argue that evolutionary biologists have long been looking for monogamy in places where it doesn't exist: "Many species of birds have long been believed to be monogamous because two parents are needed for the 24/7 labor in incubating eggs and feeding nestlings. As with humans, investment-minded theorists assumed males would help out only if they were certain the young were their own. But the recent advent of affordable DNA testing has blown embarrassing holes in this story, too. Although a pair of bluebirds may build a nest and rear the young together, an average of 15 to 20 percent of the chicks are not sired by the male in the partnership … . And bluebirds aren't particularly slutty songbirds. DNA studies of the chicks of some 180 bird species previously thought to be monogamous have shown that about 90

percent of them aren't" (*Sex at Dawn: The Prehistoric Origins of Modern Sexuality* [New York: Harper, 2011], 136–7).

3 Stephen Mitchell, *Can Love Last? The Fate of Romance Over Time* (New York: Norton & Co., 2003), 67. Further references to Mitchell are from this source.

4 Mitchell specifies: "We can experience emotions like anger, anxiety, and sexual excitement only because we have the neural equipment that generates such emotions. Yet these emotions themselves generate brain states, the chemistry of which affects neural pathways and function. We can compose life plans because we have the neural equipment that makes possible such cognitive projects. Yet the plans themselves (exercising, taking medicinal and recreational drugs, meditating) affect neural pathways and neural function, influencing the kinds of plans we may compose in the future" (73).

5 See Anne Fausto-Sterling, *Sex/Gender: Biology in a Social World* (New York: Routledge, 2012).

6 As one of David Buss's critics, Linnda Caporael, sums up the matter, "In a society that feels a stronger obligation to correct inequities arising from imperfections in the social system than to correct those resulting from differences in natural endowments, the attribution of evolved sex differences takes on new meaning: Why should the resources of a society be used to provide women with good financial prospects of their own when their 'natural' preference is for men with such prospects?" (See the commentaries to David Buss, "Sex Differences in Human Mate Preferences: Evolutionary Hypotheses Tested in 37 Cultures," *Behavioral and Brain Sciences* [1989], vol. 12, 17–18).

7 David Buss, *The Evolution of Desire: Strategies of Human Mating* (New York: Basic Books, 2003), 14. Buss contradicts his own argument later in his book when he admits that there is a great deal of diversity to human mating behavior: "Although more men than women are inclined to pursue purely casual sexual relationships, some men remain exclusively monogamous for life and some women find casual sex preferable to monogamy. Some men seek women for their economic resources and some women seek men for their looks" (215). If so, why even bother to talk about "the only mating psychology we have"? Further references to Buss are from this source.

8 Wright, for instance, concedes that "most human beings don't live in an environment much like the one for which their minds were designed. Environments—even the environments for which organisms *are* designed—are unpredictable. That is why behavioral flexibility evolved in the first place. And unpredictability, by its nature, cannot

be mastered" (*The Moral Animal: Evolutionary Psychology and Everyday Life* [New York: Pantheon Books, 1994], 106). One must ask, then, why he, like Buss, keeps insisting that, when it comes to mating behavior, modern men and women act just like their ancestors. And how are we supposed to know what our ancestors were like to begin with? As Miller admits, "If we could look at the Earth through an extremely powerful telescope a million light-years away, we could see how our ancestors actually formed sexual relationships a million years ago. [But] until NASA approves that mission, we have to combine evidence from less direct sources" (*The Mating Mind: How Sexual Choice Shaped the Evolution of Human Nature* [New York: Doubleday, 2000], 186). By Miller's own admission, such "less direct sources" involve thought experiments that are "simplistic, unrealistic, and cartoon-like" (196). Further references to Miller are from this source.

9 Miller also writes: "If evolutionary psychologists like me could make solid predictions about exactly what stimulation patterns would optimally excite the human brain, we could just move to Hollywood and become highly paid entertainment industry consultants. But we cannot do much better than ordinary film producers, because a general understanding of typical human reactions to ancestrally normal events does not allow us to predict the human brain's exact reactions to any possible novel stimulation" (155).

10 As Miller states at the end of his book, "This book has argued that both human sexes have evolved many ways of displaying creative intelligence and other aspects of fitness through storytelling, poetry, art, music, sports, dance, humor, kindness, leadership, philosophical theorizing, and so forth" (429). Throughout his discussion, Miller stresses that many of our uniquely human traits, such as our complex language skills, high level of intelligence, artistic inventiveness, and ethical predilections are too ornate, too costly, to be useful in the struggle for survival, so that it is likely that they emerged in part as a way to attract mates.

11 Helen Fisher, *Anatomy of Love: A Natural History of Mating, Marriage, and Why We Stray* (New York: Ballantine Books, 1992), 189. Further references to Fisher are from this source.

12 See Virginia Woolf, *A Room of One's Own* (Oxford: Oxford University Press, 2008).

13 Sarah Hrdy, *Mother Nature* (New York: Pantheon Books, 1999), xviii.

Chapter 4

1   Christopher Ryan and Cacilda Jethá, *Sex at Dawn: The Prehistoric Origins of Modern Sexuality* (New York: Harper, 2011), 118. In this context, Ryan and Jethá quote *New Yorker* journalist Louis Menand: "The sciences of human nature tend to validate the practices and preferences of whatever regime happens to be sponsoring them. In totalitarian regimes, dissidence is treated as a mental illness. In apartheid regimes, interracial contact is treated as unnatural. In free-market regimes, self-interest is treated as hardwired" (117). Further references to Ryan and Jethá are from this source.

2   See Chapter 9 of Fisher's *Why We Love: The Nature and Chemistry of Romantic Love* (New York: Henry Holt and Co., 2004). See also Chapter 15 of Fisher's *Anatomy of Love: A Natural History of Mating, Marriage, and Why We Stray* (New York: Ballantine Books, 1992). Further references to Fisher are from *Anatomy of Love*.

3   Fisher notes that the high incidence of female adultery in societies where the double standard doesn't exist suggests that "women avail themselves of illicit lovers with relish, perhaps even as avidly as men" (93).

4   Fisher maintains that "divorce is common in societies where women and men *both* own land, animals, currency, information, and/or other valued goods or resources and where *both* have the right to distribute or exchange their personal riches beyond the immediate family circle... . Where men and women are not dependent on each other to survive, bad marriages can end—and often do" (103).

5   Quoted in Ryan and Jethá, 250.

6   Here Ryan and Jethá are drawing on historian Rachel Maines's book, *The Technology of Orgasm: "Hysteria," the Vibrator and Women's Sexual Satisfaction* (Baltimore, MD: Johns Hopkins University Press, 1999). They specify that, according to Maines, "female patients were routinely massaged to orgasm from the time of Hippocrates until the 1920s ... . *The Health and Diseases of Women*, published in 1873, estimates that 75 percent of American women were in need of these treatments and that they constituted the *single largest market for therapeutic services*" (247).

7   Ryan and Jethá report that "The Hamilton Beach Company of Racine, Wisconsin, patented the first home-use vibrator in 1902, thereby making it just the fifth electrical appliance approved for domestic use. By 1917, there were more vibrators than toasters in American homes" (248).

8 The claim about women's lesser sexual needs is from page 305 of
   *Mars and Venus Starting Over: A Practical Guide for Finding Love
   Again After a Painful Breakup, Divorce, or the Loss of a Loved One*
   (New York: Perennial Currents, 2005). Unless otherwise specified,
   subsequent references to Gray are from this source.

9 John Gray, *Mars and Venus in the Bedroom: A Guide to Lasting
   Romance and Passion* (New York: Harper Perennial, 2005), 171.

10 Many of the readers who were disappointed by Gray's *Mars and
   Venus in the Bedroom* reported having liked Gray's 1992 *Men Are
   from Mars, Women Are from Venus* because this earlier text was not
   so biased toward men. But if one reads the 1992 text carefully, it's
   obvious that the male bias was there from the beginning of Gray's
   thought. For instance, Gray insists that women can't expect men to
   talk when they don't want to. At the same time, he insists that women
   must *always* respect men's need to withdraw to their man-cave –
   that women should never violate a man's solitude no matter how
   upset they might be. That is, men are not invariably expected to give
   women what women want but women are invariably expected to give
   men what men want. When it comes to men and women in Gray's
   universe, the story is always the same: men have the right to refuse
   but women don't.

11 See Ryan and Jethá, 272–4. The study in question is by Meredith
   Chivers. Ryan and Jethá add, "If you aren't confused already,
   consider that research psychiatrist Andrew Anokhin and his
   colleagues found that erotic images elicit significantly quicker
   and stronger response in women's brains than either pleasant or
   frightening images without erotic content... . The women's brains
   responded about 20 percent faster to the erotic images than to any
   others. With men this eager responsiveness was expected, but the
   results among the supposedly less visual, less libidinous women
   surprised the researchers" (274).

12 Fisher, *Why We Love*, 174.

13 Interestingly, but perhaps not surprisingly, one of the earlier studies
   based on the binary between emotional and sexual infidelity was
   conducted by David Buss. Ryan and Jethá explain that a researcher
   named Christine Harris "measured the bodily responses of people
   being asked Buss's questions, she found that 'women as a group
   showed little difference in physiological reactivity,' but they still
   predicted, almost unanimously, that the emotional infidelity would
   be more disturbing for them. This finding suggests a fascinating
   disconnect between what these women *actually* feel and what they
   think they *should* feel about their partner's fidelity" (144). David

Lishner and his colleagues "honed in on another weak point: the fact that subjects are given only two options: either thoughts of sexual infidelity hurt more or thoughts of emotional infidelity do. Lishner asked, what if both scenarios made subjects feel *equally* uncomfortable? When Lishner included this third option, he found that the majority of respondents indicated that both forms of infidelity were equally upsetting, throwing further doubt on Buss's conclusions" (145).

14 The study in question is by Terry Fisher and Michele Alexander.

15 The study in question is by Joey Sprague and David Quadagno.

16 Ryan and Jethá write: "Our cultivated ignorance is devastating. The campaign to obscure the true nature of our species' sexuality leaves half our marriages collapsing under an unstoppable tide of swirling sexual frustration, libido-killing boredom, impulsive betrayal, dysfunction, confusion, and shame" (2). Along related lines, if the nuclear family is so deeply embedded within our nature, why are so many people these days opting out of it? Ryan and Jethá report that "in the United States, the percentage of nuclear family households has dropped from 45 to 23.5 since the 1970s. Married couples (with and without children) accounted for roughly 84 percent of all American households in 1930, but the latest figure is just under 50 percent, while the number of unmarried couples living together has mushroomed from about 500,000 in 1970 to more than ten times that number in 2008" (110).

17 Laura Kipnis, *Against Love: A Polemic* (New York: Vintage, 2003), 24.

18 I'm here paraphrasing the title of Freud's book *Civilization and Its Discontents*, ed. James E. Strachey (London: Norton & Co., 1961).

Chapter 5

1 Bobbi Carothers and Harry Reis, "The Tangle of the Sexes," *The New York Times*, April 21, 2013, 9.

2 John Gray, *Men Are from Mars, Women Are from Venus: The Classic Guide to Understanding the Opposite Sex* (New York: Quill, 2004; originally published 1992), 13. Unless otherwise specified, subsequent references to Gray are from this source.

3 This statement is from Gray's *Mars and Venus Starting Over: A Practical Guide for Finding Love Again After a Painful Breakup*,

Divorce, or the Loss of a Loved One (New York: Perennial Currents, 2005), 208.

4 Lauren Berlant, *Cruel Optimism* (Durham, NC: Duke University Press, 2011), 170. Further references to Berlant are from this source.

5 See Barbara Ehrenreich, *Bright-Sided: How Positive Thinking Is Undermining America* (New York: Picador, 2009).

6 Lee Edelman, *No Future: Queer Theory and the Death Drive* (Durham, NC: Duke University Press, 2004).

7 Michel Foucault, *The Birth of Biopolitics: Lectures at the Collège de France, 1978–1979* (New York: Picador, 2010).

8 Antonio Gramsci, *Selections from the Prison Notebooks*, ed. Quintin Hoare and Geoffrey Nowell Smith (New York: International Publishers, 2012), 304–5.

9 See Herbert Marcuse, *Eros and Civilization: A Philosophical Inquiry into Freud* (Boston: Beacon Press, 1955). Further references to Marcuse are from this source.

10 There are many critics in my field—contemporary critical theory—who would argue that such rewards and pleasures are yet another ruse of biopolitical control—or disciplinary power in Foucault's sense—designed to conceal the coercive aspects of marriage.

11 Laura Kipnis, *Against Love: A Polemic* (New York: Vintage, 2003), 79. Further references to Kipnis are from this source.

12 Michael Cobb, *Single: Arguments for the Uncoupled* (New York: New York University Press, 2012), 3. Further references to Cobb are from this source.

13 Bella DePaulo, *Singled Out: How Singles Are Stereotyped, Stigmatized, and Ignored, and Still Live Happily Ever After* (New York: St Martin's Griffin, 2006), 2. Further references to DePaulo are from this source.

14 DePaulo informs us that there are over a thousand places in federal law where marriage confers benefits that are not given to those who remain unmarried. But why, she asks, "should you have to be any kind of couple to qualify for the cornucopia of perks, privileges, and benefits that are currently available exclusively to couples who are married?" Why not create a society "that is equally respectful and supportive of all its citizens, regardless of whether they are single or married, uncoupled or coupled?" (253).

15 Sara Ahmed, *The Promise of Happiness* (Durham, NC: Duke University Press, 2010), 6. Further references to Ahmed are from this source.

16 Ahmed writes, "Feminist genealogies can be described as genealogies of women who not only do not place their hopes for happiness in the right things but who speak out about their unhappiness with the very obligation to be made happy by such things. The history of feminism is thus a history of making trouble" (59-60).

17 Quoted in Ahmed, 69.

18 As Ahmed notes, "It is hard labor just to recognize sadness and disappointment, when you are living a life that is meant to be happy but just isn't, which is meant to be full, but feels empty. It is difficult to give up an idea of one's life, when one has lived a life according to that idea. To recognize loss can mean to be willing to experience an intensification of the sadness that hopefulness postpones" (75).

19 As Ahmed expresses the matter: "We hear the term 'happy families' and we register the connection of these words in the familiarity of their affective resonance. Happy families: a card game, a title of a children's book, a government's discourse; a promise, a hope, a dream, an aspiration. The happy family is both a myth of happiness, of where and how happiness takes place, and a powerful legislative device, a way of distributing time, energy, and resources" (45).

Conclusion

1 Christina Nehring, *A Vindication of Love: Reclaiming Romance for the Twenty-first Century* (New York: Harper, 2009), 7. Further references to Nehring are from this source.

2 Jacques Derrida is perhaps the one most closely associated with this line of thinking.

3 Adam Phillips, *Darwin's Worms: On Life Stories and Death Stories* (New York: Basic Books, 2000), 74.

INDEX